ALL I WANT IS LOVING YOU

ALL I WANT IS LOVING YOU

Popular Female Singers of the 1950s

STEVE BERGSMAN

Foreword by CAROL CONNORS

University Press of Mississippi / Jackson

All I Want Is Loving You: Popular Female Singers of the 1950s is part of a two-book set that looks at the great female singers of the 1950s. The second companion volume, *What a Difference a Day Makes: Women Who Conquered 1950s Music*, is about the Black female singers of the fifties who conquered the record charts with a mix of jazz, blues, R&B, and rock 'n' roll. Due to the types of music they sang and, of course, race issues, the two groups of singers had completely different career arcs.

The University Press of Mississippi is the scholarly publishing agency of the Mississippi Institutions of Higher Learning: Alcorn State University, Delta State University, Jackson State University, Mississippi State University, Mississippi University for Women, Mississippi Valley State University, University of Mississippi, and University of Southern Mississippi.

www.upress.state.ms.us

The University Press of Mississippi is a member of the Association of University Presses.

∞

Library of Congress Cataloging-in-Publication Data

Names: Bergsman, Steve, author. | Connors, Carol, writer of foreword.
Title: All I want is loving you : popular female singers of the 1950s / Steve Bergsman, Carol Connors.
Other titles: American made music series.
Description: Jackson : University Press of Mississippi, 2023. | Series: American made music series | Includes bibliographical references and index.
Identifiers: LCCN 2023026623 (print) | LCCN 2023026624 (ebook) | ISBN 9781496840974 (hardback) | ISBN 9781496848796 (trade paperback) | ISBN 9781496848802 (epub) | ISBN 9781496848819 (epub) | ISBN 9781496848826 (pdf) | ISBN 9781496848833 (pdf)
Subjects: LCSH: Women singers—United States—Biography. | Popular music—United States—1951-1960—History and criticism.
Classification: LCC ML82 .B43 2023 (print) | LCC ML82 (ebook) | DDC 782.42164092/52—dc23/eng/20230629
LC record available at https://lccn.loc.gov/2023026623
LC ebook record available at https://lccn.loc.gov/2023026624

British Library Cataloging-in-Publication Data available

Nineteen Fifty One through Nine

Everyone was doing fine
In Nineteen Fifty One through Nine
In Nineteen Fifty One through Nine
The universe was in different time.

Afternoon at Mickey's club,
Buffalo Bob and the Flubberdub
Shari Lewis you were my very first love

Stickball in the neighborhood
Chivalry was understood
Parents kept their kids in line
In Nineteen Fifty One through Nine

The Late Show and I Kid You Not
Perry solved each and every plot
The Toast of The Town and What's My Line
In Nineteen Fifty One through Nine

My Little Margie and Desilu
Father Knows Best for me and you
Dino and Jerry and Kovacs and Bud and Lou

Happy Trails and Beat The Clock
I've Got A Secret with the girl down the block
Audrey Meadows you were the Queen for a day

In Nineteen Fifty One through Nine
A shirt and tie and shoes that shined
Lassie, Fury, Rin Tin Tin
In fifty-five ol' Brooklyn wins

Ozzie and Harriet's Travelin' Man
Hoppy and Zorro and Superman
Give 'em hell Harry and Ike had respect in the land

Benny and Bilko, Your Show of Shows
Make Room For Daddy and Jimmy's Nose
Miltie and Allen you started something big.

—MICHAEL PALERMO, 2004

CONTENTS

FOREWORD

CAROL CONNORS

When I was growing up in the 1950s, my favorite singer in the whole world was Doris Day, which was partly because my favorite song at the time was *Secret Love*. Doris Day sang that tune in the 1953 movie *Calamity Jane*. I watched that movie eleven times, a feat only surpassed by my obsession with *West Side Story*, which I saw thirteen times.

I so wanted to be Doris Day that when I decided to change my name from Annette Kleinbard, I opted for the double-consonant letters of Carol Connors.

My attachment to Doris Day and *Secret Love* was so strong that when I was attending Louis Pasteur Junior High School in Los Angeles, I signed up for a talent show with the intent on playing the record on the turntable and then imitating Doris Day's performance from the film. Today, that's called lip syncing, but back in the 1950s it was just considered weird. I belonged to an a cappella choir led by Mrs. Duffy, yet I intended not to sing. In the end, I realized lip syncing was not a category that would win a talent contest, but in the heat of the moment I thought my creation was brilliant. I watched *Calamity Jane* so many times I could copy Doris Day exactly, from hand movements to the smelling of the flowers. I think all my schoolmates were horrified.

Except one.

A high school boy named Phil Spector watched the show and told me my lip sync was right on. Not much later, my friend Donna was dating Phil and whenever they wanted alone time I was given the job as lookout. It wasn't the most exciting thing I did, so to ward off the boredom I would sing the tunes that were those great hits by the female singers at the time. These were songs I loved: "You Belong to Me," by Jo Stafford, "Why Don't You Believe Me" by Joni James, "Music! Music Music!" by Teresa Brewer, and others. I mean, I sang these songs all the time.

One day, Phil said to me that he loved my voice and would write a song for me. There was a catch, however. I would have to come up with $10, which would be my share of the cost to make a recording. My family was poor and $10 was a lot of money back then. I said to Phil, "I'm sixteen and a half. I don't even have 10 cents to my name."

Phil was adamant so I went to my parents and asked for the money. My mother had a beautiful singing voice and when she was young was supposed to study at the Warsaw Conservatory of Music. My father, Julius, was tone-deaf and had been a jockey. But, he knew what it was like to take chances and he said to my mother, "Gail, let's hear her out." I was precocious and persistent and said wacky things such as "I'm going to have a #1 record, we are going to live in a mansion and I'm going to buy dad a racehorse." Afterward, my mother said, "Annette-ta-la, go do your homework." My father said to my mother, "Gail, give her the $10."

Phil Spector was as good as his word. He wrote me a song, and he, Marshall Leib, and I went to Goldstar Studio to record "To Know Him Is to Love Him" with me in the lead. We called ourselves the Teddy Bears and the song went all the way to #1 in 1958.

Years later, when I was more famous as a songwriter than a singer, I got to meet the object of my teenage affections, Doris Day. This all goes back to the first hit record I penned, "Hey Little Cobra." Although it was officially sung by a group called the Rip Chords, the actual singers were Terry Melcher, Doris Day's son who was head of A&R at Columbia Records, and Bruce Johnston, one of the Beach Boys. That was in 1964. Three years later after appearing in a bunch of absurd, teenage beach movies, I found myself on the set of *The Glass Bottom Boat*, starring Doris Day. I was to do a bit part and that's when I finally got to meet her.

In the 1970s, I got to meet another one of the great female singers of the 1950s, Gogi Grant, who sang one of my all-time favorite tunes, "The Wayward Wind." It was the kind of song that would bring tears to my eyes. Anyway, Gogi Grant was long past her prime as a pop singer, but I was excited to see her and told her "you were my idol when I was young." Aging singers never want to hear those words, and that included Gogi Grant, who quickly brushed me off. When long past my own ingénue stage of life, I came to understand those feelings. Now, it doesn't bother me at all when people express those sentiments because I know I made an impression on their lives.

Today, music is everywhere and can be accessed through any medium. When I was growing up, if I wanted to hear these songs I would listen to my transistor radio or watch *Your Hit Parade* on television, a show I watched religiously. Songs such as "Wheel of Fortune" by Kay Starr, "Cross Over the Bridge" by Patti Page, "Hey There" by Rosemary Clooney, or "Jambalaya" by Jo Stafford were such big hits they were always played.

That's why this book is so important, because it brings back these great singers and their wonderful songs, which have mostly been forgotten. These songs touched the heart and were the fabric of our lives. By extension, the contributions of the 1950s female singers affected my generation of rock 'n' rollers, who influenced the next generation of female singers, who were the backbone of succeeding generations and on and on until we end up where we are today.

—CAROL CONNORS, twice Oscar-nominated songwriter wrote/cowrote such popular tunes as "Hey Little Cobra," "With You I'm Born Again," and "Gonna Fly Now" (theme from the movie *Rocky*), and, of course, trilled "To Know Him Is to Love Him" as part of the Teddy Bears. Carol almost attained an EGOT of almosts; achieving nominations for an Emmy, Grammy, and an Oscar, but not a Tony.

ALL I WANT IS LOVING YOU

TENNESSEE WALTZ

FRANK SINATRA—LOUISE HARRIS MURRAY—
PATTI PAGE—TERESA BREWER

In October 1950, Patti Page recorded a Christmas song, "Boogie Woogie Santa Claus," hoping to score a big seasonal hit. For the B-side, she and her agent Jack Rael wanted an obscure song that would not detract from the A-side. Nothing sold at that time of year unless it was a Christmas song, so the idea was to get the disk jockeys to concentrate on "Boogie Woogie Santa Claus" instead of anything else. At the time, Rael kept an office in the Brill Buildings at 1610 Broadway in Manhattan and about the time of the "Boogie Woogie Santa Claus" recording he bumped into Jerry Wexler, who worked at *Billboard* magazine. Rael explained to Wexler what he was up to with Patti Page and Wexler in turn told him about a song he just reviewed, Erskine Hawkins' cut of "Tennessee Waltz." From what Wexler had said, it seemed to Rael that he had found the perfect, unknown (to listeners of pop music) and unobtrusive B-side tune for his singer's coming release.

The next day Patti Page was back in the studio to record the B-side to "Boogie Woogie Santa Claus" and four other tunes. Since "Tennessee Waltz" was the last song in and only recently chosen, it was to be the final recording of the day. The song was such a last-minute decision there was no arrangement made for the recording session, so Rael and Page asked their trumpet player, jazz musician Buck Clayton, "to come up with something." Joe Carlton produced the recording session and Joe Reisman conducted the orchestra. (The record label reads Orchestra Conducted by Jack Rael, which was the usual record industry ploy to grab royalties due to others).

"We liked the way it turned out but nobody had high hopes for it," Page recalled. "To tell the truth, I quickly forgot about 'Tennessee Waltz.'"[1]

At the time, Page, who in 1949 had had a big hit with "With My Eyes Wide Open, I'm Dreaming" (rising as high as #11 on the best-seller chart), was opening at the Copacabana for comedian Joe E. Lewis. On one of the nights after her last number, she was walking back to her room through the Copa's kitchen to an elevator and people kept stopping her to say, "Do the waltz" or "You should do the waltz." She was perplexed. What the heck were they talking about? So when she saw Rael later that evening she told him about people requesting she sing the waltz. He responded, "What waltz?" And Page said, "I was hoping you'd know." Although it was late, Real immediately got on the phone and called his source at Mercury Records distribution. He signals Page to come closer to the receiver to listen to the conversation. The disembodied voice was in dismay: "You gotta be kidding," the man exclaimed at their lack of knowledge. "We've ordered three times already, Jack! In two weeks! And each order was 200,000. You better get your head out of the sand."

Skip Press, a writer who helped Patti Page write her memoir, annotated her book with this curiosity:

In 1951, there were about 151 million people living in the United States. Many didn't have record players and played records only on jukeboxes. Yet on January 3, 1951, barely six weeks after the release of "Tennessee Waltz," sales had passed 1.4 million copies. . . . by March, the record sold 2.5 million copies. That meant that within three and half months of the record's release there was a copy of "Tennessee Waltz" owned, on average, by roughly one out of every 60 people in the country. For the whole of 1951, total sales of all records in the United States were nearly 200 million. Patti Page's "Tennessee Waltz" sold about 4 million copies in that period . . . it accounted for one out of every 50 records sold in the country in 1951.

The song ended up as #1 on the pop, country, and R&B charts, the first song ever to attain that accomplishment.

What happened to "Boogie Woogie Santa Claus"? Page wrote in her memoir, "Though some DJs may have heard 'Boogie Woogie Santa Claus,' I don't know one who ever played it." She did put "The Waltz" into her regular stage act, but that was after the Copa. Her next gig was in Miami and she premiered the song there.

Since the record was released at the end of 1950, it was only the #18 best seller for year, but a quick perusal of all the major hit records of 1950 shows it is clearly one of the very few standout classics, if not essential, tunes from that year. The only other song of equal importance and endurance is Nat King Cole's exquisite "Mona Lisa." A few versions of Lorenz Hart & Richard

Rodgers's "Bewitched, Bothered and Bewildered" were big hits in 1950, but the song was introduced in the 1940 theatrical production *Pal Joey* and the fondly remembered version was done by Doris Day the year before.

As with any civilization throughout history, all important things are put in place by adults, whether it is politics, societal governance (implied or otherwise), or culture. However, there have always been moments where the young, not necessarily teenagers, set the tone for society and even sectors of culture. In literature and music, for example, consider the 1920s, when young adults of the *This Side of Paradise* ilk in the United States and the Bright Young People in the United Kingdom ripped up the old models and drank and danced their way to hedonistic pleasure. In the United States, their model for living was the Fitzgeralds, F. Scott and Zelda, and their cultural connect was jazz music.

This still wasn't a teenage world. One had to be old enough to drink and go to nightclubs. And that jazz music wasn't necessarily by the still unshaven. The big bands employed the seasoned musician as well as the young Turk. Maybe in the big cities and among the sliver of the population that had amassed some degree of wealth there was free time to gather with friends and listen to that new technological development, the radio, but most of America was still just getting by and teenagers very quickly entered the work world because their income was needed to help support the mostly rural American family.

Things would not get easier for America's teens. By the 1930s, the United States' economy had collapsed into a depression and it was all hands on deck to find employment and help feed the family. The teenager years meant early entry into the workforce. Then the United States began the 1940s as a combatant nation in a world war. Older teenagers went off to the conflict and younger teens waited until it was their turn to be trained, armed, and shipped overseas.

Meanwhile, back on the home front there were some strange things afoot—actually on the feet. Teenage girls adopted a style of sock, generally white, ankle length or if longer, folded back to the ankle. These foot coverings were worn with shoes and were known as bobby socks, the wording of which was transformed into the phrase "bobby sox" and the teenager girls who wore them were known as bobbysoxers. This casual fashion phenomenon coincided with a big change in popular music, the rise of the vocalist. This merger of teenage fashion and music was a prelude to the big cultural change America would experience in the 1950s.

From the mid-1930s to 1941, the big swing bands dominated the best-seller record charts, mostly jazzy instrumentals such as, for example, Benny Goodman's great 1937 recording of "Sing, Sing, Sing." During this period, twenty-nine of the forty-three records that sold over a million copies were from the big bands of the time, wrote Charlie Gillett, author of *The Sound of the City: The Rise of Rock and Roll*. But in the middle years of World War II, the bands with a distinctive vocalist, whether male or female, began to rise in popularity. Soon, most every band shifted away from the unified, orchestral mode to one of supporting the vocalist, who sometimes became a star in his or her own firmament.[2]

The bandleaders didn't know it, but after dominating the airwaves through the 1930s, that sound was becoming old, especially to the teenagers of the 1940s. By offering up a vocalist, often a young troubadour, the bands were deploying a rearguard action, which worked for a time, but the strategy had a built-in flaw: the vocalists became more prominent than the bandleader, as was the case with Frank Sinatra, who became a much bigger star than the bands that once employed him, and this became an ongoing trend line. This (as well as the economics of keeping a big band together) was partly why the popularity of big bands faded.

Frank Sinatra began singing with Harry James and his band in 1939 and then moved on to the Tommy Dorsey band. In 1941 he was named the top band vocalist by *Billboard* and two years later he was on his own. In 1943, Sinatra was twenty-eight years old but it was clear from his years singing with Dorsey that he was an attraction to young women, so by the time he was just Frank Sinatra, the singer's publicity machine aimed straight for the teenage crowd, who were becoming the new influencers in the world of music. The Sinatra marketing team encouraged bobbysoxers to form their own fan clubs, hold meetings, and write letters to the local newspaper about their hero. In a unique marketing ploy, a mass radio interview was held with 200 high school newspaper editors, who were allowed to do a live interview with Frank Sinatra. Although hordes of bobbysoxers would attend a concert, it was all amped up by further marketing with local contests. Marketing even employed young girls to scream when Sinatra sang.[3]

Not to take anything away from Frank Sinatra and his unique skills as a singer—at the start of his solo career he was probably the first teen idol (a celebrity with a teen fan base), although crooners such as Bing Crosby and Rudy Vallee had their moments at a time when radio began to be the prime media for the dissemination of music to America.

Sinatra opened the way for crooners like Perry Como and Vaughn Monroe, who became major chartbusters in the later 1940s. Although neither Como nor Monroe were youngsters, both were in their thirties at the time of their initial success as a singer not associated with a big band. This didn't prevent Como, for example, from singing "When You Were Sweet Sixteen," the nineteenth best-selling song of 1947, or "Dig You Later (A Hubba-Hubba-Hubba)," the thirty-seventh best-seller the year before.

When Frank Sinatra left Tommy Dorsey's orchestra, he was replaced by a good-looking, young (but nevertheless music veteran) Dick Haymes, who would also eventually go off as a singles act. In 1938, Haymes had been thirty years old but with a big hit for the young market, "Little White Lies," the seventh best-selling song of the year. Haymes would have his own radio show, act in a number of movies, marry six times, and make hit records into the early 1950s.[4]

Pop radio was a man's world at the end of 1940s. In 1949, the last year of the decade, twenty-two of the top thirty songs for the year were by men and six were by men in a combination with a female, a sister act, or with a stylized big band sound: Jimmy Wakely and Margaret Whiting; Gordon Jenkins with the Andrews Sisters; the Stardusters and Evelyn Knight; Johnny Mercer and Margaret Whiting; Gordon MacRae and Jo Stafford; and Perry Como and the Fontane Sisters. The only two women to have Top Twenty-Five hits of their own that year were Dinah Shore with "Buttons and Bows" and Evelyn Knight with "Powder Your Face with Sunshine."[5]

With every new decade change is expected, which, of course, is not how things actually work. Just because one decade ends and another begins there is no reason to think that next year is going to be radically different than the year before. If changes were coming in the 1950s, the seeds of societal alterations could be found in the prior years. The Cold War years of the fifties began almost immediately after the end of World War II in 1945. A shift to a more conservative America under Republican president Dwight Eisenhower was an eventual reaction to the long years of progressivism under Franklin Roosevelt and Harry Truman. Even the new technology of television was unveiled in the 1940s.

The outlier in this discussion was the music world. Something did change with the singers who were now rising to the top of the best-seller charts: suddenly there was more space for women. In the twentieth century, popular music in the United States was dominated by men, but there were extraordinary periods where women as a group made significant contributions to style and the choices of what was played on radios, sold in record stores or, back in the mid-twentieth century, played on a jukebox. The latter was a machine placed in a bar or restaurant that for a small bit of change—nickel, dime, or quarter—played a song you wanted to hear.

The most well-known period where ladies crushed the record charts was at the beginning of the 1960s in the era of the girl groups. But there was an earlier time in which this female phenomenon happened—although it is an era with no official name. The time was the early to mid-1950s, the period of the female crooner. Ladies, many of whom graduated out of big bands in the 1940s, reached the charts in a huge way. They were the last bastion of traditional-pop music, the last warriors of swing, and they would fall out of favor relatively quickly with the coming of rock 'n' roll. But they had their moment.

And it all began in 1950, a surprising year in pop music because many trends that would rise in the next decade could be seen in what records sold big that year. It was certainly no shock to see that many of the big hits were in the post–big band vernacular or done by male crooners, some with well-known names like Bing and Gary Crosby with "Sam's Song" and "Play a Simple Melody," Guy Lombardo with "Third Man Theme," or Tony Martin with "There's No Tomorrow." However, the #1 song of the year was "Goodnight Irene," a folkish song originally sung by blues singer Huddie "Lead Belly" Ledbetter recorded by both Gordon Jenkins with the Weavers. This was an important song for a couple of reasons. While Jenkins was a veteran arranger and composer, the Weavers were a solid, if not radical, folk group that included Pete Seeger. This song, and the Weavers, would help usher in a folk music revival in the 1950s. Secondly, the source of this record was not the usual Tin Pan Alley or Broadway musical songwriter, but a lesser-known African American blues singer. Beginning in the early 1950s, blues or rhythm & blues would entice the pop musicians like boogie-woogie dancers to a jumpin' jive.

For the most part, *Billboard* segregated its best-selling record charts, which by the early 1950s were called Popular, County & Western, and Rhythm & Blues. African American musicians generally were charted in Rhythm & Blues. In 1950, two Black singers made the crossover to the pop chart: Billy Eckstine with the #28 top seller of the year, "My Foolish Heart," and Nat King Cole with "Mona Lisa" at #2. Both Eckstine and Cole were more jazz oriented than rhythm & blues and their sound was palatable and nonthreatening to white audiences.[6]

While Gordon Jenkins successfully combined pop and folk music, Red Foley did the same with country music, laying a boogie-beat over a country twang to produce "Chattanoogie Shoe Shine Boy," a Top Ten record in 1950. Country was also the path of entry for female pop singers invading the airwaves.

Going back to the 1930s, only a few of the big bands (such as those led by Duke Ellington) wrote and produced their own songs, but as the solo artist became more popular they needed new songs and were even more dependent on the Tin Pan Alley world of established songwriters or established publishing houses for material, a trend that would become even more important through the 1950s and into the early 1960s.

Starting in the late 1940s, the major record labels noticed the country music market was expanding and record sales of that genre of songs were exploding. The major labels figured there were numerous ways of exploiting the country sound: promote country songs as a "novelty"; get a country singer to bridge the gap to popular music styles, as with "Chattanoogie Shoe Shine Boy"; team a country singer with a pop singer; or simply find a pop singer to record a country song with a more mainstream sound. By some quirk of nature, male crooners initially weren't on board with adopting country songs, which left the market wide open for women and is one reason why the ladies were able to storm the best-selling record charts. The young pop music audience liked these songs. So, in 1950, one sees an old fiddle tune called "Bonaparte's Retreat" revived and given lyrics by Pee Wee King and becoming the twelfth best-selling record of the year for Kay Starr. Starr, in a duet with country singer Tennessee Ernie Ford, also sang the #20 best-seller that year, "I'll Never Be Free."

Back in 1946, Pee Wee King, a terrific country-songwriter, together with lyricist Redd Stewart created a heartbreak song called "Tennessee Waltz." It would be released to the country stations in 1948 and remained popular with radio deejays, sometimes redone by other singers.

It was such a versatile song that Alabama jazzman Erskine Hawkins and his orchestra substituted the country strings for a tinkling piano and transformed the song into a jazzy melody suitable for a small club or lounge. R&B fans dug the tune and it ended up as a Top Ten R&B hit in 1950 on Coral Records. It's this version that was brought to Patti Page, suggesting she make a pop cover of an R&B song that was a cover of a country song. The Patti Page version of the song, also released in 1950, would become the classic and the one still remembered today.

Louise Harris Murray was born in 1939 and was a member of the Hearts, one of the first two female doo-wop groups to have a hit record. Their song "Lonely Nights" was a Top Ten R&B record in 1955. After dropping out of the group, she came back in the 1960s to sing with the Jaynetts on their hit single "Sally Go 'Round the Roses." In 1950 she was eleven years old, mostly living with her grandmother, who kept the radio on in her house day and night (as yet there was no television in the house), and she remembered all the great female singers of the 1950s. "I loved those songs, I really did," Murray said. "I used to sing those songs all the time. I knew most of them by heart."[7]

She added, "Of course I can remember 'Tennessee Waltz.'" Over eighty years old when asked about the song, she immediately began singing it. She couldn't recall all the words exactly, but she was able to imitate with exactitude Patti Page's distinctive intonation and ellipses.

"Going back to when I was five or six, if I heard a song I was able to learn it quickly," Murray said. "I had no idea what was going on in school, but I always had a song in my head or I was writing new songs."

Her skills were boosted by the importance of the radio, which kept many an isolated home- or apartment-dweller company. "My grandparents had the radio on all the time and then when I was moved back to my mother's place, she had the radio on constantly as well," Murray reminisced. "My mother also knew all the songs and she would sing along. She was a good singer until she began having lung problems."

Asked if she ever met any of the 1950s female crooners, who were white, Louise said no. In fact, even when she appeared in concert (part of many multi-act shows) at, for example, the Apollo in Harlem, the R&B music world was so male oriented she could recall but one other female singer on the same bill as the Hearts and never the major, female R&B singers at the time such as Ruth Brown, Dinah Washington, or Etta James.

Nonetheless, she remembered all the songs from her early teenage years: Eileen Barton's "If I Knew You Were Coming I'd've Baked a Cake," Joni James's "Why Don't You Believe Me," Teresa Brewer's "Till I Waltz Again with You," and, of course, "Tennessee Waltz."

A year after the ladies were abysmally represented on the best-selling record charts, 1950 became the renaissance year when the distaff side of the song business came alive. Counting down in the Top Thirty, bottom to top, for that year: Patti Page was at #21 with "All My Love"; Kay Starr and Tennessee Ernie Ford at #20 with "I'll Never Be Free"; the Andrews Sisters with Gordon Jenkins at #19 with "I Wanna Be Loved"; Patti Page at #18 with "Tennessee Waltz"; Kay Starr at #12 with "Bonaparte's Retreat"; Eileen Barton at #11 with "If I Knew You Were Coming I'd Have Baked a Cake"; and the biggest-selling record by a female in 1950, Teresa Brewer at #6 with "Music! Music! Music!"

Teresa Brewer and "Music! Music! Music!" are important outliers in that group for two reasons. First, most of the female hits of 1950 were unendurably (by today's standards) slow, gushing, love ballads done up in post–swing band style, or as some might say, in a genre of female crooning. Eileen Barton gets a pass because "If I Knew You Were Coming I'd've Baked a Cake" was a novelty song, but even Barton, like the other singers, was an old pro by 1950. The Andrews Sisters were the supreme female act of the mid-twentieth century, although by 1950, the steam seemed to have gone out of their more ebullient and jazzy best-sellers such as "Boogie Woogie Bugle Boy," which was recorded in 1941, or even their lighthearted, calypso-inspired "Rum and Coca Cola," a song that spent ten weeks at the top of the record charts in 1945.

"Teresa Brewer was the first female artist to make it on her own as a solo act without starting out as a big band vocalist. Kay Starr, Patti Page, Peggy Lee, Doris Day all began singing with bands," notes Bill Munroe, a friend of Teresa Brewer and a Brewer musicologist.[8]

What also made Teresa Brewer different from the other gals was her age. The Andrews Sisters were born between 1911 and 1918, so in 1950 they were positively ancient in that they were in the thirty-years-of-age range. Starr, Page, and Barton were all born in the 1920s, so they were in their twenties that year—they weren't old, but not necessarily youthful.

Teresa Brewer was the only teenager in the best-selling female set and that was important because teenagers would dominate the record-buying market in the 1950s and beyond. She was eighteen when she recorded "Music! Music! Music!" although she would turn nineteen before the year was over.

The United States, as well as other industrialized countries, experienced a huge jump in the birth rate in the years after World War II, as soldiers came home, settled down, and established families. In the United States, according to the Census Bureau, the number of children aged zero to four increased to 16.4 million in 1950 from eleven million in 1940. These numbers would peak at 20 million in the 1960s. This was the baby boom generation. However, the forgotten statistic in all of this is that the United States' population had been steadily growing throughout the forties. In 1940, the US population stood at 131.7 million; ten years later in 1950 it was 150.7 million. Of that latter number, the amount of children under the age of nineteen rose to fifty-one million in 1950. That was a large demographic waiting to be serviced culturally, and what they were hearing on the radio was mostly a kind of rehashing of their parents' music.[9]

The teenagers of 1950 twisting the radio dial seeking something more youthful, more relevant to their own age, would have discovered Teresa Brewer, who was not only a teenager, but standing just over five feet in height she looked like a young kid. With a slight twang to her singing voice, she sounded youthful, especially on "Music! Music! Music!" which had a bouncy, syncopated rhythm that was different from most anything else on the radio that year.

It's hard to say if her record company, London Records, wanted her to appear older or younger. Her full, dark hair was always reasonably set, not too long and not too short; her eyebrows were perfectly tweezed, make-up moderate, and her lips colored in a dark gloss. In early publicity photos she wore a strand of pearls tightly slung around her neck. Yet, she was also saddled with an outlandish corsage, which is pinned to her dress as if she was headed to her high school prom—an ironic look considering she dropped out of high school before the end of her senior year. (Years later, when asked about quitting school, Teresa huffed, "I quit two months before graduation because I could not stand it . . . everyone is still saying how stupid I could be. What would I learn in those two months? All I'd have is a slip of paper that said they wanted to give me an honorary diploma.")[10]

In 1950 with a hit record, no one needed to know whether or not Teresa Brewer got her diploma. What was important was whether they could hear her on their AM radio at home and in their parents' car. By 1946, an estimated nine million cars boasted an AM radio. In 1949, 95 percent of American homes had at least one radio and by 1954, 70 percent had two or more.[11]

Or, they could hear music using that new technology, vinyl records. The older 78 rpm records were made of, or with, shellac. Then in June 1948 Columbia introduced the new vinyl, 12-inch, 33 1/3 rpm, long-playing (LP) record. Eventually, it would be called an "album." Nine months later, the competition, RCA Victor, unveiled the vinyl, seven-inch, 45 rpm, with a larger center hole. Eventually, this would be referred to as the "single" with an A-side and B-side.

Phonograph (record player) manufacturers soon were delivering a product that could play all speeds.

Teresa Brewer arrived on the music scene with the coming of the new technology and she was someone a thirteen-year-old in Des Moines or Denver, a fifteen-year-old in Pittsburgh or Portland, or a seventeen-year-old in Sacramento or South Florida could love. She was America's first teenage singing star, as if teenagers had just been invented.

CHAPTER ONE

mu∫ic! mu∫ic! mu∫ic! (1950)

PHIL HARRIS—TERESA BREWER—EILEEN BARTON

Like Teresa Brewer, singer/actor Phil Harris (Wonga P. Harris) didn't finish high school. His family had moved from Linton, Indiana, to Nashville, Tennessee, and he walked into his new school and then walked out again. He somewhat knew where he was going because, again like Teresa, his entertainment career began at an early age when his mother entered him into an amateur show. Then he began playing at movie houses as a teenager when cinema was just silent films, and musicians played alongside the movies and/or entertained between reels. Eventually he formed his own five-person group that played Dixieland jazz. He was always on the verge of breaking big through the 1930s and into the 1940s and never quite getting there. He did snag a good break when he became a regular on the very popular Jack Benny radio show. Harris had done movies and some recordings; then in 1950 he stepped into a studio to warble a novelty song called "The Thing."[1]

Sounds ominous, right? But the listener never quite knows what the "thing" is. Harris sings, "Ooh, I discovered a [drum beating or foot stomping sounds] right before my eyes." So there always a musical cutoff right after the line "I discovered a. . . ." The rhythm sounds like something a marching band would have played in 1935.

Harris, who was born in 1904, wasn't handsome in a classic way. His stocky body held up a side of roast beef kind of head, which was cut by heavy eye lids and full cheek demarcations that ran from each side of his nose to each side of lips. His smile always looked under constraint. Although not a great singer, his shtick was so strong that he was the voice of Baloo in *The Jungle Book*, which meant he sang the fine, fun tune from the movie, "The Bare Necessities."

"The Thing" moved into the #1 slot of the *Billboard* chart on December 2, 1950, and it would stay for four weeks before being eclipsed by Patti Page and "The Tennessee Waltz." "The Thing" would be the fifteenth best-selling song of that year, squeezing in between two of the most schmaltzy melodies of 1950, the harrowing "There's No Tomorrow" ("Love is a moment of life enchanting / let's take that moment, that tonight is granting") by Tony Martin and "Sentimental Me" by the Ames Brothers, who were at the peak of popularity in 1950 despite sounding like a barbershop quartet with music.

There is really no encompassing description of a novelty record. Its purpose is to be humorous, whimsical, or even nonsensical. In America these songs had been taking slices of a particular kind of tuneful interlude since the mid-1800s because Broadway, vaudeville, road performances, tent meetings, minstrel shows, and beer joints needed something light and fun to get the crowds excited. The novelty song as written by the professionals, Tin Pan Alley songwriters, attained radio popularity in the 1920s, although the progress of jazz musicianship and big bands dominating the airwaves caused the novelty song bubble to lose gas. The concept came back with a vengeance in the 1950s and stayed strong well into the 1960s with gleeful tunes such as "The Chipmunk Song" by David Seville, a #1 hit in 1958, and "Itsy Bitsy Teenie Weenie Yellow Polkadot Bikini" by Brian Hyland, which rose to #2 two years later. Perhaps singer/westerns actor Sheb Wooley was thinking of "The Thing" when he recorded "Purple People Eater," which was another #1 novelty song in 1958. At least we got to know what the creature looked like: it was one-eyed, one-horned, and purple. The grape-colored thing not only could fly but it could rock. Indeed, the creature wanted to get a job in a rock 'n' roll band.

The radio stations and record stores were globbed up with novelty songs in 1950. Phil Harris had to fight off a slew of his male counterparts, including the Ames Brothers, who had a monster hit of their own called "Rag Mop," a nonsensical form of novelty record in the light jazz vein. Most of the lyrics are simply the spelling of the song's title. It was originally written by Johnnie Lee Willis, a bandleader who combined swing with western music, and steel guitarist Deacon Anderson. Apparently, they both needed more schooling because in the song "rag" is spelled with two Gs and "mop" with two Ps.

Perry Como, who was known as a crooner, had a fondness for novelty records and he came on willfully in 1950 with "Hoop-Dee-Doo" a polka tune ("Hoop-Dee-Doo, Hoop-Dee-Doo / I hear a polka and my troubles are through").

Both were incandescent songs, but when it came to male singers in 1950, neither the Ames Brothers nor Perry Como could touch "The Thing." Como's "Hoop-Dee-Doo" was the twenty-fifth best-selling record in 1950, two slots behind "Rag Mop," but the latter took the #1 best-seller position for one week in February of the year.

What Harris, Como, and the Ames Brothers couldn't do, however, was transcend two female singers who boasted the best and most popular novelty records of the year, if one doesn't count Red Foley's "Chattanoogie Shoe Shine

Boy," which could or could not be considered a novelty record depending on one's interest in, or interpretation of, this western-swing composition.

So, it was Teresa Brewer versus Eileen Barton, "Music! Music! Music!" versus "If I Knew You Were Comin' I'd've Baked a Cake."

Oddly, both Brewer and Barton had similar histories in that their careers began a very young ages, although it was not unusual for female singers who attained stardom in the early 1950s to have become hoofers before getting out of elementary school.

Brewer and Barton started their careers before kindergarten. The big difference between the two was the year of their birth. Brewer was born in 1931 and Barton in 1924 (although Barton's publicity machine often listed her as a 1929 birth). Those seven years between the two singers made a big difference.[2]

When Teresa Brewer (Theresa Veronica Breuer) was born, her family was living in the Birmingham section of Toledo, Ohio. She was the first of five children of Helen Kasap and Ludwig Breuer Jr. Her father was a glass inspector for Libbey-Owens and mother was a housewife. Perhaps sensing her daughter had entertainment skills, mama Helen enrolled Teresa at the Linville School of Dancing and Dramatic Arts in East Toledo. Her first performance was at the age of two, when she sang "Take Me Out to the Ballgame" on *Uncle August's Kiddie Show*, which ran on WSPD, Toledo's leading radio station. The sponsor of the show was a local bakery and Brewer was paid in cookies and cupcakes.

After winning an appearance on the *Major Bowes Amateur Hour* in New York, at the age of seven she was a regular on one of Major Bowes's traveling vaudeville shows.[3]

Edward Bowes, better known as Major Edward Bowes, or just Major Bowes, boasted an immensely popular radio show in the 1930s and 1940s called the *Major Bowes Amateur Hour*. In support of the show, he also ran national tours that would perform, among other venues, at movie theaters between film reels. Brewer was part of this show for five years, from the age of seven to twelve, mostly traveling in the company of her aunt. More often than not, these Major Bowes shows involving Brewer were one-night stands throughout the Midwest. Brewer would go out for a short spell, come home and do homework, and then go out on the road again accompanied by her aunt Mary Kasap or, on the rare occasion, her mother. It was a little boring for a young girl, and Teresa would recount watching Alan Ladd in *This Gun for Hire* (1942) over and over and over again.

However, she loved singing and being on the stage. In fact, if she misbehaved, her mother would punish her by not letting her go on tours.

Brewer told an interviewer, "There were 16 of us in the unit, and I was the only child . . . the only trouble I had was that various school boards (in the cities where the show would set up) would inquire about my schooling."[4]

While Brewer always claimed her years with Major Bowes were "fun," the truth is there is almost no record of Brewer ever uttering a disparaging word about anything. In 1956, she told an interviewer her Major Bowes troupe often traveled in their own rail car, but it was an awful grind for a young kid. By her reckoning, while with Major Bowes she visited thirty-eight states and most of Canada before she hung up her dancing shoes at age twelve.

One has to ask if this was letting a talented girl be all that she could be, or if it was about exploiting the skills of a child. Teresa did love to sing. On the other hand, she was earning $100 a week being on the road. In the 1930s, during the Depression, $100 was a lot of income and would certainly have come in handy for a family of seven where the father was the only wage earner in a blue-collar job.

Eileen Barton was born in Brooklyn, New York, into a vaudeville family. Her parents, Ben and Elise Barton, starred in Ben Barton and his Californian Collegiates (the title of the show often changed). Ben led the band, but the real talent was the mom, who sang, danced, and played the fiddle. Barton joined the family business at age two and a half singing "Ain't Misbehavin." By three and half, she was a regular vaudevillian, playing with a guy named Ted Healy. The Three Stooges were also on the bill. Then came radio shows with Eddie Cantor, Rudy Vallee, and Milton Berle. By the age of eight she had a program on WMCA in New York called *Arnold's Dinner Club*. In 1944, reportedly at fifteen years of age (in reality she was twenty), she was in Los Angeles with a nightclub routine and also doing guest turns on radio shows, including *Johnny Mercer's Music Shop*. In an interview in which she recalled her career, Barton explained what happened next: "Johnny had a guest star every week and I was the guest one week. At the same time, a big ad agency, McCann-Erickson, was playing records of folks to audition for this new show with Frank Sinatra. They played my record from *Music Shop* and picked me and I got the show," which was called *Frank Sinatra in Person*, a CBS show.

She stayed a year before moving on to host her own Saturday show called *Teen Timers*—after all, the bobbysoxers needed a show they could call their own. On November 24, 1945, *Billboard* noted: "Current airing *Teen Timers*, with Eileen Barton, will be dropped . . . former show will continue on NBC as sustained under the moniker of the Eileen Barton Show."

She started recording for Capitol Records in 1948, and in 1949 she went into the studios to sing "If I Knew You Were Comin' I'd've Baked a Cake" for the National label. She recalled the experience: "I was playing a theater and Al Trace and his band were on the date. He kept playing this cockamamie song and asked, 'I've got a record date, will you do it?' But I thought it was a terrible song, so I turned him down. When I got back to New York and was dickering with MGM to record, my father told me, 'Eileen—don't wait for somebody that wants to dicker with you. If this other guy wants to do a record, do it.' So, I said all right; I went in and cut 'Baked a Cake.'"[5]

The chorus of the song goes like this: "If I knew you were comin' I'd've baked a cake, baked a cake, baked a cake / If I knew you were comin' I'd've baked / How-ja do. How-ja do. How-ja do," with subsequent stanzas replacing *baked a cake* with *hired a band*, the "grandest band in the land." While the lyrics seem insubstantial, there were some serious names behind this song, in particular the two veteran songwriters; bandleader Al Trace attached his name to the song under the pseudonym Clem Watts, Al Hoffman (wrote Patti Page's "Allegheny Moon," among others), and Bob Merrill (wrote Barbra Streisand's "People" and many more).

The Al Trace Band musicians played behind Barton but were called "The New Yorkers" on the label, as if the wispy record needed a veneer of sophistication. The record was released in April 1950 and rapidly moved into the #1 best-seller slot on *Billboard*, ruling America (also #1 in the UK) for two weeks. The song it displaced was Teresa Brewer's "Music! Music! Music!," which had reigned for four weeks.

For Teresa Brewer, the year 1950 began in novelty record mode and the genre engulfed her like a thick miasma with no visible means of escape. Like it or not, London Records was determined to make the young singer the exemplar of novelty song recordings. That strategy succeeded for awhile.

With 1950 barely two weeks old, in a year of doltish songs London Records pushed into the market one of Brewer's silliest sounding tunes, "I Beeped When I Shoulda Bopped," a parody of "hip" or "cool" jazz lingo. Bop was short for bebop, an improvisational jazz style recorded by such hipsters as Dizzy Gillespie or Louis Prima, none of whom sounded like Teresa Brewer.

"I Beeped When I Shoulda Bopped" was intended as the B-side to another novelty song "Ol' Man Mose," which, although sung by such clean-cut acts as Teresa Brewer and Betty Hutton, bragged a bawdy, accidental history. In 1938, singer Patricia Norman, backed by the Eddy Duchin band, began a recording of "Ol' Man Mose," a not-very-serious song about a gentleman who passed away. Somewhere Norman loses track of the lyrics and one supposes she just filled in the lyrics like this: "(We believe) He kicked the bucket / (We believe) Where's the man? Fuck, fuck, fuck it." People claim she actually did not curse in the song, but one can listen to a recording of the song on the Internet and it sounds pretty obvious.[6]

Needless to say, that wasn't Teresa Brewer's version "Ol' Man Mose," which wasn't even released as an A-side. On January 14, 1950, *Billboard* polled a selection of the country's disc jockeys as to what songs would soon be hit records. It was a regular feature in the magazine at the time. The disk jockeys usually got it right about 50 percent of the time. For this issue they tagged

Gordon Jenkins's "My Foolish Heart" and the Ames Brothers' "Rag Mop" as future hits; both became major best-sellers in 1950. In that same column, the disk jockeys' fourth-highest vote-getter for a bright future was "I Beeped When I Shoulda Bopped."[7]

Billboard's competition, *Cash Box* magazine, boasted a regular feature called "Disk Jockeys' Regional Record Reports," where it would survey about fourteen different deejays around the country as to what were the Top Ten records being played in a particular week. In the January 4, 1950, issue of the magazine, one deejay listed "I Beeped When I Shoulda Bopped" as its #10 play. The disk jockey was named Willie Bryant and he worked at WHOM in New York.[8]

At this moment in time, "cool jazz" was replacing the old swing jazz and the center of that world was New York City, so a song that parodied hipster talk would be appealing in that particular market and even to surrounding cities in the East. Cool jazz had not yet in a major way penetrated across the rest of America and this was a problem for this particular record; it had limited geographic appeal. Through January, the record was still in Top Ten play in New York City and Albany, New York, and even Newark, New Jersey, but nowhere else.[9]

The second thing to happen to "I Beeped When I Shoulda Bopped" was that it got run over by "Music! Music! Music!"—at first, in unexpected ways.

Remember, "I Beeped When I Shoulda Bopped" made its first appearance on the *Cash Box* disk jockey report the first week of the year. Also making its premiere appearance, in Pittsburgh, was "Music! Music! Music!" but by a singer named Etienne Paree. By the third week in January, with "I Beeped When I Shoulda Bopped" charting in New York and Newark, "Music! Music! Music!" reappeared on the regional charts, this time in Boston, and by a new singer, Eddie Miller.

"'Music! Music! Music!' was already out by Eddie 'Gin' Miller, I believe, he did it with sort of a German accent," Brewer recalled. "I heard the record and thought, 'I can't do that song.' 'There's nothing to it,' they [her label] said. 'Oh, do it.' When I listen, then and now, to my original version of the song, I think that it was done too slowly. The tempo is just too slow. But, I'm glad I did it."[10]

After the Eddie Miller release, London Records was getting antsy and it paid for a vertical, half-page promotion in that same issue of *Cash Box* touting Teresa Brewer and her recording of "Music! Music! Music!" with "Copenhagen" on the B-side. One month later, in the February 25, 1950, issue of the *Cash Box*, "I Beeped When I Shoulda Bopped" is still a Top Ten record in New York; the Eddie Miller version of "Music! Music! Music!" stood at #6 in Jacksonville and #3 in New York, but Teresa Brewer's version of the song was steamrolling across America, #4 in Washington, DC, #2 in Pittsburgh, and #1 in Boston and Chicago.[11]

"I heard it played for the first time on December 31, 1949," Brewer told *TV Show* magazine in 1953. "We were at a New Year's Eve party at my mother-in-law's up in the Bronx and we had *Mile Man's Matinee* tuned in. I didn't notice what was on. I was in a rosy fog because that very afternoon I'd had word from my doctor that I was pregnant with Kathleen, our first baby. Well, anyway my brother-in-law was listening and he said, 'Well that's great. You'll never have another like it though.'"[12] So much for passive-aggressiveness from an in-law!

"Music! Music! Music!" begins with an antiquated reference: "Put another nickel in / In the Nickelodeon / All I want is having you / And Music! Music! Music!"

Even in 1950, the word *nickelodeon* was obscure, or frankly unknown, because it referenced the very earliest of movie projectors for commercial purposes. In 1905, to see this newfangled technology called motion pictures people would go into an amusement hall where you put a nickel in the slot, leaned over a machine, and watched a brief "movie." Of course, motion pictures got bigger and huge halls were built to show these amusements on big screens, and thus the movie theater came into being. The nickelodeon disappeared around 1915.

The songwriters of "Music! Music! Music!" are listed as Stephen Weiss and Bernie Baum, an odd couple if there ever was one. Weiss was Austrian composer who generally wrote operettas before immigrating to the United States in 1938. In 1949, he turned fifty years of age.[13] Baum was a twenty-year-old up-and-comer. He would later be associated almost exclusively with Elvis Presley, writing many tunes for his movies.[14] How closely these two gentlemen actually worked together is not known and it's possible that Baum heard an existing Weiss composition and added lyrics to make it seem modern.

For "Music! Music! Music!" they conflated the old term *nickelodeon* with the public record-playing machines called jukeboxes found in diners, bars, and almost anywhere else people gathered to eat, drink, and cavort. The songwriters probably used the word because in the 1940s it cost a nickel to play a song or a quarter for six songs. By the late 1950s, inflation got to jukeboxes and one song would cost a dime, or for a quarter one got three songs.

In the modern world, it's hard to envision how popular jukeboxes were, except to say it was the contemporary equivalent of getting your songs streamed on the internet today. In 1934, there were an estimated 25,000 jukeboxes placed in public areas across America. Six years later, that number had increased to 500,000.[15] The jukeboxes were very popular during the war years, when soldiers came home on leave and longed to hang out with friends or meet new people, especially women, before being shipped out. Jukeboxes were very important to the budding record industry for two reasons. First, a lot of records were bought just to be played on these machines. Second, although jukeboxes did not make money for the performers, the exposure to songs was exponential. Jukeboxes were so important that even into the 1950s, music trade publications such as *Billboard* had separate charts for jukebox plays.

Dixieland music was also very popular at the end of 1940s. London Records employed the Dixieland All-Stars to back Brewer on "Music! Music! Music!," which was intended to be the B-side to the song "Copenhagen," a Dixieland jazz number delivered with zest by Brewer. Indeed, in one of the first mentions of "Music! Music! Music!" in *Billboard*'s "Record Reviews" column, "Copenhagen" is the featured song. The reviewer wrote "The fine young stylist pipes the seldom-heard lyric of a two-beater with an engagingly raffish old-time shout quality. Plenty of 'kicks' on this side. . . . Top Dixie sidemen in support."[16] Indeed, the Dixieland All-Stars included such fine musicians as Max Kaminsky, who played with the Tommy Dorsey and Artie Shaw bands, plus such jazz greats as Sidney Bechet, Willie "The Lion" Smith, Jack Teagarden, and Danny Perri, who became a much in-demand session guitarist playing behind everyone from Ella Fitzgerald to Screamin' Jay Hawkins.

As for the B-side, "Music! Music! Music!," the reviewer really didn't have much good to say about the song, although the singer got an enthusiastic thumbs-up: "A gay, corny, feed-the-nickelodeon novelty is sung with infectious vitality, backed with an old-fashioned thumping. Should be a good one in the boxes [jukeboxes]."

Among the other women singers in review for that issue were Kitty Kallen with "You Missed the Boat," Kay Starr with "Tell Me How Long the Train's Been Gone," Nellie Lutcher with "Little Sally Walker," and Fran Warren in a duo with Tony Martin on "I Said My Pajamas (And Put on My Pray'rs)." The reviewer called the latter song a "novelty nonsense ballad," but of the songs mentioned here, it was the one that became a hit.

Sometimes reviewers are so perspicacious it's frightening. The key phrase in the review, "Should be a good one in the boxes," is exactly what happened; the record was placed in jukeboxes in a time of dispiriting, mock-operatic ballads sung by the likes of a Vic Damone or Tony Martin. The jaunty tune, chirped by a cheerful "thrush," was immediately popular. It happened quickly as recorded by *Billboard*. In its February 11, 1950, issue, the column "Record Possibilities," where insiders guessed what's going to be a future hit in different categories from radio activity to store sales to jukebox plays, the jukebox operators' number one prediction for a future hit was Teresa Brewer's "Music! Music! Music!"[17] The song was not mentioned by retailers, disk jockeys, or even the *Billboard*'s panel of experts, only by the jukebox operators. That wasn't just by chance or operator brilliance.

"Music! Music! Music!" was recorded the year before and London Records intended to drop it in 1950, so the company quickly looked for opportunities to tie Teresa to jukeboxes. On January 21, 1950, *Cash Box* reported: "A majority of the music trade quartered on Gotham's [New York City's] Coin Machine Row this past week to witness the showing of AMI's new Model 'C' Phonograph [jukebox]. On hand to partake in the festivities were . . . Teresa Brewer, Bobby Wayne, Eddie 'Piano' Miller . . . New machine features forty selections and was received by the trade with much enthusiasm."[18]

Promotion-wise, the year ended as it began. The November 11, 1950, issue of *Cash Box* featured two photographs under the headline "Wurlitzer Entertains Artists." The underneath caption, dateline New York, read: "Here are some of the guests who attended a cocktail party given by Ed Wurgler, General Sales Manager of Wurlitzer, before the MOA dinner, Top photo left to right: Teresa Brewer, her husband, Bill Monahan . . ."[19]

On March 18, "Music! Music! Music!" was *Billboard*'s #1 best-seller in the country and it would camp at the top of the charts for four weeks. The record would go on to sell over a million copies.

"I recorded 'Music' for London Records, a British company that was then just starting to sign American artists," Brewer told interviewer Bill Munroe. "The records were still being pressed in England, however. There was a big strike over there at the time and there were problems getting all the records pressed. As it was, the record sold over a million copies, but it would have sold much, much more if there hadn't been the strike."[20]

David Laing, in his Teresa Brewer obituary for UK newspaper *The Guardian*, wrote that "Music! Music! Music!" was "a million-selling hymn to the power of the jukebox."[21]

What did Brewer think of her breakout song? *Hit Parader* magazine caught up with her in 1954 and asked Brewer that very question. At that time, she was twenty-three, married, a mother, and inexplicably this is how she began her response: "I guess you could say I am a very lucky little girl."

She continued, just being a little confused: "It's just a few years ago that the wonderful Coral people released a record by an unknown singer [referring to herself] called 'Music! Music! Music!'" (The song, of course, was issued by London Records.) "Fortunately for me, the public liked the tune, and overnight I found that I was a singing star. I have always felt that 'Music' was the key to quite a bit of the success that has come my way."[22]

On the strength of "Music! Music! Music!" London Records quickly rushed to market a follow-up record, another novelty song—a juvenile inanity called "Choo'n Gum." Take your pick of the most puerile stanzas: either "My mom gave me a nickel / To buy a pickle / I didn't buy a pickle / I bought some choo'n gum" or "choo, choo, choo, choo, choo, choo'n gum / How I love choo'n gum / I chew, chew, chew."

But Teresa Brewer was hotter than a firecracker, so the future-hit-record column "Record Possibilities" in the March 25, 1950, issue of *Billboard* selected

"Choo'n Gum" as a strong possibility to become a hit. Although the record was not nearly as good as "Music! Music! Music!," suddenly reviewers were completely on board with Teresa Brewer. The *Billboard* reviewer, higher than a junkie on New York's Bowery, called "Choo'n Gum" "a wing, zingy slicing of a spirited novelty." Calming back down, the reviewer added the song was "built around the traditional 'My Ma Gave Me a Nickel' child chant. Live two-beat band backing socks it home with winning earmarks."[23]

Not be outdone, *Cash Box* in its "Record Review" column chose "Choo'n Gum" as its "Disk of the Week." The in-depth review didn't hold back on the gush-factor: "You can count on this fresh Teresa Brewer waxing [record] for a smash hit in the phonos [jukeboxes]. 'Choo'n Gum' will rival the gal's click rendition of 'Music! Music! Music!' . . . There's no doubt about it—this biscuit is going to mean big profits in every music machine in the country. Top deck [A-side] has Teresa taking a standard school-day lilt, adding a bit of spice and zest in her vocal delivery and set on the table is a tasty dish of sparking silver for the jukebox trade. Arrangement and piano solo supplied by Jack Pleis and his Dixieland All-Stars, the chirp turns her dynamic singing personality into high gear to bring back this nostalgic oldie hotter than it was before."[24]

Eddie "Gin" Miller might have gotten out-muscled by the petite, young Teresa Brewer in regard to "Music! Music! Music!" but he still made something of a modest hit out of the song, so, he too, rushed back with a follow-up, this time, no dancing around the subject, overtly focused on the jukebox. *Billboard*'s "Record Possibilities" also chose his "Juke Box Annie" as a future hit. That review went like this: "Another of those . . . novelties with a catch gimmick, which figures to pick up attention and fast action. Could even be the sequel to 'Music! Music! Music!'"

On April 22, 1950, a headline on page 12 of *Billboard* read "London's Brewer Disk of 'Music' Hits Million Sale." The story noted that, on station WNEW, radio personality Martin Block presented the eighteen-year-old "thrush" with her gold copy. According to London Records, the article stated, the song had sold an additional 500,000 to date in England, Europe, and Canada.

Finally, the story concluded, "Miss Brewer's latest cutting, 'Choo'n Gum,' released three weeks ago, is the current pace-setter at London."[25]

Once again, Eddie "Gin" Miller got hit in the head by the young lady. "Juke Box Annie" had no juice, while "Choo'n Gum" became a tasty morsel, rising to #17 on the music charts. In 1950 alone, three other stars took a shot at the song: Don and Lou Robertson, the Andrews Sisters, and, as unlikely as it may seem, Dean Martin.

London Records kept the Teresa Brewer marketing theme steady and ready throughout 1950, continuing to tie "Music! Music! Music!" to the jukebox industry while pushing "Choo'n Gum." The May 20, 1950, issue of *Cash Box*, in what is clearly a staged photo, shows a pensive, if not moonstruck, Teresa Brewer sitting on a bar stool before a jukebox, chin resting in cupped hands, as she contemplates the complexities of life. The cutline, with a New York dateline, reads: "Young thrush [female singer] Teresa Brewer, currently clicking like sixty, strikes an enthralled pose, as she listens to her London recording 'Choo'n Gum' on the new Wurlitzer Model 1250 phonograph [jukebox]. The London Records star dropped in for a visit with a local jukebox op [operator], with the above pic [picture] resulting. Music ops are well familiar with Miss [she was actually a Mrs.] Brewer's antics on 'Music! Music! Music![,] currently topping popularity lists."[26]

Just as London Records kept steady on its marketing of Teresa Brewer, it also would not budge from the novelty record approach chosen for its new star. She stood somewhere between five feet and five-feet two inches tall, depending on which press release was being issued at the time, and her weight was about ninety-eight pounds. She looked like a young teenager and that was the market London Records was aiming for.

Before 1950 came to a close, London would unleash yet another silly record by Brewer—although by this time the returns were severely diminished. The record was called "Molasses, Molasses" and the lyrics were viscous: "Molasses, Molasses / It's icky sticky goo / Molasses, Molasses / It always sticks to you." Despite a hard push by London Records, it would disappear, not quite without a trace as it was a bit gooey at the start.

In a weak moment, Brewer conceded these records were "icky" in and of themselves. Never one to publicly utter a profanity, Brewer also referred to her time in novelty record purgatory as her "ootsy-poo" period.

"That's all they gave me. 'Choo'n Gum,' 'Molasses,' everything was icky-sticky," she said. "Now, they were hits, but they should have been children's records. I did many, many of that type of song. I was locked into it. 'Molasses' was my favorite song to sing my children to sleep. I used to bounce them on the bed or rock them to sleep, so that was great. That was one of the first songs my girls ever knew."[27]

Brewer had to be a good soldier because she wasn't in control of what she sang; London Records was.

The "Record Possibilities" column in the October 28, 1950, issue of *Billboard* showed the disk jockeys choosing "Molasses, Molasses" by Teresa Brewer as their fifth choice for future stardom. Right behind it as the sixth choice was "Molasses, Molasses" by Lenny Carson and the Whiz Kids. The retailers chose "Molasses, Molasses" by Teresa Brewer as their second choice for tomorrow's big hit and by Lenny Carson/Whiz Kids as its tenth choice. The more prescient jukebox operators didn't even choose Brewer's version of the song, only listing the Lenny Carson version (the seventh-best choice for becoming a hit).[28] Once again the jukebox folk were right about Brewer's recording of "Molasses, Molasses"; it didn't deserve a mention, but they were wrong about Lenny Carson. Not even the Whiz Kids could save that juvenilia.

One theory about the morass of novelty records at the start of the new decade was that pop music was suffering from a lack of imagination, creativity, and direction. Many of the hit songs in 1950, if not by Gordon Jenkins pushing pop versions of folk songs or novelty cuts, were post-swing vocals, heavy on the romantic drama. That was one reason why "Music! Music! Music!" and "If I Knew You Were Coming I'd've Baked a Cake" stood out; those songs had zest and vitality. No offense to the versatile Kay Starr, who had a good year in 1950, but her hit songs (the buoyant "Bonaparte's Retreat" and, with Tennessee Ernie Ford, the semi-country "I'll Never Be Free"), although romantic, were charmless.

Nevertheless, musicologist Larry Birnbaum, author of *Before Elvis: The Prehistory of Rock 'n' Roll*, declared "I'll Never Be Free" to be "torchy," but important for other reasons. First, the songwriting team of Bennie Benjamin and George David Weiss was interracial when, in the heart of the Jim Crow era, almost nothing was. Secondly, it was a crossover record, becoming a Top Five hit on both the country and pop charts.[29] Finally, due to Bennie Benjamin's investment in the composition, Birnbaum thought the song "smacks of rhythm & blues." His commentary is incisive here, because numerous Black musicians took on the song, including Dinah Washington, Ella Fitzgerald, Lucky Millinder, and Aretha Franklin.

If the theory that the proliferation of novelty songs meant a dearth of creativity in pop music at the start of the new decade seems implausible, here's another hypothesis: there were so few good, new pop songs that were tuneful and with prospects that there was at the time this crazy, stampede by A&R men to get their singers into the mother lode when one good, or at least interesting, song did appear. It was like a redux gold rush, circa 1849. A good song would attract singers like a crowd of prospectors when some yelled "Eureka! It's gold."

How weird were things in 1950? When music website playback.fm figured the top 100 songs of that year, this is what it included: two versions of "If I Knew You Were Comin' I'd've Baked a Cake"; two versions of "Hoop-Dee-Doo"; two versions of "Chattanoogie Shoe Shine Boy"; two versions of "Goodnight Irene"; three versions of "Music! Music! Music!"; four versions of "Mona Lisa"; four versions of "Tennessee Waltz"; four versions of "Harbor Lights"; five versions of "Rag Mop"; and six versions of "Bewitched, Bothered and Bewildered."

On March 18, 1950, when *Billboard* listed the "Nations' Top Ten Jukebox Tunes," it included every single version of each song that made it to a jukebox. So, on that date, the top four songs (in order and from the top) were "Music!

Music! Music!," which had a total of ten versions; "Rag Mop" with an astounding fourteen versions; "Chattanoogie Shoe Shine Boy" with ten versions; and even the very weirdly titled "I Said My Pajamas" had five versions.[30]

So, if there was a creativity desert in pop music, where could singers go for inspiration?

In 1950, the answer to that question was country & western.

The B-side to "Choo'n Gum" was "Honky Tonkin'," a song written and released by Hank Williams three years before.

This wasn't a good cut for Brewer. For one thing, Jack Pleis and his Dixieland All-Stars had no feel for the country song. Brewer shoots for the high notes on the accentuations and it's a little undisciplined.

As noted, the "Disk of the Week" column in the April 1, 1950, of *Cash Box* reviewed "Choo'n Gum." It also reviewed "Honky Tonkin'," saying it was almost as good as "Choo'n Gum," which wasn't saying much. The reviewer added, "The flip [B-side] features the chirp [female singer] in an old-fashioned shouting delivery, with a middle chorus of real low-down blues. Both ends [record sides] are blue-ribbon winners. Music ops [operators] should hop on the bandwagon—but pronto!"[31]

The difference between Hank Williams and the pop vocalists of the late 1940s and early 1950s was that he wrote his own songs, as did other singers in the genre. In 1952, when Roy Acuff introduced Hank on the *Grand Ole Opry*, he said of the singer that Hank was "a fellow that writes just as many songs, as most anybody in the country and sings them just as well when it comes to the country style of singing."

Ed Ward, in *Rock of Ages: The Rolling Stone History of Rock & Roll*, discussing the roots of rock 'n' roll music, noted, "white music was changing, too, although it's fruitless to look on the pop charts, which listed tuneful but insipid songs . . . for the evidence of rock 'n' roll birth. The folk [country] charts, however, were rife with change."[32]

Other music historians have adopted similar themes. Charlie Gillett, who wrote *The Sound: The Rise of Rock and Roll*, observed: "With country and western, when the majors [record companies] found that a substantial section of the potential popular music market was listening to the radio stations that were playing such music and was requesting from local record stores the records it heard, the companies responded by heavily promoting various songs performed in versions of country and western style."[33]

Most of the record companies were based on the East Coast or the West Coast and favored the sophisticated or urban sounds of jazz-pop, but there was a whole section of America that found the popular music stations weren't playing music that was all that enticing. In the South and Southwest, for example, where there was an affinity for music called "folk," "hillbilly," or, eventually, "country," once stations of this genre began to pop up and excite listeners, it was time to take a look at what was going on elsewhere in the country.

The first #1 hit of 1950 was "Rudolph, the Red-Nosed Reindeer," a holiday-novelty song by western singer Gene Autry, and this type of western-novelty song became one of the main approaches to the genre. "Chattanoogie Shoe Shine Boy" fits this category.

Another approach was pairing of country and pop singers such as Kay Starr and Tennessee Ernie Ford.

A handful of singers could actually bridge the two genres and the most successful of the lot was Frankie Laine, who made a career with these types of songs. His most famous tunes include "Mule Train" in 1949, "High Noon" in 1952, and in 1950, "The Cry of the Wild Goose."

At the start of the new decade, the most successful adaptations of the country genre were by the female crooners such as Kay Starr with "Bonaparte's Retreat" and Patti Page with "Tennessee Waltz."

In 1951, former big band singer Anita O'Day (Anita Belle Colton) took a soft-jazz swing at the "Tennessee Waltz." She intro'd the song by scatting against a delicate xylophone sound. This version became a moderate hit as well. Anita O'Day was not without a strong fan base. Beverly Warren, who sang with Ellie Greenwich in the girl group the Raindrops ("The Kind of Boy You Can't Forget," a Top Twenty hit in 1963) was big on Anita O'Day. "I had her albums," Warren said. "She had a real easy but sassy way about her. She was on the bill of one of the early Newport Jazz Festivals and knocked it out of the park. What a singer!"[34]

The irony of female singers taking on country songs is that the heavy romanticism of pop music at the start of 1950s, especially with the female singers, was sometimes put in contrast to the inherent assets of country music, which were more earthy lyrics without being risqué. The opening lines to "Honky Tonkin'" reads: "When you are sad and lonely and have no place to go / call me up, sweet baby, and bring along some dough," which was another way of saying, "young lady, if you are either lonely or horny, call me up and we'll party or more," which sounds normal by today's standards but was an unmentionable occurrence back in the day. In 1950, women didn't call men on the phone; women didn't ask men out; and women didn't suggest a hook-up. None of that was respectable.

Writer Gillett summed up the dichotomy this way: "The styles of female popular singers—Rosemary Clooney, Kitty Kallen, Doris Day—were even more respectably pleasant. The general tone of this style and the songs that belonged to it denied the physical nature of sexual relationships and expressed trite emotions about simple events with almost no reference to any shared experiences. But the country singers, although in overall effect often even more sentimental, brought in a wider range of experience in their songs, and a slightly different vocabulary. The country singers, in however small a way, were indication that there were alternatives to the standard popular-music product."

The male crooners finally came on board the following year. In 1950, Hank Williams boasted a #1 record on the country charts with "Cold, Cold Heart." Mitch Miller, Columbia Records A&R executive (Artists & Repertoire, who decided which songs a musician records), quickly pushed its own crooner Tony Bennett into the studios with an orchestra under the stewardship of Percy Faith to record a pop version. A listener would know from the start that this was not a Hank Williams kind of "Cold, Cold Heart." The opening violins were a big hint. Another clue was the soft horns floating behind a trilling voice.

Released the following year, it went to #1 on the pop chart on November 3, 1951, and reigned supreme for seven weeks.

"A young sounding Tony Bennett croons over light orchestration on his recording, making 'Cold, Cold Heart' sound like an old Neapolitan or Sicilian ballad that was translated into colloquial English," sums up Allmusic's Bill Janovitz. "That a young Italian singing waiter . . . could find common ground with a country singer . . . is a testament to Williams' skill as a writer and to Bennett's imagination and artist's ear."[35]

Mash-ups worked.

Here's how important country was to the pop charts in 1951: A pop version of a country song held the #1 slot for over a quarter of the year. Patti Page's "Tennessee Waltz" hit the market at the very end of 1950, but its real penetration was at the start of the following year, where it was the #1 record for eight weeks. By the way, in 1951 "Tennessee Waltz" was the #1 play on jukeboxes for twelve straight weeks.

CHAPTER TWO

COME ON-A MY HOUSE (1951)

TERESA BREWER—BILL MONAHAN—DINAH SHORE— LES PAUL—ROSEMARY CLOONEY—WILLIAM SAROYAN AND ROSS BAGDASARIAN—MITCH MILLER

The word "teenager" was created in the 1950s due to the tremendous population of those in this age category and because teenagers started gaining more independence and freedoms. Teenagers were able to buy more things like food, clothes and music because of an increase in spending money, as well as using cars more often than before, increasing freedom. Teenagers were also becoming more independent in the type of music they preferred to listen to, no more listening to what their parents liked, teens flocked to the new music of the decade.[1]

That's a recent commentary on the Internet explaining the derivation of the term "teenager." It sounds good, but it's not accurate. The word "teens" referring to the years between thirteen and nineteen had been in use since the 1600s. Derivatives of the word such as "teenager" began to be used in the 1930s and 1940s, according to the Oxford English Dictionary. However, that may not be right either, as someone recently discovered the word in a book published in 1922.

The word "teenager" really took on cachet in 1950s, not only because there were so many of them but because their behavior was perceived as different from prior generations. They were less reverential, less obedient, and certainly less interested in what their parents thought they should be pursuing, especially when it came to music, which was due to a number of factors: a flood of new radio stations since the World War II years; the importance of the deejay who played recorded music; new technologies such as better phonographs, hi-fis, and portable radios; and accessibility to a wider range of music genres.

Teresa Brewer arrived at the moment in time when youth turned to youth. Yet she was, perhaps, the wrong choice of singer to be the idol of American teenagers. Although still in her teen years, she made the decision to be an adult before those years were over. By the time she recorded "Music! Music! Music!" she was already married and as the song burst across the airwaves, she was many months pregnant with her first child. She was years into her career as an entertainer in adult nightspots. What she wasn't doing was hanging out at soda fountains, ice skating rinks, drive-in movies, or making out with boyfriends in basement dance parties or the backseats of cars. She wasn't rebelling against teachers and her high school curriculum such as those unhappy boys did in "Blackboard Jungle," she didn't ride motorcycles like Marlon Brando in "The Wild One," and she didn't drag race like the kids in "Rebel Without a Cause." In fact, after the birth of her first child, staying home with her husband and daughter was perfectly okay with her.

A lost childhood and all those years traveling away from her family when she was just of elementary school age left her yearning for a kind of normalcy she hadn't known. What she wanted was a family life. Technically, Teresa Brewer may have still been a teenager in 1950, but she was an old soul. Years later she would have a big hit with the song "A Sweet Old Fashioned Girl," which tidily summed her up at the beginning of the 1950s.

The entertainment rags had been kind to her at the start, talking around her pregnancy. A column in the May 6, 1950, issue of *Billboard* briefly commented, "Teresa Brewer, London's 'Music! Music!' thrush, has canceled all personal appearances until September," thus completely avoiding the fact she was looking quite large.[2]

Even *Billboard* had to catch up when things were obvious. On September 16, 1950, the magazine reported, "London [Records] thrush Teresa Brewer (Mrs. Bill Monahan) gave birth to a girl September 4 at the Westchester [New York] Square Hospital . . ."[3]

As late as 1956, there was still confusion as to who Teresa Brewer was and who was her audience. Writer Dan Jerome of *TV Star Parade* magazine began a story about her this way: "Her teen-age fans think of her a 'girl friend' and older women feel she's their own daughter. Girls think she's cute. Little boys think of her as an older sister and are shocked when they discover she has a six-year-old daughter."[4]

It was a long leap of conviction for Brewer and family from her days with Major Bowes to becoming a recording sensation. In reality, Brewer's mother retired her from show business when she was at the ripe old age of twelve. Brewer settled down to school life back home in Toledo, but she continued to act in school plays and perform on local radio stations, including a feature spot on *The Pick and Pat Show*, and eventually starring on her own local program billed as "Toledo's Miss Talent." At age sixteen in January 1948, Teresa, along three other Toledo entertainers, won a local competition and were flown to Manhattan to appear on the Adams Hat *Stairway to the Stars* talent show with Eddie Dowling. She stayed in New York, winning more accolades and awards on such shows as *The Big Break* and Mutual's *Talent Jackpot*. Among her winnings at *Stairway to the Stars* was a week's stint at the famous Latin Quarter nightclub in New York to work with Ted Lewis, who had been one of the most popular big band leaders in the 1920s. He even had a signature phrase, "Is everybody happy?" Swing jazz had become passé, but he kept a small orchestra together and was the under-card and a kind of special events emcee at the Latin Quarter.[5]

Brewer came to New York chaperoned as always by her Aunt Mary. Apparently, there was enough cachet attached to being at the Latin Quarter, even as a teenage award winner, that she was able to pick up other gigs in New York, including singing at a club called the Sawdust Trail, which one magazine at the time called "one of the less elegant spots off Times Square." This was the kind of club that would put a loudspeaker on the sidewalk outside the front entryway hoping people passing by would be intrigued enough by the music to come in for a drink or two. According to Brewer legend, this ploy worked because a fellow named Ritchie Lisella strolled by, heard what *Look* magazine called Brewer's "educated hiccup and nasal twang," and walked in. Anyone who had an interest in music would have done the same because Brewer had a very distinctive voice and when she sang she sounded like no one else. Writers went in all directions when trying to describe her sound; her voice was low, her voice was high ranged, her voice was twangy, her voice was brassy, and so on.[6]

Lisella was certainly intrigued. He had been looking to break into the music business as a talent scout or agent and he really liked her distinctive sound. He called her over. They talked but nothing came of it because Brewer had been using another agent at the time, which was how she got the gig at the Sawdust Trail.

It was always a struggle to make it in New York and work was becoming less steady the longer she was away from her Latin Quarter win. Time was running out for her and she knew it. A few weeks after the Sawdust Trail gig, she had been visiting with songwriters in the Brill Building when she bumped into Ritchie Lisella again. It turns out Teresa Brewer was giving up and planning to head back to Toledo. Personally, Ritchie really liked the pleasant, convivial Brewer; professionally, he enjoyed her sound and was confident he could put her across, thinking more in the line of a record contract than any more second-rate club venues. He asked Brewer and her aunt to give him two weeks and as an added incentive he would stake her during that period of time. He was as good as his ambition, getting her a contract with London Records.

Decca Records, a British musical enterprise, established its US label in the mid-1930s, only to sever the two companies as World War II approached. With the war over, the British Decca established a new North American subsidiary called London Records in 1947 with its headquarters in New York.[7] The new label hadn't quite gotten established yet when Richie Lisella came to it with a new talent. It bit and Teresa Brewer signed with London, which quickly got her into the studio to record three records, six tracks. These were 78s and the first pressing on the blue London label read "A New Star is Born." Below the wording continued: "Teresa Brewer sings 'When the Train Came In' by songwriters Pleis-Young" and further down on the label, "accompanied by Jack Pleis and his orchestra." Pleis was one of London's A&R men and he brought in the Dixieland All-Stars to back up Brewer. The B-side was "A Man Wrote a Song."

The second recording was "Copper Canyon," a duet with a singer named Bobby Wayne that was the title song of a 1950 western movie starring Ray Milland and Hedy Lamarr. The B-side of the record was "Way Back Home," which was a minor hit that same year for Bing Crosby and Fred Waring & His Pennsylvanians. The oddity of the B-side was that it was originally recorded in 1935 by the Boswell Sisters, America's first girl group to score a series of hit records and attain a kind of early twentieth-century pop stardom.

"Copper Canyon" was, indeed, a lighthearted, novelty western tune, sung with infectious joy by a young Teresa. As Bobby Wayne sang, "down in Copper Canyon people are mighty gay," to which Teresa responded, "Look at her, look at him, look at Sally and Slim / why they're real glad they came / and down in Copper Canyon they all feel the same."

This record was a tiny breakthrough for Brewer. It didn't chart in the United States, but it got good airplay north of the border, becoming a Top Twenty-Five record in Canada.

The third recording was "I Beeped When I Shoulda Bopped" with "Ol' Man Mose" on the B-side. The fourth recording was the one that made Teresa Brewer a star, "Music! Music! Music!" with "Copenhagen" on the B-side.

It has been reported that Brewer was sixteen when she auditioned for the *Stairway to the Stars* show, but she probably didn't come to New York immediately. She turned seventeen on May 7, 1948, so she was "underage" when her agent got her the gigs performing in nightclubs. In October 1948, according to Brewer, she was working at the Latin Quarter when she spotted a tall, handsome young man in the audience. As Brewer told a reporter. "I thought he was the older brother of my current boyfriend. He came every night to see the show, and he finally came backstage and was introduced to me by a mutual friend." His name was Bill Monahan, and he walked her home that night.

Bill Monahan was four years older than Brewer. He worked with his brother in a road construction business (in other interviews it is a building contracting business) located in the Bronx. Brewer told a couple of slightly different stories as to how the romance came on. In 1953, she informed a *TV Show* reporter, "I wasn't impressed. He was just a big blond guy in a brown suit," but she warmed up to the idea of dating him when he suggested they go up to his mother's for Sunday dinner. Two years later, in an in-depth interview for *TV Star Parade*, she told this lengthy tale: "He saw me home every night. We'd walk . . . or we'd stop for coffee. By the time the first month was up, he had given me a ring. When I was booked into a small New York club, the Sawdust Trail, Bill kept coming around every night. I usually didn't finish working until 3 a.m. and Bill insisted on walking me home . . . Finally Bill said, 'We'd better get married if I'm ever going to get some sleep.'"[8]

Brewer turned eighteen in May 1949 and they were married in November of that year. They honeymooned with her family in Toledo and then came back to live with Bill's parents in the Bronx. When first child Kathleen came along they moved into a small house in suburban Scarsdale, just north of the Bronx.[9]

According to Bill Munroe, the couple was madly in love and when she had to go on the road, he always went with her. They were inseparable. The media appeared quite stunned that the diminutive singer (she always looked younger than she was) was married and had children, and early stories always seemed to focus on her family and how grounded she and Bill were. Although these types of stories were standard fare at the time, the entertainment magazines just could not drop the whole happy family storyline no matter how many years on Teresa remained a star performer and no longer a youngster.

In 1962, on his twentieth birthday, Teresa Brewer fan Bill Munroe traveled to a small coastal town north of Boston for the Salisbury Beach Frolics, which brought in popular acts throughout the summer. Everyone from Patti Page to Liberace to the Kingston Trio performed that summer, but Munroe wanted to see Teresa Brewer. He was going to meet two friends and arrived early, so to kill time he strolled along the seashore outside the game arcade. Standing in front of him was a man he recognized from magazine photos, Bill Monahan, who was also killing time before his wife's show. Not being very shy, Munroe walked up to Monahan and introduced himself. Munroe told him he had come down from Maine to see the show and Monahan invited him into the Salisbury Beach Frolics bar for a drink. Munroe was underage and since no one inquired he ordered a beer. When his friends arrived, Monahan bought them a beer as well. After a while, Monahan excused himself as he had to go help Brewer. Munroe and his two buddies went into the main showroom, where they had reservations, and much to their surprise, they were moved to the front row. Monahan had arranged it. Said Munroe, "He was a very nice guy."[10]

The photos of Bill Monahan in those early years of marriage when Brewer was a new, bright luminary in the celestial void, shows a thin, handsome young man, almost always in a sports jacket of some kind. He is never completely in style, but not out of style either. Whether sporting a formal shirt with tie or something more leisurely underneath the jacket, he never completely emerges from under his 1950s blue collar upbringing as he generally wears white or light argyle socks with formal black shoes. Brewer had a wide, inviting smile, while Bill mostly tried to look serious because when he attempted a smile for the camera it always looked strained.

For a while in the early to mid-1950s, Brewer wore her hair in the popular bob cut, a style made popular by June Allyson in the movies. Other singers of the time, including Rosemary Clooney and Gisele MacKenzie, also adopted the bob.

A writer described her this way in 1953: "Her eyes are large and brown and they slant up at the corners. They're her most arresting feature. . . . She highlights her lashes with a little mascara. A light pancake and lipstick complete her make-up. No nail polish, no eye shadow, no streaks in her hair, no henna . . ."

In what is a timeless showbiz story, when an average Joe marries a successful female entertainer, whether she is an actress or singer, he tends to gate-crash her career. The first step happens when average Joe, no matter what business he was in before, decides he could manage his wife's career better than a professional manager. It was no different in Brewer's marriage. An article in *TV Show* magazine highlighting her domesticity, headlined the whole spread "Just Plain Bill's," the wording sitting above a picture of their six-room, two story cottage in Scarsdale, as plain-looking a structure as you could find in any suburb in America at the time. The story concludes with this note, "Bill doubles as her road manager."[11] According to another magazine, he officially became her manager in 1952.[12]

That's the general story. However, in a 1956 photo-heavy article about Teresa Brewer, one of the most telling shots is a picture of Brewer sitting next to Ritchie Lisella with a serious looking Bill Monahan standing, but leaning over her shoulder looking down at the paper she is holding. The caption read: "Ritchi LiSella [sic], Teresa's manager, discusses future bookings with his cute client and her handsome husband Bill Monahan." Ritchie Lisella discovered her, became her manager, and unless he took a long vacation, seven years into her career he was still her manager. However, the masquerade that Bill Monahan was her actual manager continued. *TV-Radio Mirror*, in a September 1959 story about Brewer titled "She Follows Her Heart Home," showed a picture of Bill intently scrutinizing Teresa in a new dress. The fawning cutline read: "Teresa's satin gown with hand-beaded flowers is intended for club dates, but she gets a bigger kick out of dressing up for special audience-of-one—Bill Monahan, who admires its beauty even more as her husband than as her manager." Inside the article runs this additional comment: "Married to Bill Monahan, who has been her manager since 1952."[13]

According to press reports, Bill established a music publishing business, which made sense if Teresa wanted to retain the rights to her songs. *Compact: The Young People's Digest*, in its December 1956 cover story on Brewer, wrote, "Teresa, whose husband now publishes her songs . . ."[14]

That same year, a magazine called *Songs That Will Live Forever* spotlighted Brewer. The author wrote: "Teresa's husband, Bill Monahan, is mainly a building contractor; but he is also a music publisher—his two companies have published some of the songs that Teresa has made famous." However, since most of Brewer's songs came from other songwriters, and if she didn't get additional songwriting credit, there was a limited amount of Teresa Brewer songs that would fall into Monahan's "two companies."

Even with all that effort to prop up Bill in her life and the wonderfully schmaltzy view of Teresa the homemaker, subtle cracks began to show.

In one of those take-it-or-leave-it-as-is comments, in a 1953 magazine article Brewer says of her husband, "Actually Bill's sort of stage-struck. He likes to think he's a red-hot singer, but really he can't sing a note . . . but he loves the business."[15]

Why not? Which option was more fun, paving roads in the Bronx or meeting celebrities while traveling America with his wife?

An interview with Brewer around the time of their tenth anniversary made note that Bill was in the construction business until he gave it up to handle Teresa's affairs and be free to go with her wherever her work took her. "I wouldn't travel without him . . . Bill looks after everything for me," she said.

And that's the other issue of being married to a celebrity. Bill decided to take on the job as "road manager" and travel companion, which essentially meant he would do for Teresa what her Aunt Mary used to do for her when she was young. For someone as notoriously "nice" as Teresa Brewer, in the role of performer, celebrity, star, perhaps even diva, she would have a lot of demands: "I need water" or "my hem is loose, can you get some pins," or "there's a problem with lighting, can you talk to so-and-so" or "can you call home for me." There is no equality when married to a star. That's even more apparent in social situations. Other stars, reporters, associates, only would want to talk to Teresa. They had no interest in chatting will Bill Monahan. If Teresa brought him around, hung lovingly on his arm, introduced him to everyone with great excitement, in the end he would still mostly be ignored.[16]

There was always an undercurrent of differences between the star and her husband. For one thing, the income disparity was huge. A 1956 article in *Look* reported she did six weeks of touring and earned $200,000; worked six television appearances that netted her $30,000; had four weeks' work in a nightclub that garnered $50,000; and one week of work recording brought in another $120,000. Bill's contribution: nil, unless he took a salary as his wife's road manager, but there's no record of that happening.[17]

Secondly, to be a star didn't come cheap. In the mid-1950s, Brewer's clothing allowance was $700 a month, mostly for custom gowns for all her touring, nightclub, and television appearances.

In 1956, Bill acerbically quipped to a reporter, "Her hobby is shopping. She just can't stop buying stuff." One year later, he continued on this theme, telling another writer that Teresa's extravagance is clothes while "I go to the Salvation Army."[18]

By that time, Bill and Teresa had four girls (Kathleen, Susan, Megan, and Michelle) and were living in a ten-room house on two acres in New Rochelle, New York.

Someone once said of Teresa Brewer that after "Music! Music! Music!," she had a Top Ten record every year through the advent of rock 'n' roll. That's not quite accurate. From 1950 through 1957, she boasted a Top Twenty record every year except 1951. It wasn't for lack of trying on the part of London Records in 1951, which tossed into the market every Teresa Brewer recording it had except the kitchen sink—and if there had been a song about kitchen sinks, London would have recorded that as well. One of Brewer's releases, "If You Don't Marry Me," was a #3 record in the United Kingdom, but did not chart in the United States. "Longing for You" scored with deejays, becoming Teresa's only hit record in 1951, climbing as high #23 on the chart.

The weakness of Teresa's recording career one year after "Music! Music! Music!" can't be fully attributed to London Records' lack of understanding of the American market. The year 1951 was problematic for the recording industry due to a number of sublimated factors. First, after a boom time for female singers in 1950, a new chasm developed, creating a large distance between the success, or popularity, of male and female singers.

In 1951, the *Billboard* chart for the top thirty songs of the year showed only three female singers as a solo act in the listing: Rosemary Clooney with the highest rated song "Come On-A My House," the #4 best-seller; Dinah Shore scored with "Sweet Violets" at #18; and the indefatigable Patti Page boasted three best-sellers, the fabulous "Tennessee Waltz," which began the new year as the #1 song, and also "Mockin' Bird Hill" at #14 and "Would I Love You (Love You, Love You)" at #26. The odd note about Page's #14 song was that at #13 was also "Mockin' Bird Hill" but by Les Paul and Mary Ford. The husband-and-wife duo's biggest hit that year was "How High the Moon" at #3.

Also scoring with a mixed-gender presentation were Debbie Reynolds and Carleton Carpenter with "Aba Daba Honeymoon," which was featured in the 1950 film *Two Weeks with Love*, and the Fontane Sisters teamed with Perry Como for "You're Just in Love," a #27 best-seller.

Just a note about Dinah Shore (Fannye Rose Shore). She was an old hand at show business by 1951. Thirty-five years of age at the time, Shore had been a star since 1940, when she scored with her first hit "Time to Smile." She married actor George Montgomery and entertained the troops during World War II. Shore appeared in movies, continued to have hit records such as "Buttons and Bows" in 1949, and hosted a radio show, the latter proving to be a good training ground, because with the rise of television, Shore began hosting her own television show in 1956.

The veteran Dinah Shore and the still teenaged Teresa Brewer ended up going head to head in 1951. That year, *Cash Box*, in its regular column "Record Review," which looked at new releases and hoped to find a winner, picked the same song by Dinah Shore in a duet with Tony Martin and Teresa Brewer teaming up with Snooky Lanson. In the competition, *Cash Box* chose the Dinah Shore/Tony Martin song "A Penny a Kiss" for its featured "Disk of the Week." The reviewer wrote: "A terrifically appealing new novelty serves to unite Dinah Shore and Tony Martin on records and their first disk together turns out to be a winning one. Throughout the number there's the sound of coins dropping in a jug and ops [juke box operators] who get going with this one are gonna hear a lot of coins dropping themselves—in their machines. The tune has a wonderfully cute set of lyrics and a simple air that makes its possibilities great . . . this one is bound to be big."[19]

The Teresa Brewer/Snooky Lanson version was cut with a different title, "A Penny a Kiss—A Penny a Hug." Despite his juvenile name, Snooky (Roy Landman) was not a teenager. He was thirty-six years old but looked young enough to match up with Teresa and to cohost the NBC television show *Your Hit Parade*, which was geared to teenage viewers. A reviewer liked this cut as well, writing: "A winning novelty done in duet style is offered on the upper level [A-side] by Teresa Brewer and Snooky Lanson. Accompanied by Jack Pleis and the orchestra, the pair makes this one sound real cute." Actually, the reviewer preferred the B-side, a song called "Hello," adding, "the bottom half [B-side] is a very happy souding [sic] novelty that will draw an awful lot of nickels into the boxes . . . this is definitely one to get with."

Neither the A-side nor the B-side of the Brewer/Lanson record charted. The Shore/Martin version was a Top Ten record. Shore's label released an astounding seventeen singles by her in 1951, five of which charted.

The Playback.fm chart of the top ninety-nine records of 1951 counts only Rosemary Clooney as the lone single female act in the top twenty; then at #21, #22, and #23, Dinah Shore with "Sweet Violets," Teresa Brewer with "Longing for You," and Anita O'Day with her version of "Tennessee Waltz."

Things looked so dire for female singers in 1951 that the May 5, 1951, issue of *Cash Box* ran a long exposé with a headline in large-size, crimson-colored type screaming "What's Happened to the Girl Singers?"

This is the way it began: "Where are those smash records from Kay Starr, Doris Day, Dinah Shore, Fran Warren, Jo Stafford, Margaret Whiting, Peggy Lee, Teresa Brewer and all the others? Except for Patti Page, the girls seem to have taken a back seat in the pop record picture."

Then the article posed these rhetorical questions: "Is it that the proper material just isn't being written for them? Are the A&R departments funneling all the likely tunes to the male singers? Are the girls failing to receive the proper concentrated promotion from the diskeries [record companies]?" The answers, according to the article, were yes, yes, and yes. Going into depth on the subject of "promotions," the article, after a study of record company ads, confirmed that since the beginning of the year, the record companies had been pushing male singers as "opposed to the girls" and some ads listing record firms' top disks didn't have even one by a female singer.[20]

Interestingly, the article pointed out that there were millions of "boys" in the military throughout the country who in spare moments were hungry for entertainment. The nearest form of musical diversion was the jukebox located in all sorts of bars and dance halls. These "boys" wanted to hear music whenever they could, the article stressed, "and what's more they wanted to hear female singers."

Bravely going where no publication had gone before, the article concluded: "The important thing is that there's a market for our great girl singers. And we have gone through a drought long enough. Let's get them to work turning out those best sellers."

Whether it was because there was so little space for female singers or that the songwriters had run dry, 1951 was a dreadful year for pop music. Two African American singers, Nat King Cole with "Too Young" and Billy Eckstine with "I Apologize," managed to crash the pop charts, but the male singers were stuck in a post-swing, overly dramatic, if not soap opera, screech of ballad-mongering. It was a big year for Tony Bennett, but his songs weren't memorable, and the same can be said for the milquetoast singers Perry Como, Mario Lanza, Vaughn Monroe, Tony Martin, and even in this grim year, Frankie Laine.

Scanning the top records of the year, from this graduating class of pop songs, there is only one classic to be had: "How High the Moon," by the married couple of guitarist Les Paul and singer Mary Ford. The song topped the pop record chart for nine weeks in 1951; it also went to #1 on the R&B chart, which no white act had ever done before.

Besides just being one helluva a good song, it also highlighted technological advances pioneered by Paul. He created what he called "sound on sound." Basically it was a layered, overdubbed recording that highlighted not only Les's guitar prowess but also the true capabilities of multi-tracking, which revolutionized the recording of music. As writer Richard Buskin wrote for soundonsound.com, the song was "a multi-layered, souped-up recording that highlighted not only the jazz guitarist's quick-fingered virtuosity, but also, thanks to his technological and innovative brilliance with recording, the creative possibilities that lay beyond merely capturing a straightforward live performance."[21]

"How High the Moon" was a true outlier in an atrocious year for pop music. So, if there was a creativity drought in pop, where could performers turn for their next great song? As noted, country & western was one option, but there was even more fertile ground to be found somewhere else—on the rhythm & blues chart, which was blossoming like a field of sunflowers in the spring.

After World War II, two structural-cultural changes affected the rising tide of rhythm & blues music in the United States. In some regards these were what one might call mercantile factors: the rise of independent record producers and rhythm & blues programming on radio stations ended up being related. As author Philip H. Ennis wrote, "the appearance and rapid growth of the independent record labels after 1945 paralleled the growth of black-oriented stations. Both were crucial for the development of rhythm & blues."[22]

With the major recording companies ignoring not only country & western but also rhythm & blues, entrepreneurial efforts to record the latter sprung up all over the country, because it was a relatively easy operation once advances in recording technology made the business cheaper. One person could find the local talent, make recordings, promote to radio stations within a moderate geography, and do well enough to make another record. Again, the expenses were minimal; it could cost $1,000 to record and press 500 copies of a record. Hundreds of independents proliferated, but because not all records sold, most of these labels quickly faded, and less than 100 were left by 1950. Some of the strongest specialized in R&B. From 1942 through 1952, about thirty independent record companies were established mostly to record African American singers and musicians. Almost all these independents were in key markets such as New York, Los Angeles, or Chicago. Even Sun Records in Memphis, which first recorded Elvis Presley, Jerry Lee Lewis, Johnny Cash, and Carl Perkins, started out recording Black musicians.[23]

Of *Billboard*'s fifty best-selling R&B records between 1949 and 1953, less than 10 percent were from major labels.

All these rhythm & blues records needed to be played somewhere, and by the late 1940s, the country experienced a growth in programming time for R&B and radio stations dedicated to that sound. In 1948, John Pepper and Burt Ferguson, two white owners of WDIA, a Memphis radio station, decided to program entirely for the city's African American population, thus becoming the nation's first all-Black radio station. WDIA, with a powerful transmitter, claimed its spread went far, far beyond Memphis and reached "1.2 million Negroes," which would have been 10 percent of Black America at that time. In the early 1950s, other stations made similar proclamations. WOKJ of Jackson, Mississippi, declared it was "the only way to the 107,000 Negroes" of that community, or WXLW in St. Louis proclaimed it was "serving and selling 328,000 Negroes in the St. Louis area since 1947."

Rhythm & blues covered a wide spectrum of music, from swing to country-novelty, to jump-blues combos, to pre-rock 'n' roll rhythms, to flashy country guitar-gods, to wild saxophone-laced blues, to the new vocal-harmony sound that would become doo-wop.

In 1942, *Billboard* created its first rhythm & blues chart, called the "Harlem Hit Parade" because it was initially based on the sales returns from six record stores in Harlem, New York. In 1945, the magazine revised the chart to also cover jukebox plays and called it Race Records, but "race" was a controversial adjective, so in 1949 the chart was renamed Rhythm & Blues.

The lackluster pop songs in 1951 were smothered by over-orchestrations as if each song was a prelude to a motion picture of great consequence. These were perfect times for guys like Mario Lanza, who craved songs that were structured and sounded like mini-operas. His big hit of 1951, "Be My Love," after the swooping violins, began this way: "Be my love, for no one else can end this yearning / the need that you and you alone create." That is why songs such as "How High the Moon" stood out so dramatically.

Most of the other real classic and enduring recordings of 1951 could be found on the R&B charts. It would be very hard to find a fan of "Be My Love" today, but there are still millions of listeners who get a thrill from The Dominoes' ribald novelty-blues hit "Sixty Minute Man," where the introductory lyric is all sexual performance: "Look here girls I'm telling you now, they call me Lovin' Dan / I rock 'em, roll 'em all night long, I'm a sixty-minute man."

Probably the most important song of the year wasn't even "How High the Moon" but Jackie Brentson's (actually Ike Turner and his Kings of Rhythm) "Rocket 88," which has often been called the first rock 'n' roll record.

For something smoother, Tommy Edwards unleashed his wonderful "It's All in the Game"; Amos Milburn carried the traditional blues-booze song into 1950s with "Bad, Bad Whiskey"; and finally, one of the early, great doo-wopizations of an American classic, "The Glory of Love" by the Five Keys, with the unforgettable refrain: "You've got to give a little, take a little, and let your poor heart break a little / That's the story of, that's the glory of love."

Sadly, the R&B charts that year treated the ladies even worse than did the pop charts. No woman singer as a solo act made the Top Twenty, and only Ella Fitzgerald ("Smooth Sailing," #22), Dinah Washington ("Cold, Cold Heart," #33), and Ruth Brown ("I'll Wait for You," #35) were in the Top Forty.

The best song of 1951 may not be eternal in terms of listener appreciation or even importance as were a handful of ditties that year, but in a dour year for pop tunes it was like a January thaw in a long, hard winter—and it belonged to a song-belle, Rosemary Clooney. The standout record for 1951 was the unlikely hit "Come On-A My House."

Yes, its origination was as another novelty number, but Clooney transformed it into a sexy zinger of a tune. Two years on, in the movie *The Stars Are Singing*, her film character is first given a copy of the lyrics to sing and she asks, "how do you want me to do this? What kind of tempo?" and she is told "be happy, smile, it's up-tune. The last girl in here made it sound like a funeral march." The dubious Clooney character swings it. Afterward, she tells the bandleader, "this isn't for me . . . it [the song] won't sell a record." "Come On-A My House" sold more than a million copies. It reached #1 on the *Billboard* chart on July 28 and stayed there for six weeks throughout the summer until bounced by Tony Bennett and "Because of You" on September 28.

The song originated in the minds of two antithetical sources, William Saroyan and Ross Bagdasarian. Saroyan was well known at the time as an author and playwright, winning a Pulitzer Prize for his 1939 drama *The Time of Your Life*. He also notched an Academy Award for writing *The Human Comedy*, which was not comedic but sentimental. Saroyan's countenance and literary output was the stuff of hopefulness, not necessarily frivolity. His songwriting partner was his cousin Ross Bagdasarian, a waggish, somewhat zany character who would become well known at the end of the decade for creating two wildly successful novelty songs, "Witch Doctor" and "The Chipmunk Song," both of which spent weeks in the #1 slot. If you were ten years old in 1958, even if you couldn't do your multiplication tables, you could remember "oo-ee, oo-ah-ah, ting-tang, walla-walla bing-bang," the earworm chorus of the song that was credited to Bagdasarian's alter ego, David Seville.

The two men of Armenian descent were driving across the Southwest and to pass the time wrote "Come On-A My House," which was based on an Armenian folk song. The concept poked fun at the fractured lingo of Armenian American immigrants and the old custom of spreading an array of goodies on the table when guests arrived. The song was included in the Saroyan/Bagdasarian Off-Broadway play *The Son*.

The first to record the song was Kay Armen (Armenuhi Manoogian), an Armenian American singer who had a moderately successful career as a singer and radio host. It went unnoticed by everyone, everywhere except for one very important person—Mitch Miller, who was then head of A&R at Columbia, one of the major record producers in the country. According to Bagdasarian, the song was rejected by everyone for being too ethnic. The problem was the crude parody of speech patterns, which made some people uncomfortable.

For example, the title doesn't read "Come on over to my house," it's "Come On-A My House." Cultural rights or wrongs were no problem for Miller, who, Bagdasarian said, "liked the song."

The witty Clooney recalled the song: "William Saroyan and songwriter Ross Bagdasarian . . . cooked it up on a cross-country drive, supposedly inspired by the bounty and variety of the American landscape they were traveling through; in my opinion they'd had a little too much time on their hands."

Clooney admitted she had no appreciation for the song's slightly tongue-in-cheek, self-lampooning edge and in her opinion the lyric ranged from incoherent to just plain silly. "The tune sounded more like a drunken chant than an historic folk art form, and I hated the gimmicky arrangement," she wrote in her memoir. The song, produced by Miller, had a tinny, jazzed-up harpsichord attempting a kind of calypso rhythm.

Clooney was trying for a more sophisticated image and wanted to sing the lame, lovestruck themed tunes popular at the time, especially with male singers. "I was afraid once people heard it, they wouldn't take me seriously as a singer capable of more than 'I'm gonna give-a you candy.' Maybe I took myself a little too seriously then, I wanted to sing death-defying love songs . . . not weird novelty fluff."

Mitch Miller thought otherwise. Something sensual in the verbiage appealed to him and he envisioned a young and pretty Rosemary Clooney singing it. She couldn't get behind the song at all and flatly told him it was not for her.

Young women singers in the 1950s did not write their own songs and mostly were not responsible for the tunes they sang; the A&R men were. If they became more successful, subsequent contracts could include provisions for the singer to choose X amount of songs they wanted to sing.

Miller was very successful with young male singers at the time—guys like Tony Bennett, Johnnie Ray, and Guy Mitchell—because his conservative tastes matched their style of music. He was also good with bandleaders like Percy Faith and Ray Conniff, because he was one at heart and by profession. However, he had no idea what to with a strong talent such as Frank Sinatra, whose career nosedived under Miller's direction. Columbia boasted a number of female singers under contract, and for them Miller steered a lot of country-crossover songs in their direction, such as Hank Williams's "Jambalaya" for Jo Stafford. With the coming of rock 'n' roll in the mid-1950s, he moved in another direction entirely, producing a steady stream of saccharine, if not outright corny, *Sing Along with Mitch* albums.

In 1951, Miller was the management and he wielded a big baton. Young Rosemary Clooney was labor. She said no to his suggestion that she sing this novelty song. Miller said yes and they got into a roaring argument, which was pretty brave of her considering she was making just $50 a recording session. In the end management won out, as Clooney recalled Miller simply said to her: "Know what I think? I think you'll show up because otherwise you will be fired."

Clooney had two hurdles to overcome. The first was the cheesy harpsichord that Miller was determined to use in the orchestration. Miller didn't have a harpsichord in house, so he rented one from the Juilliard School and brought in someone to play it, an aspiring comedian, Stan Freeman. Clooney went straight to Freeman and asked him how he was going to play it and the response was "like a piano," which was something Clooney could understand even though the instrument had two keyboards and sounded like an organ.

Secondly, she couldn't find the proper tone for the silly lyrics. After the fourth take in the recording studio, Miller told the band to take a break. He knew what the problem was because there was a reason he chose Rosemary Clooney for this song. As she recalled, Miller put his arm around her shoulders and said, "Look at this way. You are asking this boy over to your house because you are going to marry him."[24]

Clooney, like many other female singers at the time, had been in the show business swirl since she was a child. Showbiz people had their own set of rules when it came to the opposite sex, which was that there really were no rules. Whether, as Teresa Brewer said, she had "boyfriends" before Bill Monahan, or were more frank about it like Rosemary Clooney, who admitted she had "affairs" before her marriage to actor José Ferrer in 1953, these women, despite the nice girl image of their public persona, were sexually experienced and understood male-female relations. When Miller said to her, "Think of the song this way. You are asking this boy over to your house because you are going to marry him" what he actually implied was more like "You are inviting some guy over to your house because you want to screw his brains out."

That made all the difference in the song, because Clooney gives every line a nuance, and every phrase sounds like an enticement. What was a clumsy novelty song became something very provocative. It was, in its own way, a very progressive song, and more importantly, it offered an aggressive message for women at the time it was recorded. Pop music as sung by the ladies in 1951 could be all about romance, but it could never, ever be about sex. If, on the other hand, you were smart enough to hide the sexuality in a novelty song, well, good for you.

The song begins with this line, "Come on-a my house, my house, I'm gonna give you candy," which as a novelty song means nothing more than here, have some candy, but as sung by a woman looking to reel in a guy, the word "candy" can mean anything in your imagination. And the song ends with her singing, "Come on-a my house, my house, I'm gonna give you everything, everything, everything." Once the listener is keyed into the sexuality of the song, the ending was the cherry on the cake, so to speak.

Rosemary Clooney had nailed the song and Mitch Miller knew what he had. After the fifth and final take, as Clooney recalled, Miller jumped up on a chair, flung his arms out wide and trumpeted, "I'll get them to ship a hundred thousand of these in three days." That was June 6, 1951.

By the end of July, *Billboard* reported "Come On-A My House" was the third most-played song on jukeboxes, one ahead of a Guy Mitchell/Mitch Miller composition, "My Truly, Truly Fair," which was the kind of song Miller really loved, something that you could envision on the big screen being sung by twenty singers and dancers in a big production number. Other than "My Truly, Truly Fair," for 1951 July was a competitive moment. The #1 song was Nat King Cole's "Too Young," which would end up as the #1 best-seller for the year. At #2 was "Jezebel" by Frankie Laine, and at #5 was "How High the Moon," already seventeen weeks on the chart.[25]

By the first week in August, *Billboard* reported "Come On-A My House" was the #1 song for two weeks in row as the most played tune by radio disk jockeys. That week it was also the most played song on US jukeboxes. At #16 that week was Kay Starr's version of the same song. The pileup had begun, and not just for this record. Dinah Shore's "Sweet Violets" was the fifth most popular song played by disk jockeys. The twenty-first most popular song that week was also "Sweet Violets," by Jane Turzy. "Good Morning, Mr. Echo" by Margaret Whiting rolled in as the fourteenth most popular song. Meanwhile, at #26 was Georgia Gibbs's version of the same song.[26]

Rosemary Clooney was born in 1928 to Frances Guilfoyle Clooney and Andrew Clooney in the town of Maysville, Kentucky. Frances was nineteen, Andrew was eight years older and already had problems with alcohol. Her parents' marriage fell apart quickly, and she and her sister often were left with the Guilfoyle grandparents. Pill and alcohol abuse ran through the Guilfoyle family like an underground stream. Rosemary showed talent at a very early age and her Aunt Olivette, who was a singer, brought Rosemary on stage at the local Russell Theater when she was just three years old. Olivette would later overdose on pills.

In the 1940s, WLW in Cincinnati was one of the few radio stations in the country broadcasting at 500,000 watts, the legal limit at that time. On a good night, it could be heard in Calgary or even Argentina. Like many major stations at the time, music programming was very important and the station had its own full orchestra and jazz combo. One of the local girls who sang at the station was Doris von Kappelhoff, who left town and changed her name to Doris Day.

It was still common for radio stations to support the local community through open auditions, and Rosemary and young sister Betty arrived there in 1945 as the Clooney Sisters. After singing "Straighten Up and Fly Right," they were offered a steady gig at the station. As Clooney recalled, "I began singing for a living in April 1945. I was sixteen; Betty was thirteen. The Clooney Sisters were paid $20 a week. Apiece." That was good money at the time.

The sisters were also singing locally, usually at a high school gym with a friend's band. Barney Rapp, a Cincinnati bandleader who had discovered Doris Day, heard about the Clooney Sisters and signed them to his band. Suddenly they were singing at all the big stops in town, which often boasted remote broadcasts. When Tony Pastor, who fronted a nationally renowned band, was coming to town, he sent his road manager Charlie Trotta to scout ahead. As it turned out, Pastor was losing his female vocalist and Rapp recommended the Clooney Sisters. Trotta listened to the girls, signed them up, and told them since they were underage, they needed somebody in the family to travel with them. Rosemary and Betty recruited their Uncle George, who was recently home from the war. Like Teresa Brewer, Rosemary Clooney dropped out of high school just short of graduation. Her sister ended her schooling as well. The year was 1946 and the first stop on the road was Atlantic City.

After the sisters had been on the road for three straight years, Uncle George, who had become their manager, booked Rosemary as a single act on *Arthur Godfrey's Talent Scouts*. Among the other acts competing that night was Anthony Dominick Benedetto, better known as Tony Bennett. Rosemary won. In 1949, on her twenty-first birthday, Rosemary Clooney signed a record deal with Columbia Records, having been recruited by the head of A&R at the time, Manie Sacks. Clooney remembered:

> This was a good time for singers. Large orchestras were less and less feasible economically—it was getting to be too expensive to take all those people on the road—and television was beginning to encourage a closer, more intimate focus. With the light starting to go down on the big bands, vocalists were emerging on their own, like butterflies from cocoons: Peggy Lee from Benny Goodman's band, Jo Stafford out of Tommy Dorsey's . . . I was starting on my own at the right time. The competition was tough . . . with her wildly successful "Tennessee Waltz," Patti Page won the Best Record in a *Cash Box* poll. Nevertheless, I was sure of myself and my own talent; sure I'd made the right choices.[27]

Clooney had begun recording with the Tony Pastor Band (sometimes with sister Betty) as early as 1946, but her first record as solo act, "Cabaret"/"Bargain Day," wasn't until 1949. Some of her early recordings charted, but not "Cabaret." Her first hit as a solo act under her new Columbia contract was "Lover's Gold." In 1950, she even did a duet with Frank Sinatra on a song called "Peachtree Street." And like Teresa Brewer at London Records, Clooney had to sing her fair share of juvenile novelty records, such as "Me and My Teddy Bear," in 1950. By one count, she sang over two dozen children's songs in a five-year period.

As Clooney noted, "I couldn't pick and choose the songs I recorded, but that was all right; I was happy to be singing and loving it."[28]

On the subject of 1950s female singers, Louise Harris Murray, of doo-wop group the Hearts and girl group the Jaynetts, picked Ruth Brown, a star on the R&B charts, as her favorite lady vocalist when she was young, but right up close to Brown came Rosemary Clooney. "I used to try to sing like her," Louise said.

Like other record companies at the time, when Columbia executives thought they had a hot commodity, they would inundate the market. In 1951, the label released nine Rosemary Clooney records. The first seven were all Top Thirty hits, beginning with "You're Just in Love," a duet with Guy Mitchell, who was one year older than Clooney. Mitch Miller was high on Mitchell, who would have a very successful career, the peak coming in 1956, when his recording of "Singing the Blues" squeezed in between two Elvis Presley #1 hit records, "Love Me Tender" and "Too Much" to take the reign. Mitchell would hold on to that spot for an astounding ten weeks, which for decades was the song spending the longest time at #1 except for Elvis's two-sided "Don't Be Cruel"/"Hound Dog."

Next for Clooney came "Beautiful Brown Eyes," which climbed to #11 on *Billboard*, and finally "Come On-A My House." Other Clooney songs to chart that year were "Mixed Emotions" (#22), "I'm Waiting for You" (#21), "If Teardrops Were Pennies" (#24) and "I Wish I Wuz" (#27). So 1951 was a very good year for Rosemary Clooney.

The August 4, 1951, issue of *Billboard* published its "Music Popularity Chart," which it did by looking at fourteen different markets around the country. "Come On-A My House" was #1 in ten of those markets.[29] Normally, the chart would dominate a page of the magazine, but for this issue a promotion was spread across three of five columns, from top of the page to bottom. In various forms of typescript, the advertisement screamed in descending word placement:

LONDON RECORDS

BUT ONLY

LONDON RECORDS

HAS

LONGING FOR YOU

BY

TERESA BREWER

WITH JACK PLEIS AND THE ALL STARS

BACKED BY *JAZZ ME BLUES*

While London got very lucky when it signed Teresa Brewer, the New York office was mostly about male singers. "Music! Music! Music!" was a monster record, but after that it was diminishing returns for its star singer. One of the problems was limited vision on the part of London Records honchos. It really didn't know what to do with Brewer. When the novelty record concept fell flat, it was obvious she needed to sing more of the heavily romantic tunes popular at the time. A lot of these songs were real downers, although everywhere on the radio. London Records, on the other hand, was determined to use Dixieland jazz, a more upbeat type of music, and they tried to infuse the two strands together for Teresa Brewer, which is best seen in its release of "If You Want Some Lovin'" early in 1951.

The bouncy song, a musical aggregation of pop, western, and Dixieland, began with a jovial Brewer singing, "I've always had a way with the fellas, they seem to come to me with open arms / I never had the heart to refuse them, so I let them fight it out for my charms." It was almost a perfect Teresa Brewer song.

Cash Box's "Record Review" column on February 3, 1951, thought so too, and awarded the song its "Sleeper of the Week" designation, muscling out new songs by Les Paul, Harry Belafonte, and Billy Eckstine, among others. The reviewer, waxing ecstatic, wrote: ". . . Teresa Brewer comes through with a disk that looks like it's gonna be a great big hit. Doing it in her high-powered style, Teresa sends a lot of rhythm though this and makes it extremely listenable. Ops [jukebox operators] won't go wrong getting with this one immediately because it's certain to have tremendous drawing power in the boxes. Featuring a good set of lyrics, this jumpy version of a western ditty will have no trouble at all breaking through. Not only does Teresa turn in a grand volal [vocal] but she gets some wonderful backing."[30]

Feeling strong after giving birth to her first child about six months before, London put together a short tour for Brewer in high-powered venues. The first stop was three weeks at a club called the Versailles in New York. A week after the *Cash Box* record review of "If You Want Some Lovin'" she was at the Copa in Pittsburgh. This was followed by the Oriental Theater in Chicago and, to top it off, the Last Frontier in Las Vegas.

Sadly, none of the hoopla worked; the song sank into a sea of disappointment. By the end of February, London tossed up "Counterfeit Kisses" with "Lonesome Gal" on the B-side. This song didn't even make "Sleeper of the Week," or any other designation, and got tossed in the junk bin with other releases. The *Cash Box* review was a bit painful: "Thrush, sounding much like Patti Page here, fashions a glowing accounting of a contrived pop-style country item." Also in the pile were songs by Guy Mitchell and Rosemary Clooney, still with the Tony Pastor Band. Probably the biggest insult was the huge London Records promotion dominating the page, which was not for Brewer but for labelmate Al Morgan.[31]

"Counterfeit Kisses" evaporated as well. While 1951 was not a great year for female singers, in March it was a fabulous time for Patti Page and Rosemary Clooney. According to *Billboard*, the best-selling pop singles at the end of March included three Patti Page cuts, "Tennessee Waltz," "Would I Love You," and her version of "Mockin' Bird Hill." Just outside the Top Ten at #13 was Rosemary Clooney's first hit on Columbia, "Beautiful Brown Eyes."[32]

Finally, in August London found itself a Teresa Brewer winner when it released "Longing for You" into a crowded market for the same song. Indeed, the *Cash Box* issue of August 4, 1951, chose two new records as its "Disk of The Week" in its "Record Review" section. Both tunes were "Longing for You," one by Vic Damone and the other by Teresa Brewer. Somehow Sammy Kaye's version didn't get a nod. For Vic Damone, the review wrote that the singer "has another hit on his hands as a follow up to his recent success 'My Truly, Truly Fair'" . . . Vic dishes the tune out in a wonderful manner and makes sound go right through." The B-side was the cut "The Son of a Sailor."[33]

As for Brewer, her reviewer noted, "here is a tune that seems tailor made for Teresa Brewer . . . this top deck [A-side] is a lovely waltz number that can't miss. Teresa pipes the lyrics in a meaningful and appealing manner. Jack Pleis and his orchestra, with the assistance of a choral group, set the musical backing in a fine fashion. The combined effect is one to make ops [jukebox operators] take notice and stock up fast." The B-side was "Jazz Me Blues."

They all slugged it out over "Longing for You." In a year for male singers, the fellows did better: Damone's version reached #12, Sammy Kaye's #16, and Brewer's settled for #23.

The song was based on "A Waltz Dream" by Oscar Straus and it really wasn't very interesting pop music despite all the attention from music companies. More interesting was Brewer's B-side, a jazz standard written by Tom Delaney in 1921 and recorded by many great jazzmen from Bix Beiderbecke to Art Pepper. Unfortunately, even attempting a song with a strong jazz pedigree, Brewer got the usual, tedious, Dixieland treatment from the house orchestra led by Jack Pleis.

Another music company had been tracking Brewer and saw she was not being given the best material with which to work. So, it should have come to no one's surprise that when her contract was over with London Records, she quickly moved on.

Decca and its subsidiary Coral records had been stalking Brewer and got their girl. The headline in *Cash Box* on September 29, 1951, read "Coral Signs Teresa Brewer; Decca Acquires New Artists." The story, with a New York dateline, read: "Coral, after prolonged negotiations, has signed Teresa Brewer to a recording contract. Teresa, who was formerly on the London label, came to the public's attention with her waxing of 'Music! Music! Music!'" London Records also lost Brewer's labelmate Al Morgan, who signed with Decca.[34]

Decca, looking for female singers, also picked up Jeri Southern and June Hutton and the Madcaps. The latter singer was another trouper. In 1934, Hutton left home at fifteen years of age to join her older sister Ina Ray Hutton singing with the big bands. Ten years later she replaced Jo Stafford in a popular singing group called the Pied Pipers. She only stayed one year at Decca. Jeri Southern was in her mid-twenties when she signed with Decca and stayed with the company through 1958, never quite catching on despite earning a solid reputation as a pop/jazz singer.

The Coral subsidiary ended up with Teresa Brewer and a much better deal.

CHAPTER THREE

YOU BELONG TO ME (1952)

JOHNNIE RAY—EDDIE FISHER—KAY STARR— JO STAFFORD—PAUL WESTON—GISELLE MACKENZIE— ROY HOGSED—TERESA BREWER

As the *Cash Box* article of 1951, about the lack of female singers on the record charts, attested, one of the long-held beliefs by music industry executives was that young girls were the driving, commercial force of the industry, because pre-teen and teenage lassies were the ones dropping nickels, dimes, and quarters into restaurant and bowling alley jukeboxes and buying those newly introduced vinyl records called 45s to be played on home phonographs. And what the young girls wanted to hear were songs from their favorite male singers. This trope was given a reasonable level of credence in 1952 with the arrival of two young men on the music scene, Johnnie Ray and Eddie Fisher.

While male singers such as Tony Martin, Johnny Desmond, Perry Como, Al Martino, Vaughn Monroe, and Tony Bennett were already big stars selling millions of records, there were two unrealized issues going on. First, these crooners weren't pushing the evolution of pop music forward in any manner; basically these singers were just warbling through the radio-safe and industry-standard approach to pop music, which had been popular for twenty years. It was like leading the wagon train into a box canyon while the hostile elements of country & western and rhythm & blues were circling and introducing exciting new emanations. Second, none of these singers created the mass spectacle of thousands of young listeners, mostly girls, stampeding concert halls and screaming for their favorite singer, such as the bobbysoxers had done with Frank Sinatra in the mid-1940s and wouldn't do again until the mid-1950s with the arrival of Elvis Presley.

Again, we are not talking about the changes going on in those lurking country & western and rhythm & blues genres, but only about the pop radio stations, which still dominated American airwaves, resulting in the most record sales and jukebox plays. To point out the importance of the latter medium, in January 1952 *Billboard* reported jukebox disk purchases had climbed to fifty million record sales a year. The story noted, "recent disk industry estimates of the importance of sales to coin machines include a 40 percent increase in sales during the past two years."[1]

As the records turned, 1952 would get a big boost by two young men who had absolutely nothing in common except for their appeal to young female listeners. The phenomenon of mass teenager crush fell on the unlikelier of the two men, Johnnie Ray. In the history of teen heartthrobs, or teen idols, it seems there was a long interregnum between Frank Sinatra and Elvis Presley. That's because the Johnnie Ray havoc-causing appearances came and went so quickly and left no lasting effect, it was almost as if it didn't happen at all. But Johnnie Ray had his massive teen frenzy moment just as Frank and Elvis did and that all began, more or less, in 1952, when he dominated the airwaves and teenage girls came to his concerts to wail and scream.

Born in Oregon in 1927, Ray was somewhat of a child prodigy despite suffering a succession of hearing problems necessitating the wearing of a hearing aid. By fourteen years of age, he was working youth dances and became a regular on "Uncle Nate's Stars of Tomorrow," Portland's answer to Major Bowes. He left Oregon in his early twenties, trying to make a career in the music industry first in California and eventually ending up in the Midwest. His big break came when he got a gig at Detroit's Flame Showbar, which only hosted rhythm & blues singers. Ray had scrapped around long enough over the years to develop a lively stage presence, where he would kick away the piano bench and play standing up, something Little Richard and Elton John would eventually do as well. Ray moved on to other clubs, picking up support from fellow musicians such as Tony Bennett. For his early recording of "Whiskey & Gin" the *Billboard* review noted: "Warbler [singer] has an extraordinary sound, a cross between Kay Starr and Jimmy Scott, on this finely constructed rhythm novelty."

The review was interesting for unusual insight in the budding singer. The Kay Starr–Jimmy Scott reference was an unlikely metaphor for the private Johnnie Ray, who was still at this point in his young life very much ambiguous about his sexuality.

Ray signed with Columbia (but was assigned to the OKeh label) and in October 1951 Mitch Miller, a savant with certain recording acts, during a recording session, pulled him aside. They went into Miller's office, where he played Ray the song "Cry" by a girl singer named Ruth Casey, who recorded the song for a small, independent label. Mitch suggested to Ray that he record the song, which in the Columbia Records universe meant you record this song or you'll never work for Columbia again.

Ray, under Miller's stunned gaze, launched into a truly impassioned, almost mental breakdown arrangement of the song. It was like nothing else on the radio at the time and Miller bought the dream. Jonny Whiteside, the author of *Cry: The Johnnie Ray Story*, absolutely loses his knickers when describing the song, calling it "one of the most intense" and "emphatically powerful pop records ever made" and Johnnie Ray took the "lyric soaring into blue strata of hopelessness, then plunged them into a vermillion pit of blood-churning emotion."

Whiteside also harps on the Kay Starr influence, or Johnnie Ray's professional yet female persona, writing that Ray "stretches, bends and dominates the lyric in a tumultuous release of desperate psychic information. And it is put across not only by a voice charged with anguish and emotion, but by a dramatic shift in rhythmic patter. That is the Kay Starr influence."[2]

In March 1952, a radio disk jockey named Alan Freed, who had initiated late-night rhythm & blues programming on a popular Cleveland radio station, decided to promote his show by offering hometown listeners a concert by some of the performers with airplay on his station. The Moondog Coronation Ball, which would become known as the first rock 'n' roll concert, was to be held at the Cleveland Arena. By some estimates as many as 20,000 teenagers showed up for the concert and the local police department panicked, quickly shutting down the show after just a couple of performances. Four months later, in Boston, a red-hot Johnnie Ray entered the stage before a sold-out crowd of 4,000 teenagers when once again the local police department panicked and a tear gas canister was tossed onto the orchestra floor, resulting in a stampede for the exits. Luckily, no one died and only four women were injured in the melee.

Johnnie Ray's big hit "Cry" was released at the end of 1951, with the major sales and charting occurring in '52. The B-side, "The Little White Cloud That Cried," also became a hit record. Of *Billboard*'s top thirty records of 1952, Ray bagged four slots: "Cry" came in at #3, "Little White Cloud that Cried" #18, "Walkin' My Baby Back Home" #24, and "Please Mr. Sun" #30.[3]

The only other performer to have this kind of impact on record sales and the record charts for 1952 was another singer hot with the teenage girls, Eddie Fisher.

It would be hard to find two singers as diametrically opposite as Johnnie Ray and Eddie Fisher. Ray was tall, gangly, almost angular, which was helpful when he contorted because it accentuated his body movement. He had a pretty face that aged quickly under a deluge of alcohol. Once his hair began to recede, his ears looked too large for his head and those little facial features that made him adorable no longer worked to his advantage. Before all that happened, women,

including many famous actresses, wanted to grasp him to their bosom, which
wasn't a place Ray particularly wanted to go. Despite a marriage, the conceit
that he was bisexual eventually faded.[4]

If Johnnie Ray had WASPy charm, Eddie Fisher was the king of his bar
mitzvah class. Short in height, he boasted a full head of dark, curly hair that
he wore as a perfect pompadour over his very handsome face. Girls didn't just
want to hug Fisher to their bosom, they wanted to cover the young man in
kisses and unlike Johnnie Ray, Fisher was not ambiguous about the opposite
sex. Born in 1928, Fisher was one year younger than Ray. He was a city boy from
South Philly. There is a tale by Myrna Greene, who wrote *The Eddie Fisher Story*,
of Fisher getting his career started in his hometown. He was performing on a
local show sponsored by the Pet Milk Company, which placed posters of Fisher
at front of trolley cars. Lips, drawn in lipstick, began appearing on the promos.
His marriage to, and divorce from, Debbie Reynolds followed by his marriage
to, and divorce from, Elizabeth Taylor, were gossip fodder in newspapers and
magazines for years. In 1967 he married actress Connie Stevens, which, alas,
failed as well.

Fisher's climb to success was a series of starts and stops. Finally, by 1950
he began picking up recognition and *Billboard* that year called him the most
promising male vocalist of the year. In 1951, Fisher was in concert at the
Paramount Theater in New York, which was also premiering the Dick Powell
and Rhonda Fleming movie *Cry Danger*. Fans lined up outside the theater for
tickets. As author Greene writes, the people in the line weren't coming to see
the movie, "they were coming to see and hear Eddie Fisher, the new singing
sensation."[5]

Fisher spent a lot of time in the recording studio, and these songs would
finally be released in 1952. Like Johnnie Ray, Fisher had some kind of year and
he also boasted four Top Thirty songs: "Wish You Were Here" at #7, "Anytime"
#12, "I'm Yours" #20, and "Tell Me Why" #28.

With that kind of success by Ray and Fisher, one would think they would
have an immense crossover appeal. They didn't. Ray was a dramatic performer,
who sang lachrymose songs that were manifestations of his active stage
presence. Fisher was just another crooning gunslinger, offering the usual fare
of boring balladry.

With Ray and Fisher stomping around the recording world in 1952 like
Lilliputian giants, according to recording executive lore and conviction there
should have been little room on the record charts for the ladies, because those
hordes of teenage girls buying records were simply ga-ga for the guys. So much
for common wisdom as none of this happened at all; 1952 was another year
where the ladies crashed the party big time. Despite all the hoopla around "Cry"
or "Wish You Were Here," of the top five records in 1952, female singers took

three slots. Expanding the count to the Top Ten songs that year, women boasted five of the biggest hits: Kay Starr's "Wheel of Fortune" at #2, Jo Stafford's "You Belong to Me" at #4, Vera Lynn's "Auf Wiederseh'n Sweetheart" at #5, Rosemary Clooney's "Half as Much" at #6, and Patti Page's "I Went to Your Wedding" at #8. One position out of the loop was Georgia Gibbs's "Kiss of Fire" at #11.

In 1952, women held the #1 record slot on the *Billboard* chart for thirty-two weeks. Even more noteworthy, starting on June 12, when Vera Lynn's "Auf Wiederseh'n Sweetheart" became #1 until December 20 when Joni James's "Why Don't You Believe Me" ended its reign at #1, women held the top slot for every week except one.

Even with all the excitement for Johnnie Ray and Eddie Fisher, the two could claim none of the most consequential or classic pop recordings of the year. "Cry" was too idiosyncratic for expanded consciousness and Fisher's recordings, in retrospect, were so of the moment, they were like fresh baked bread that when left around too long solidified and became inedible. The only record by a pop male singer that has lived on past 1952 was Frankie Laine's recording of "High Noon," the theme song to the famed Gary Cooper movie of the same name. Fans of western movies can't leave *High Noon* without humming the opening lines to the theme song, "Do not forsake me, oh my darlin', on this, our wedding day."

So, once again, it came down to the women, who sang two of the most important pop songs of the 1950s. Kay Starr grabbed the silver ring with her version of "Wheel of Fortune," which, hands down, would have been the best song of the year if not for Jo Stafford's elegant recording of "You Belong to Me."

"Wheel of Fortune" is not without its fans. When Beverly Warren of the the Raindrops was growing up in the 1950s, her taste in music was more rhythm & blues. The standout song of her youth was Frankie Lymon and the Teenagers' 1956 hit "Why Do Fools Fall in Love" and as the 1950s turned into the 1960s, it was the Patti LaBelle and the Bluebelles version of "You'll Never Walk Alone." Perhaps, even greater in her memory is Kay Starr, who she exclaimed is "unfathomable on 'Wheel of Fortune.' I loved that song and always wanted to sing it the way Kay Starr did it. I can still recall the melody. What Starr did with 'Wheel of Fortune' was unbelievable! Back then there were no gimmicks, not auto-tuners. You went into the studio and just sang."[6]

Actually, Kay Starr's "Wheel of Fortune" did have gimmick, a clicking sound at the beginning of the song that was supposed to be the noise of a roulette wheel turning. Then came the horns of the band, the clicking again, back to the band and finally we hear Kay Starr singing, haltingly without a rush, "The wheel of fortune, goes spinning around" (stretching out the last sound of the word); "Will the arrow point my way? Will this be my day?" (again stretching the last word).

Starr gives a slight nod to the country side of music, which wasn't unusual since the song was by the same songwriters, Bennie Benjamin and George David Weiss, who wrote "I'll Never Be Free," Kay Starr and Tennessee Ernie Ford's big hit from two years before. The versatile Benjamin, a Black man born in the Virgin Islands, was able to find common ground with such white songwriters as Weiss, Sol Marcus, Ed Durham, and Ed Seiller, cowriting such tunes as the 1938 hit "I Don't Want to Set the World on Fire" and even modern, harder stuff such as "Don't Let Me Be Misunderstood," a big hit for the British group the Animals in 1965.[7]

"Wheel of Fortune," indeed, turned true for Benjamin and Weiss; numerous versions of the song were already recorded before Starr took a turn at it early in 1952. According to musicologist Larry Birnbaum, Starr adhered closest to a rendition by interracial performers, white singer Sunny Gale backed by African American Eddie Wilcox and his orchestra. A number of "Wheel of Fortune" songs charted, but nothing came close to Starr's version. Birnbaum writes, "Starr makes the song wholly her own, belting the lyrics with stirring conviction. Although it's a ballad without a back-beat or boogie-woogie bass line, parts of it (especially the bridge, where Starr overdubs her own backing harmonies) have a slow-motion rock 'n' roll feel."[8]

"Wheel of Fortune" wiped away Johnnie Ray's tears, knocking "Cry" out of the #1 slot on March 15 and keeping hold of that cherished throne for ten weeks until early May. "You Belong to Me" began its run at #1 in September.

Tim Weisberg, the host of Midnight Society talk radio, is a big fan of "You Belong to Me," the Top Ten hit by the Duprees in 1962. This was the Italian doo-wop version of the song made famous by Jo Stafford in 1952. Weisberg, a doo-wop aficionado, counts "You Belong to Me" as one of the top five songs of that genre. Many people who were teenagers in the early 1960s would concur.[9]

The Duprees were five young men from Jersey City who got together to sing doo-wop. They were discovered by George Paxton, a former big band leader, who with Marvin Cane formed Coed Records in 1958. Coed was based in the New York's hothouse of songwriting talent, the Brill Building. The original group was called the Parisians and they dropped off a demo of "My Own True Love," without a phone number. Paxton liked the song but had to wait until the group came by again to bring them in for an audition. The song did well, and it was time to make the next record. The group's specialty was to redo old standards and remake them in doo-wop harmony as the Flamingos had done with "I Only Have Eyes for You." In the next recording session, they did a couple of songs such as "As Time Goes By," which the group wanted as an A-side, but Paxton liked "You Belong to Me."

"Joey Vann [Joey Conzano], our lead singer, had older sisters, who bought lots of records including those by the female recording artists of the 1950s,"

Tom Bialoglow, an original member of the group, explained. "He knew these songs and singers, Jo Stafford, June Valli, etc. and it was his idea to sing 'You Belong to Me.' I used to listen to the radio a lot when I was a kid and knew the Jo Stafford song well because it had a vibraphone in the recording."

In the recording studio, the backing musicians were all from the *Tonight Show*. "The band was all well-known professionals and our arrangement was pretty," Bialoglow added. "The song was popular and Joey, the lead, really sold it. We did thirty takes before deciding number nineteen was the one."[10]

Well, if you're going to tap pre-rock pop standards, there is probably no better song than Jo Stafford's excellent "You Belong to Me."

Patti Page's "Tennessee Waltz" of 1950 was written by Pee Wee King and Redd Stewart, who coauthored "You Belong to Me" along with another songwriter, Chilton Price. Of the three, King is the most fascinating. Pictures of him circa 1940s showcase the cowboy songwriter, complete with the big cowpuncher hat, hand-knotted tie, and showy rodeo shirt.

This guy's presence just screamed, "I'm an ol' cowhand from the Rio Grande"— except he wasn't. He was born Julius Frank Anthony Kuczynski in Wisconsin and began his musical career playing accordion, which he learned from his father, a professional polka musician. By the 1930s, he found himself doing movies with singing cowboy Gene Autry, and his transformation was complete.[11]

Other than "Slow Poke," a major hit for himself in 1952, his best songs were huge starbursts for women: "Tennessee Waltz" for Patti Page, "Bonaparte's Retreat" for Kay Starr, and "You Belong to Me" for Jo Stafford.

A small news item toward the bottom of page 19 in the March 15, 1952, issue of *Cash Box* carried the headline, "Jo Stafford & Paul Weston Wed." The date of the wedding was February 26, and the place was St. Gregory's Roman Catholic Church in Los Angeles. The story highlighted the blissful coming together of two veteran musical talents and the copy read: "Jo Stafford and Paul Weston have long been a hit-making musical team. In addition to collaborating on Columbia Records, they have appeared together on numerous radio programs . . . currently high on best-seller and popularity lists is the Jo Stafford recording of 'Shrimp Boats,' co-authored and arranged by Paul Weston." The story also noted that Weston was a Columbia recording star in his own right with a string of best-sellers and had his own hit record at the time, "Charmaine."[12]

As West Coast musical director for Columbia, Weston operated as the company's A&R representative in Los Angeles. He wasn't Mitch Miller, but he had to keep abreast of the market, find songs for the West Coast artists, and produce and arrange recording sessions. He had a good ear, especially when it came to bringing songs to Jo Stafford even before they were married.

From Stafford's 1944 hit "The Trolley Song," recorded when she was part of the Pied Pipers singing group, until 1952, Stafford was such a consistent hit-maker she could count almost fifty Top Thirty records. In 1947 alone, she pushed ten songs onto the charts, including "A Sunday Kind of Love," which was turned inside out in the 1953 doo-wop classic by the Harptones. Fran Warren's 1947 version of the song was her first to reach the music charts, but it couldn't touch Stafford's take, which climbed to #15 on the chart. Recorded for Capitol, the attribution underneath Stafford's name reads "With Paul Weston and His Orchestra."

Despite all those hits, she hit a dry spell—at least for her, which was like nobody else's dry spell. From 1949 through 1950, she charted with seventeen more Top Thirty records, but without—gasp!!—breaking the Top Five. Then in 1952, she recorded "Shrimp Boats," a jovial cross-genre song sounding like a mash-up of a Broadway tune and a native folk song. It was the kind of record Columbia excelled in producing. The song was cowritten by Paul Weston, and the attribution below Jo Stafford's name on the record reads "with Paul Weston and his Orchestra and the Norman Luboff Choir."

Weston was forty years old in 1952 when he married Stafford. He had been selling his musical arrangements in the early 1930s, which brought him to the attention of bandleader Tommy Dorsey, who hired him for this orchestra in 1936. Two years later, he convinced Dorsey to bring on the singing group the Pied Pipers for the orchestra's next tour. The Pied Pipers' lead singer was twenty-one-year-old Jo Stafford. With the coming of World War II and the breakup of the big bands, Weston worked with vocalist Dinah Shore and eventually moved to Hollywood. He was hired at Capitol Records and began working again with Stafford. When Weston moved on to Columbia, Stafford followed him to the new label.[13]

While Weston was known for creating a new trend in tunesmanship called the "mood music" genre, he was also at the forefront of a different genre, that of advancing the female crooner.

Weston and Stafford's marriage was the culmination of a professional relationship that began almost fifteen years before. Weston had worked with other female singers over the years and had that instinct for what would make a hit song, especially if sung by a woman. At Columbia Records, he had to work with a wide roster of talent and hundreds if not thousands of song sheets came across his desk. Stafford was such a big star at the time that, if he plucked an interesting tune out of the stack and slid it in her direction, it was right and natural. Considering the provenance of a song such as "You Belong to Me," where the songwriters boasted amazing success with other female singers, once Weston got his hands on the sheet music it would have first gone to no one else at Columbia but Stafford. As with past Stafford/Weston collaborations, the record label for "You Belong to Me," underneath Jo Stafford's name, reads "with Paul Weston & his Orch."

Considering the success of "You Belong to Me," it would seem to be a foregone conclusion by Columbia that this record would be a hit. That wasn't what happened at all. "You Belong to Me" was intended as the B-side with "Pretty Boy" as the A-side song; we know that because in one of the earliest reviews of the record by *Cash Box* on July 6, 1952, the focus was on "Pretty Boy." In its "Record Review" column, *Cash Box* even chose "Pretty Boy" as its "Sleeper of the Week," which wasn't a surprise considering the weak competition that week from the likes of Fred Waring & His Pennsylvanians, George Shearing Quintet, Vaughn Monroe, David Rose Orchestra, and even an offering from actress Marlene Dietrich. All other reviews were diminutive, but the "Sleeper of the Week" gets a full review alongside a photo of the singer, in this case a serious-looking Jo Stafford.[14]

The reviewer of "Pretty Boy" takes a restrained approach, writing: "Jo Stafford comes up with a wonderful waxing on an inspired fast moving calypso type number entitled, 'Pretty Boy.' The number has everything that is necessary for a hit tune. It's not the run of the mill type number, but instead a rhythmic, interesting, and different style presentation. It features cute lyrics and contains the wonderful vocal backing by the harmonic voices of the Starlighters. The captivating and melodic instrumental support is projected impressively by the zestful orchestra of Paul Weston."

As for the B-side song, "You Belong to Me," the reviewer assumed it was included simply as a good match-up with "Pretty Boy." He writes: "The underdeck [B-side] is a side handmade to supplement the top. It's a slow and lovely ballad that gets a tender and warm reading by Jo Stafford . . . Paul Weston again provides the lush background."

Here's where the reviewer goes completely wrong, noting "both sides are terrific, but the top deck [A-side] is hit material." It wasn't.

What the reviewer got wonderfully right is in the throwaway comment that Jo Stafford's "invitingly clear voice makes your spine tingle." There are two subtleties within the descriptive information that ring out. First is the observation of Stafford's "invitingly clear voice," which in this song is like melodic purity with every annunciation, pause, even the breath ringing true. No tricks, no gimmicks, just a clear voice and a song. That leads to the second cognizance, that the song "makes your spine tingle" or what happens when everything about a song rings precise, unblemished, and leaving you craving to hear it again.

If there is one gimmick, perhaps innovation, to Paul Weston's otherwise straightforward arrangement, it is in the introduction where Stafford introduces the tune with a soft, non-jazz, scatting against laid-back orchestration. It sounds something like "baa ba-ba wee wee wee boo-wee boo-wee," which looks silly written out but sounds delicious. Then Stafford launches into what is probably the best remembered opening lines of a song from the early 1950s: "See the pyramids along the Nile / Watch the sunset from a tropic isle / Just remember, darling, all the while / You belong to me."

On September 13, "You Belong to Me" became the #1 song in the country and it would stay there for five weeks until Patti Page's "I Went To Your Wedding" took the top slot on October 18. Even so, on that date, a look at *Cash Box*'s "Regional Record Report" showed Stafford's song was still #1 or #2 on stations in Chicago, New Orleans, Norfolk, Boston, Miami, Louisville, and Baltimore.[15]

In 1952, the first record chart was created in the United Kingdom and in the #1 slot for that initial listing was Al Martino's "Here Is My Heart." The second song to hit #1 in the UK was "You Belong to Me," making Jo Stafford the first female to top the UK chart.[16]

Stafford was born in 1917 in Coalinga, California, where her father hoped to find work in the oil fields. Her mother Anna York Stafford was an accomplished banjo player and often sang to her four children the old folk songs she had learned during her years in Tennessee. Stafford took piano lessons and studied voice, thinking there might be a future for herself as an opera singer. Instead she joined with her two sisters to form a pop trio, the Stafford Sisters. Their first radio gig was on a Los Angeles station when Jo was sixteen. The year was 1933, and from there the girls moved on to other radio stations even finding work in film industry as off-screen voices. All of the Stafford Sisters married by 1938 and began to drop out. Jo's husband John Huddleston was also a singer, so she kept going as a performer.

In 1938 Stafford, along with members of the Four Esquires and the Three Rhythm Kings, formed a new octet called the Pied Pipers. They were hired by Tommy Dorsey, fired, made a few recordings for Victor, were reduced to being quartet, and then hired back by Dorsey when he also took on Frank Sinatra as vocalist for his band. The group backed Sinatra on his first big hit with Dorsey, "I'll Never Smile Again."[17]

"Frank became a star within months of starting with Dorsey when he recorded 'I'll Never Smile Again,'" author Kitty Kelley wrote. "After that Tommy put Frank's name above everyone—above Connie Haines, above Jo Stafford and the Pied Pipers and above the other musicians, including [drummer] Buddy Rich, who hated Frank because of it."

Stafford told Kelley when the latter was writing her Sinatra biography that she was backstage at the Astor Hotel in New York when Rich cursed out Frank, who grabbed a heavy glass pitcher filled with water and threw it at Buddy's head, who was quick enough to duck out of the way. "If he hadn't," said Stafford, "he probably would have been killed or seriously hurt. The pitcher hit the wall so hard that pieces of glass were embedded in the plaster."[18]

Near the end of 1942, the Pied Pipers left the Dorsey band. Two years later, with Jo Stafford as the featured singer, the group had a #2 record with "The Trolley Song." After that, Capitol Records began recording her as a solo act. By the next year, recording with Johnny Mercer, Stafford grabbed her first #1 with "Candy." From then to 1955, she never left the top of the record charts, recording thirty-one Top Ten hits, and was the first female to sell 25 million records.

Stafford's popularity, craftsmanship, even endurance in some regards can be attributed to her versatility as a performer. She easily and successfully slid from pop to jazz to country to spiritual to folk. In her later performing years, she and her husband Paul Weston did a musical comedy act. In discussing the ascension of folk music in the 1950s, writer Geoffrey Stokes noted, "mainstream performers as diverse as Frankie Laine, Jo Stafford, Harry Belafonte, and Vaughn Monroe had scored occasional hits with folk (or folk-type) material . . . demonstrating only that certain performers could sell a folk song."[19]

She was never so successful she couldn't make fun of herself. On June 27, 1947, the *Santa Cruz Sentinel* got to interview Red Ingle, a comedic singer who had performed with Spike Jones and the City Slickers. The headline read "Hill-Billy Tunes Get Hot on Record Parade" and the column was about Ingle's successful hit recording with "Cinderella G. Stump," who in the real world was Jo Stafford. Ingles took an "old moody torch song" called "Temptation" and transformed it into "Tim-tayshun," a jokey fiddle tune that shot all the way to #1 on the record chart. Stafford sounded like a Carter Family singer who drank too much moonshine, or as the Santa Clara newspaper revealed, "They [Ingle and Stafford] even put out a little mechanical hocus-pocus to get a nasal twang into Jo Stafford's usually mellow tonsils."[20]

In 1953, a front-page headline in *Variety* magazine read: "Jo Stafford Inks 4-year CBS-TV $1,000,000 Deal."[21]

In the early years of television, the variety show hosted by a well-known performer was one of the most popular formats. Male crooners such as Perry Como as well as female singers such as Dinah Shore were recruited to headline shows or to be regular guests. Jo Stafford got her shot with the eponymous *The Jo Stafford Show*, which only ran one season from 1954 to 1955.

Television both extended the careers of the female crooners beyond the time of their hit-making years and provided a well-paying safe haven for those who never became the Jo Staffords or Patti Pages or Teresa Brewers of their time.

For a brief moment in radio history, the veteran Jo Stafford and up-and-coming singer Gisele MacKenzie crossed paths. They met several times during the run of a radio program called *Club Fifteen* and were photographed together in cast publicity pictures.

Starting in 1947, Bob Crosby hosted a national radio show that featured popular music. It was the *Club Fifteen* or *Bob Crosby's Club Fifteen* and it ran until 1953. The show was very popular in its time and a good place to get exposure. Crosby preferred his cohosts or regular performers to be women and those included such stars as the Andrews Sisters and Jo Stafford.

In 1951, the show, which was sponsored by Campbell Soup, was undergoing changes. The Andrews Sisters, who at that point were alternating with Stafford as Crosby's regular costar, decided to leave.

Meanwhile, up in Canada, Gisele MacKenzie (Gisèle Marie Louise Marguerite La Flèche), who was born in Winnipeg in 1927, had built up such a career she was Canada's first lady of song as a teenager in the 1940s. She quickly migrated over to radio and headlined a couple of Canadian national network shows including one called *Meet Gisele*, where famous international movie stars would chat with the host.

By 1951, Gisele realized that she needed to come to the United States if she was ever going to have any major success in the entertainment field. Bob Crosby and the promotions staff at Campbell Soup had begun looking for a replacement for the Andrews Sisters. Tape recordings of female singers were sent to Crosby, who allowed Campbell Soup employees to vote on their favorite unnamed singer. The one that struck their interest was Gisele's. From 1951 to 1953, on alternating nights she and Jo Stafford switched off as the cohost of *Club Fifteen*. At the same time, she was also working another radio show hosted by singer Mario Lanza.[22]

Looking like the next big female singer, Capitol signed her up in 1951, brought her into the studio to record a handful of songs, releasing the first early in 1952. The A-side was "Le Flacre" which got a bit of airplay and rose as high as #20 on the pop chart. The second record to be released was "Adios," which hit the market that same summer. Again, the song got decent airplay. It did better, climbing as high as #14 on *Billboard*. Then in October, Capitol released "My Favorite Song" with "Don't Let the Stars Get in Your Eyes," a hit for country singer Slim Willet, on the B-side.

On October 18, 1952, *Cash Box* issued its most recent "Record Reviews," choosing for the predictive "Sleeper of the Week" a couple of male singers who had been doing well in duets with female singers. Guy Mitchell, who teamed with Rosemary Clooney among others, was this time joined with Mindy Carson for "That's A-Why" with "Train of Love" on the B-side. "Guy and Mindy, who have outstanding voices in their own right, sound just as grand together," said the reviewer. In a rare two-choice "Sleeper of the Week," the column also picked Don Cornell, a run-of-the-mill crooner, for his song "I" with "Be Fair" on the B-side. The reviewer noted: "He had great success with 'I'm Yours' and 'I'll Walk Alone,' is going great with Teresa Brewer on 'You'll Never Get Away,' and now has a sensational piece."

The reviewer got it right, at least in terms of the Teresa Brewer duet, which became a Top Twenty hit that year.

Among the names in the also-rans of the record reviews that week were Phil Harris teaming up with the Bell Sisters, old stand-by Vaughn Monroe, R&B singers Billy Ward and His Dominoes, and newcomer Gisele MacKenzie with her record "My Favorite Song" and "Don't Let the Stars Get in Your Eyes," For the A-side, "My Favorite Song" the reviewer gave it a B rating, saying: "An up and coming biggie that's making quite stir in the music biz gets a wonderful going over by Gisele MacKenzie. The thrush sings this pretty number with a soft bounce to the backing by the Buddy Cole ork [orchestra]." The reviewer didn't think much of the B-side, giving it a C+ rating. Trying to be kind, the reviewer exclaimed: "A peppy backdrop adds a great deal of color to Gisele's happy reading of a cute bouncer with enjoyable lyrics and a fine melody. Ork credits go to Buddy and the boys."[23]

Nothing happened to "My Favorite Song" and it seemingly got lost in the shuffle, but somewhere a disk jockey turned the record over and listened to the B-side, "Don't Let the Stars Get in Your Eyes." He liked the song and added it to his playlist. By December, the record was looking like a hit. Despite a very competitive market with seasonal hit "I Saw Mommy Kissing Santa Claus" by Jimmy Boyd, Eddie Fisher tunes, and a slew of women crooners such as Joni James, Patti Page, Teresa Brewer, and Vera Lynn on the charts, Cash Box's "Disk Jockey's Regional Record Report" showed radio stations in places like New Orleans, Philadelphia, and Lawrence, Massachusetts, placing the song as #1 on the playlist.

Capitol started cranking up the promotion machine. Reporting on a jukebox conference in Los Angeles, a reviewer wrote: "They are still talking about the overflow turnout at the Dan Stewart Company for the showing of the new 1953 Rock-Ola 120 selection 'Fireball' phono.... Well over 400 music operators attended, with Spike Jones, Gisele MacKenzie, the Four Lads ... adding to the general merriment."[24]

The song looked like it was going to be a comer, getting as high #11 in sales and #18 on jukebox when it got blindsided. Perry Como released his version of the same song and it was a locomotive going downhill, blowing away every other version of the tune that may have been in the market at the time.

In 1953, MacKenzie boasted a Top Ten hit in the United Kingdom with "Seven Lonely Days," but she didn't get her first major US hit until 1955, when "Hard to Get" became a Top Five record—just in the nick to time, because by the following year rock 'n' roll would change the music business forever. That was alright because fate would have other plans for MacKenzie.

Jim Stewart, who once had been on the tour team for Joan Baez, was also a lifelong friend of Gisele MacKenzie. When he was six years old he could remember his parents listening to the Club Fifteen radio show and even then was fascinated with her. At the age of ten, Stewart, who grew up in the small Ohio town of Circleville, saw that MacKenzie was going to appear at the Ohio State Fair. For the gig, MacKenzie was staying at the Hilton Hotel in Columbus and a call went out for a local hairdresser. Stewart's aunt got the job. While doing MacKenzie's hair, the aunt said, "my nephew is just crazy about you," so MacKenzie said, "bring him backstage at the show."

"I was this towheaded kid and brought a stack of records for her to sign," Stewart laughed. The nice thing was she invited him to come to New York City in the autumn to sit backstage at her television show, *Your Hit Parade*.

The original *Your Hit Parade* was a sixty-minute radio show that played fifteen of the top songs in the country. It began on NBC radio in 1935, changed networks over the years, then returned to NBC. Among the many, many singers on the show in the 1940s were future female crooners Dinah Shore, Georgia Gibbs, and Doris Day. In 1950, the show moved to television with a similar format, playing the top songs in the country. In the modern world, the show would be unrecognizable, because it featured four vocalists who sang every song, every week, with each performance all tricked out in elaborate presentations and costumes. The show, targeted to a younger audience, was very popular and lasted nine seasons.

In 1952, the lineup of the show was Dorothy Collins, Russell Arms, Snooky Lanson, and June Valli, but that latter singer was leaving and MacKenzie wanted that spot, which she got thanks to Jack Benny.

Here's how Stewart tells the story: During the time of *Club Fifteen*, the wife of Bob Crosby's brother Bing Crosby died and Bob took some time off to be with him. Sitting in for Bob was Jack Benny at a time when MacKenzie was alternating with Jo Stafford. Benny was so impressed by her that, when *Club Fifteen* went off the air, he took Gisele to Las Vegas as his opening act. Starting in 1950, Benny hosted a very successful television show promoted by Lucky Strike cigarettes, the same sponsor as *Your Hit Parade*. When he saw June Valli was leaving *Your Hit Parade*, he invited MacKenzie on his show, with a full screen-time performance, singing and even doing comedy. In 1953, Gisele got the job.[25]

Here's how *Cash Box* played the change in its June 6, 1953, issue—badly. The headline goes "McKenzie [spelled incorrectly] Replaces Valli" and a two-sentence story reads: "Gisele MacKenzie, Capitol recording artist has been engaged for the *Hit Parade* beginning next fall. She replaces June Valli, RCA Victor artist, who appeared on the show this season."[26]

Many female crooners and even aging movie stars would have their entertainment careers extended by migrating to television, but MacKenzie got there early, and after rock 'n' roll arrived she got the bonus package: her own television show, which ran on NBC in the 1957–58 season.

She would continue doing Las Vegas, touring with Jack Benny, starring in summer stock, and performing on many television shows including some drama, soap operas, and serials.

What happened to *Your Hit Parade*? It went off the air in 1959, although it really was dead as early as 1957. "Rock 'n' roll chased *Your Hit Parade* off the air," Stewart concluded. "After Elvis, kids wanted to see the real singers and not a song put into a skit."

Like MacKenzie, Teresa Brewer would have her Perry Como–type moment, but with a rock 'n' roll twist. It, too, started in 1952 with a song that looked like it was going to be a bigger hit than it was.

The story begins with Roy Hogsed, a little-known country singer born in Flippin, Arkansas. He had been recording steadily since 1947, first as Roy Hogsed & the Rainbow Riders and then as a solo act. He would have passed through the record world unnoticed except for an unlikely tune he recorded in 1948 called "Cocaine Blues."[27] It began this way: "Early one morning while I'm making the rounds, took a shot of cocaine and I shot my woman down / went right home and went to bed, and stuck that lovin' .44 beneath my head."

Not too many people were singing about cocaine in 1948, least of all a country singer. It's not that there were less drugs circulating among country & western performers than in pop or rhythm & blues circles (just ask Hank Williams and Johnny Cash) but the outright mention of drugs was taboo—and this song was issued by Capitol, one of the bigger record companies. The song became a bit of cult classic and was reissued in 1950 and 1951. In the latter year, Hogsed's litany of new records was literally and thematically all over the place, from the patriotic "The Red We Want Is the Red We Got (In the Old Red, White and Blue)" to the spurious "Shuffleboard Shuffle." Another of his records that year was "The Snake Dance Boogie" with the sanguine "I'm Gonna Get Along Without You" on the B-side. The label for "I'm Gonna Get Along Without You" reads that the song was written by Roy Hogsed and Rex May, which isn't true. It was written by Milton Kellem, at the time was a forty-year-old songwriter from Philadelphia who more than likely sold the rights to the song to Capitol for chump change and a bus ticket to New York.[28]

Hogsed recorded the tune in a perky, country vein. There was nothing exciting or unusual about the tune, so it was assigned to being a B-side song and probably would have been forgotten if someone at Coral Records, Brewer's new record company, hadn't picked up the platter knowing about Hogsed and the infamous "Cocaine Blues." Coral was still figuring out what to do with its new star and reverted back to the juvenile silliness of her old label with a song called "Roll Them Roly Boly Eyes." For the B-side, Coral A&R, under Bob Thiele, picked up "I'm Gonna Get Along Without You," which they renamed "Gonna Get Along Without Ya Now." It was such a versatile song that the former country tune was given a big band treatment and the gender in the lyrics were switched.

On April 5, 1952, *Billboard*'s "Music Popularity Charts" selected the record for review. The A-side, "Roll Them Roly Boly Eyes," got a tepid appraisal: "Miss Brewer puts her best Gay '90s voice forward on this bouncy item with solid ork [orchestra] by Ray Bloch. Should get spins." The B-side, "Gonna Get Along Without Ya Now," received a poorer rating, but a peppier assessment, which noted: "Another bouncy tune that's just right for thrush's [female singer's] tonsils. Bloch's arrangement is outstanding."

To add insult to injurious comments, the page with the "Music Popularity Charts" was dominated by a three-column (the magazine was five columns across), top of page to bottom advertisement by Mercury Records for its big star at the moment. In random sizes of type, the promotion read: "BLAZING!; From Her Performance on Milton Berle's TV Show; GEORGIA GIBBS; Has a Smash Hit in; KISS OF FIRE."[29]

Coral didn't know what it had in "Gonna Get Along Without Ya Now," as seen two months later in *Billboard* when the company took out a full-page ad to promote two of its stars, Ray Bloch and Teresa Brewer. Bloch's picture and name was used to push an up-and-coming Coral singer and the ad read in part "Ray Bloch's discovery Buddy Nee." As for Brewer, Coral included a big photo of the singer with a promotion for a new record release "Kisses on Paper" with "I Hear the Bluebells Ring" on the B-side. Almost as an afterthought, a dark block with tinier lettering in white type was added. It read: ". . . And she's getting hotter and hotter with "Gonna Get Along Without Ya Now" and (in even smaller type) "Roll Them Roly Boly Eyes."[30]

"Gonna Get Along Without Ya Now" is a good, upbeat tune, a perfect fit for Teresa Brewer's approach to singing. The reviewers were correct; the orchestration by Ray Bloch was enthusiastic and bit innovative with what sounds like a Jew's harp at the beginning of the song. It did well, climbing as high as #25 on the pop charts. Over the years, however, the Brewer version of this song has been pretty much forgotten because in 1956, at the beginning of the rock 'n' roll era, two sisters, who professionally called themselves Patience and Prudence, recorded an updated version of the same tune.

In 1956, Brewer turned twenty-five years old, had four children, and the end of career as a major recording star was quickly coming around the bend. Patience McIntyre was fourteen years old and her sister Prudence McIntyre was eleven. They became recording stars because their father, Mark McIntyre, a veteran musician and songwriter, was also one of the owners of Los Angeles–based Liberty Records and he brought his talented daughters into the studio.[31]

The lyrics were altered one more time.

Brewer's swing time version began this way: "Got along without ya before I met ya / Gonna get along without ya now / Gonna find somebody twice as cute cause ya didn't love me anyhow / you ran around with ev'ry girl in town / and ya never cared if it got me down . . ." Then it had a chorus that ran this way: "Boom boom, boom boom, Gonna get along without ya now . . ."

Patience and Prudence's rewrite aimed to teenagers sounded like this: "Uh huh, uh huh, gonna get along without you now / Uh huh, my honey, uh huh my honey, gonna get along without you now / you told me I was the neatest thing / You even asked me to wear your ring / you ran around with every girl in town / you never cared if it got me down." The chorus went back to "Uh huh, uh huh, gonna get along without you now."

It's the Patience and Prudence version of the song that still gets played on oldies stations and is most remembered by the baby boomer generation. Even aficionados steeped in 1950s music lore don't even realize the song had been previously recorded by Teresa Brewer.

CHAPTER FOUR

TILL I WALTZ AGAIN WITH YOU (1953)

RICHARD ADLER AND JERRY ROSS—TONY BENNETT—
PATTI PAGE—TERESA BREWER—BOB THIELE—JUNE VALLI—
JONI JAMES—ANTHONY (TONY) ACQUAVIVA

Before considering the year 1953 in pop music, we first have to skip ahead to Broadway in 1954, because that year the big new musical was *The Pajama Game*, which would go on to win three Tony Awards including best musical. There are so many minor, trivial, game-show answers emanating from this show, it gets hard to stop. For example, the choreographer was Bob Fosse, who would become the most iconic choreographer in America after Martha Graham. Also having a big career after this play was the understudy to the starring actress Carol Haney. The young lady's name was Shirley MacLaine. The story is that Haney suffered an ankle injury and MacLaine had to step into the role. In the audience was a Hollywood director, who saw MacLaine's beauty and talent and quickly signed her to Paramount Pictures.

A key part of the show's success was the outstanding songs written by the songwriting team Richard Adler and Jerry Ross. A number of the melodies became hit records. Creatively, these tunes were so well-formed and rhythmic that the female crooners rushed to these melodies like mice to a block of cheese. Patti Page took "Steam Heat" to #9 on the pop chart, while Rosemary Clooney's recording of "Hey There" shot all the way to #1.

The reason we dwell on *The Pajama Game* is because Richard Adler and Jerry Ross initially came to the music industry's attention in 1953 for a song they wrote called "Rags to Riches." As with all good songs in the early 1950s, it attracted hordes of singers like ants at a picnic, but there were two outstanding renditions. The first highlight was by the R&B group Billy Ward and His Dominoes on King Records, a melding of pop and doo-wop streams. As sung by lead singer Jackie Wilson, the vocals are histrionic, yet it was a very successful song, the twentieth best-selling record on the R&B charts for the year and very popular on the jukeboxes.[1]

However, the real mastery of this particular tune is in the version by Tony Bennett, also in 1953. Bennett had been a star since the start of the decade and was no stranger to the pop charts. Even with all that success, in retrospect, those earlier songs, including #1 hits, were stifling post-swing songs that didn't outlive the year in which they were introduced. That all changed with "Rags to Riches," a song where Tony Bennett really found himself, adding an innate ebullience that heretofore seemed to be missing. Sure, the lyrics are dramatic ("I know I'd go from rags to riches, if you would only say you care / And although my pocket may be empty, I'd be a millionaire") yet you can only envision Bennett smiling throughout the recording. He nailed it.

In 1953, "Rags to Riches" was the very rare instance where something on the pop charts was better than any recording of the same song on the rhythm & blues charts, which was being crashed by new talent, creativity, and a combination of blues with doo-wop. Ruth Brown, Johnny Ace, B.B. King, and Clyde McPhatter & the Drifters all boasted Top Ten records of the year. Classic, eternal songs include The Orioles' "Crying in the Chapel," Faye Adams's "Shake a Hand," Clyde McPhatter & the Drifters' "Money Honey," and Willie Mae "Big Mama" Thornton's "Hound Dog."

The pop charts in 1953 were not centered at all, with recording trends heading off not into one dead end but to many. For example, a resurgence of instrumentals by big-band type orchestras was the most outstanding aural phenomenon of the year. The #1 song for 1953 was the instrumental "The Song from Moulin Rouge" by bandleader Percy Faith, who was having a good year: his orchestra backed Tony Bennett on "Rags to Riches." Also in the Top Ten for that year was the instrumental "April In Portugal" by bandleader Les Baxter. The popularity of instrumentals was so heightened that if it was necessary to choose a classic composition from the 1953 pop charts it would be another instrumental, "Ebb Tide" by Frank Chacksfield, a bandleader from Great Britain. The song, with lyrics, would be revived many times over the next decade with a subsequent best-known version by the Righteous Brothers in 1965.

Giving "Ebb Tide" a run for its royalty money and consideration as the only other classic pop song of the year was "I Believe" by Frankie Laine. The song was originally introduced by female singer Jane Froman on her television show, making it the first hit song ever introduced on television. Good for Froman, yet better for Laine, who with his distinctive baritone really gave gravitas to this inspirational tune ("I believe for every drop of rain that falls, a flower grows"). There have been so many versions of this song since 1953 it would take a calculator to keep track.

So for the first time in the new decade, the year's best songs were not by the ladies. In fact, 1953 was not a good year for female singers. Of the twenty most popular tunes, only two were by women, Patti Page and Teresa Brewer, who by this time were formidable veterans of the pop charts. The irony of Page and Brewer both having monumental hits in 1953 was that they were headed in opposite directions. Page purloined some thunder from Brewer, going after the novelty song crowd, while Brewer took a cue from Page and went deep into serious balladry.

Looking at *Billboard*'s Top Thirty songs of the year, a rush of thrushes eventually crowded in. Eartha Kitt, a Black singer, crossed over to the pop charts with "C'est Si Bon"; June Valli, a young singer who made a name for herself on television transformed into a pop star by covering Darrell Glenn's country hit "Crying in the Chapel"; and finally, the red hot Joni James, who boasted three Top Thirty hits that year: "Why Don't You Believe Me," "Your Cheatin' Heart," and "Have You Heard."

Perry Como totaled three Top Thirty hits in 1953, including "Don't Let the Stars Get in Your Eyes." Yet, that year, two of the country's best-known female singing stars earwormed their way deep into everyone's temporal lobes. It's odd that each of these two ladies, Page and Brewer, boasted two of their best-selling songs in 1953 but the records were such outliers in regard to their careers it's as if someone else did the records. Brewer's renown is fondly recalled through the lighter fare such as "Music! Music! Music!" or "A Sweet Old Fashioned Girl," while Page if best remembered for heart-pounding tunes such as "Tennessee Waltz" or "Allegheny Moon."

According to Page biographer Skip Press, on August 1, 1953, Patti Page was to appear at Soldier Field Stadium in Chicago as part of a promotion called "*Downbeat*'s Star Night." She had recently come out of the studio recording a children's album and decided to go with a cute little number from that session called "(How Much Is) That Doggie in the Window." The song began this way: "How much is that doggie in the window? (woof, woof) / the one with the waggly tail / How much is that doggie in the window? (woof, woof) / I do hope that doggie's for sale."

Page had been recording a children's album about a dog called Arfie and an existing tune, "How Much Is That Doggie in the Window," was going to be used. The song was based on the nursery rhyme, "Oh, where, oh where has my little dog gone." Bob Merrill, who wrote "If I Knew You Were Comin' I'd've Baked a Cake" for Eileen Barton, also gets credit for this novelty winner. The backstory is that another popular female singer at the time, Mindy Carson, was offered the song but turned it down. Big mistake, because Page's version sold two million copies and was the #1 best-selling song in the country for eight weeks.

As Page recalled the session, before recording the song no one had been thinking sound effects. However, "to a musician, it was natural to make a sound of some kind at that place because it was right on the beat, so the violin player, Max Ceppos, chimed in the barks. When we listened to it being played back, Joe Carlton, the A&R man, said, 'Oh, that sounds great. Let's keep that in there' ... then Joe Reisman, the arranger and bass clarinet player, ... put in a 'small dog' going 'yip yip,' which made it even cuter."

The song was not only popular with kids; men caught on to it as well. When Page sang the tune in concert, all the males in the audience would bark out loud and do wolf calls.

Skip Press added this interesting tidbit about the song: the Mercury Records marketing team produced even more tinder for promotional efforts, allowing side companies to produce "Doggie in the Window" stuffed toys, children's books, pajamas, and more. However, Press added, Page's manager at the time, Jack Rael, neglected to include royalties from product licensing in Page's contract, so she never received one cent for the millions of dollars received from the sale of ancillary "Doggie" goods.[2]

When singer Donna Loren (born Donna Zukor) was seven years old, her parents sat her down at the dining room table and told her that when she grew up and went to work, she could be a clerk in a five-and-dime store or cultivate a career that would support the family (parents and two brothers). As she added, "What is a child to do when faced with a decision like that?" By her tenth birthday, Loren was performing on the Mickey Mouse show. She became a successful model, The Dr. Pepper Girl; the lead female singer on the *Shindig!* rock 'n' roll television show; and finally a supporting actress in teen and surf movies in the 1960s.

It had all started very early for Loren when she was a child and her mother bribed her into performing at a children's talent competition to sing "(How Much Is) That Doggie in the Window." Loren came in second when the winner, a baton twirler, much to everyone's surprise caught the baton she tossed in the air. Today, Loren recalled, "I wasn't a big Patti Page fan, but I loved *Tennessee Waltz*, which I still sing today."

Then at the ages of nine and ten, Loren was pushed to sing live at other venues such as the Hollywood USO, where she sang tunes such as "A Sweet Old Fashioned Girl." Sardonically, Loren remarked, "that was the beginning of my Teresa Brewer era."[3]

She wasn't the only one caught in the Teresa Brewer loop. Diane Renay (Renee Diane Kushner) rose to fame in the girl group era with the catchy tune "Navy Blue." She was seventeen at the time.

Renay was born in South Philly, then a hotbed of musical talent. Unlike Loren, she wasn't pushed into the music business at an early age; that would come later.

As for her childhood introduction to music, she said, "I used to imitate Teresa Brewer when I was a little girl." By twelve she graduated to doo-wop singing with a group of South Philly boys. At fourteen years, her father thought she had talent and took her into a studio to make a demo. She sang "Zing! Went the Strings of My Heart" and a couple of other songs. Then at sixteen, Artie Singer, who coached Bobby Rydell and Frankie Avalon, took an interest in her. The next year she was a star—and it all started with Teresa Brewer.[4]

Loren and Renay were beginning their elementary school careers when Brewer moved from London Records to Coral and they all had bright futures ahead. It took a little longer for Brewer to catch up to the expectations of her new company. The hype began early. On December 24, 1951, *Cash Box* posted a picture of Brewer with her new boss, Coral A&R man Jimmy Hilliard. The headline above the picture reads, "Teresa Brewer Sings, Sings, Sings" and the caption with a New York dateline said, "Teresa Brewer, who recently signed a recording contract with Coral Records is pictured at her first session with Jimmy Hilliard, A&R chief of the diskery [record company]. Teresa's initial Coral release 'Sing, Sing, Sing' and 'I Don't Care' has both sides making a splash with juke box and disk jockey play mounting. Coral is going all out on the platter and artist."[5]

The company was still pushing the tune early in the next year. A Teresa Brewer feature in the February 1952 issue of *Popular Songs* magazine goes full bore on the song: "Now sparkling Teresa comes to the fore again with another smash pair of hits, this time on the Coral label. On one side, Miss Brewer revives the great standard 'Sing, Sing, Sing.' This number, already waxed several times in the past years, receives its best treatment in the recording by Teresa. Jack Pleis and his orchestra blend in with some fine instruments which really send the tune flying."[6]

Hilliard was not a good fit for Brewer, although he would fail upward, moving to the RCA subsidiary "X" Records and then to head of operations for Bally Records in Chicago. "Sing, Sing, Sing," the old Benny Goodman tune, didn't swing with listeners. It was a straight-to-the-reject-bin failure.

Her second song rollout was more interesting, a proto–rock 'n' roll barrelhouse blues number "Lovin' Machine" originally sung by R&B singer Wynonie Harris. Finally, someone got smart and ditched Jack Pleis, giving the arrangement and production to Ray Bloch.[7] He gets a dose of bluesy gusto from Brewer although the song is not as sexy as when Wynonie Harris wailed "Up to my house, I've got somethin' you've never seen; Well I got hip to the tip and built me a lovin' machine." Teresa's version has its fans. Singer/songwriter Billy Vera wrote, "She [Teresa Brewer] shows that she can sing anything believably. Killer tenor sax solo." The B-side was a song called "Noodlin' Rag," which didn't stand a chance because female-crooner-killer Perry Como also recorded it and his version went to #25 on the pop chart. It wasn't much of a song. "I love to hear a band that's playin' a doodle de doo / a doodlin' to the noodlin' rag (oh, the noodlin'rag)."

"Gonna Get Along Without Ya Now" did well. The opportunity to do better on the follow-up was scorched by more nonstarters, including "I Hear the Bluebells Ring" with "Kisses on Paper" on the B-side. "I Hear the Bluebells" was actually a good song, a jazzy beat handled nicely by Brewer. Perhaps it was just too old-school swing for that moment in time.

Another singer that moved over to Coral was Eileen Barton, who was saddled with covering big hits by other singers—although she did well with these covers. Her version of Johnnie Ray's "Cry" went to #10 on the pop chart in 1951, while her "Don't Let the Stars Get in Your Eyes" hit #24 on the pop chart in 1953.

Coral released a new record in 1952 with a Teresa Brewer number "Rhode Island Redhead (Here! Chick! Chick!)" on the A-side and an Eileen Barton number "En-Thuz-E-Uz-E-As-M" on the B-side. These tunes had been prize-winners on a show called *Songs for Sale*, where amateur songwriters would have their songs performed and the winner was guaranteed to be recorded. No feather in the cap for either singer. "Rhode Island Redhead" was a silly, unredeemable undertaking by Brewer.

The logjam at radio stations and on the jukeboxes was finally broken by Brewer's successful duet with Don Cornell. The week that *Cash Box* made "You'll Never Get Away" the "Sleeper of the Week," there was another duet in review, Connee Boswell and Artie Shaw with their song "Where There's Smoke There's Fire," which fizzled out quickly.[8]

In the early 1950s, record companies would push so many songs by popular artists into the market that you could almost get Tony Bennett fatigue or Rosemary Clooney fatigue or, god forbid, Frank Sinatra fatigue. However, if you got your best in-house singer to do a duet with a well-known singer of the opposite sex, it was almost as if the coupling were a brand-new entity entirely. Many of these duets were moderately successful, such as "You'll Never Get Away," which climbed to #17 on the pop chart. The B-side, "The Hookey Song," was ridiculous hokum about not playing hookey from school. The managers for Don Cornell should have let this pass. He was in his mid-thirties, had sung with the Sammy Kaye band in the 1940s, and was one of the very successful male crooners having a string of hits since 1949. He was too old and too successful to be singing about playing hookey from school, but heck, if Perry Como could sing "Noodlin' Rag" and have a hit, why not the hookey song?

Because of the duo's success, the following summer they were reunited for another couple of songs, "The Glad Song" and "What Happened to the Music." "The Glad Song" is not without fans, but today it sounds like two adults, on too much caffeine, singing too fast, and Teresa at too high a range especially on Teresa's "I'm glad," Don's "I'm glad you're glad," Teresa's "I'm glad you're glad I'm glad." All repeated too often.

As for the B-side, "What Happened to the Music"? Whew. It was only 1953 and rock 'n' roll wouldn't sweep away the detritus of the pop charts for another two to three years, but already Don Cornell, in his Bing Crosby voice, was lamenting "what happened to the music of not so long ago / where are the good old fashioned songs we used to know."

Bill Munroe concludes: "Don Cornell had a number of hits in the later 1940s and early '50s. They included . . . 'The Bible Tells Me So,' written by Dale Evans, and 'I'm Yours.' In fact, at the tail-end of 'You'll Never Get Away,' Don croons a snippet of 'I'm Yours' to Teresa. She returned the favor the following year in 'The Glad Song' by singing a few bars of 'Till I Waltz Again with You' in the song's final moments. Cute idea."

"Till I Waltz Again with You" was introduced into the record market at the tail end of 1952. It took a few weeks for radio disk jockeys to pick it out of their stacks of new releases, discover a wonderful new song, and play it endlessly. In 1953, it would end up as the sixth best-selling song of the year, reigning as the #1 song in the country for five weeks, bumping Perry Como's "Don't Let the Stars Get in Your Eyes" from the top of the charts and finally being dethroned in mid-March by Patti Page's "(How Much Is) That Doggie in the Window."

The difference with "Till I Waltz Again with You" in regard to Brewer's career is that this was a mature ballad sung maturely. Brewer's normal frantic pace of song was slowed down, not just to a waltz but to a foxtrot and her wide range was moved to the lower scales so she didn't have to sound like she had four too many cups of coffee. This song had no gimmicks, a pure ballad: "Till I waltz again with you, let no other hold your charms / If my dreams should all come true, you'll be waiting for my arms." Jack Pleis was back with his orchestra to sit in behind Brewer, and his conservative arrangements matched perfectly in this song. She easily slid into the Patti Page and Jo Stafford rarified pantheon of those who melodically conquered the romantic ballad from a female perspective.

One of the earliest reviews of the song, in the *Cash Box* column "Record Reviews" on November 1, 1952, knew it was writing about gold. It immediately highlighted the song as its coveted "Sleeper of the Week" and the unnamed reviewer got it right about the song from beginning to end of the column. In a state of music ecstasy, he or she, wrote:

Teresa Brewer came into the music world and sent it for a loop with her captivating waxing of "Music! Music! Music!" Since then, Tessie has been holding her own with some fine jobs of recording as can be noted by listening to her cutting of "You'll Never Get Away" with Don Cornell. Now a new-voiced Teresa steps up with something that should rock the wax circles again. The cute chirp softens her voice to a romantic one and appealingly lilts a lovely ballad with impressive lyrics called "Till I Waltz Again With You." The tune and the presentation are equally outstanding. It's a pleasant surprise to hear Teresa sing in such a warm and tender style. On the flip end [B-side] the thrush is the same old wonderful self . . . but we're crazy about the top half [A-side].[9]

The recording of the song is a credit to Brewer. In 1952, Brewer and husband Bill Monahan were visiting the Brill Building when they entered the elevator. Sydney Prosen also stepped through the closing doors, an unknown songwriter who came down to the Brill Building to promote tunes he had written. When he recognized Brewer, he asked if she would listen to one of his songs. (Gregory Merwin in a *TV-Radio Mirror* magazine story of September 1959 wrote up the anecdote in a latently sexist way: "Sidney Prosen, then unknown, asked if Bill and she would listen to the song as if Bill had any say in what Brewer would sing.") Teresa was pleasant, polite, and said she would indeed listen. The *TV-Radio Mirror* article quoted Brewer: "He didn't have a demonstration record and he didn't play the piano. But he started then and there to sing it, with a hillbilly beat I didn't like. I felt that, if it were sung straight, it would be good."[10] She told Bill Munroe, "He sang it and it was done in a country tempo, with a fifth bar, and I said it just doesn't work . . . I thought the song was beautiful, so we put it in a pop tempo, recorded it."

The song was "Till I Waltz Again with You." Prosen confessed that Mitch Miller had turned it down, which meant it didn't go to Columbia's stable of female singers including Rosemary Clooney. Brewer found it appealing and so very different from anything she had done and wanted to sing it. There was one problem; Coral was still thinking about Brewer only as a performer who should be singing those bouncy, fun songs that created her career. Coral, with Jimmy Hilliard as head of A&R, fumbled Brewer's momentum at the label from the start. As a magazine feature on Brewer noted, "She had switched over to Coral Records, the head of recording there did not think that 'Till I Waltz Again with You' was the right song for Teresa, but this time she was in favor of singing it."[11]

Normally, A&R had such tight control over fifties recording acts, especially at the big recording companies, that there would be little discussion as to what a singer might or might not sing. Brewer had been a name performer at London Records, and on that strength Ritchie Lisella would have negotiated some leeway in her contract as to Brewer being able to choose some, not all, of the songs she would be recording. Brewer understood she had a certain style that her public liked, what she called "bouncy, rhythm-type songs," but she told

Hit Parader magazine in 1954, "there is always an exception to the rule . . . this exception concerns Sidney Prosen, who had a tune that he thought I would like. It was a nice song, a little on the slow side. I recorded it, crossed my fingers and waited to see what the reaction would be."[12]

"Till I Waltz Again with You" won the *Cash Box* disk jockey poll award as the most programmed record of the year. It sold over a million records, probably the most sales of any song Brewer ever recorded,[13] and, again, as she told Munroe, "it's my favorite of all of them."

There is an interesting anecdote to the song. According to a number of Elvis Presley biographers, one of the first songs he performed in public was "Till I Waltz Again with You" and one night in 1972 after a Teresa Brewer show in Las Vegas, she was informed that Elvis wanted to come back to her dressing room to say hi. Brewer's first thought was, "What was Elvis doing watching my show?" Teresa recounted the event to Munroe: "Sure enough, he came back with his whole entourage and the first thing he said was that he enjoyed my singing. For about a half hour, he told me his life story, sort of rambling on; he seemed so lonely. When he was through, he snapped his fingers and he and his entourage left. He seemed like a very lonely man; he just wanted to talk."[14]

Brewer discovered "Till I Waltz Again with You" and pushed it on Coral Records, despite deep resistance. Although she never said there were issues with the company's management of her career, after the success of "Till I Waltz Again with You," numerous management changes took place at Decca and Coral. Most importantly, a real go-getter named Bob Thiele took over as head of A&R for Coral.

Thiele was born in Brooklyn in 1922. His family's claim to fame was that it operated the famous Lundy's Restaurant. At fourteen years old he was promoting his own radio show, and at seventeen in 1939, started his very first label, Signature Records, which recorded mostly hot jazz (not swing) musicians such as Coleman Hawkins. Later he recorded the crooner Alan Dale. After Signature folded, he began working with Coral Records in 1953 as assistant to Milt Gabler, who took over as head of Coral A&R when Jimmy Hilliard achieved his first fail-upward elevation to head of A&R at the parent Decca Records.

Thiele wrote in his autobiography, *What a Wonderful World: A Lifetime of Recordings*, "Teresa was already a major recording star when we both arrived [she signed with Coral in 1951] at Coral and began our professional relationship. Almost immediately we [Coral Records] hit #1 with 'Till I Waltz Again with You,'" which remained on the singles charts for half the year.[15]

The trade press story about the changes at Decca can be seen in the *Cash Box* issue of June 6, 1953, which in big type announced: "Milt Gabler Named A&R Head of Decca; Bob Thiele Takes Over at Coral." The paragraphs read: ". . . Milton Gabler last Thursday was named A&R head of Decca, replacing

Jimmy Hilliard . . . Gabler moves over from Coral, Decca's subsidiary, where he was also A&R head. Replacing him at Coral is Bob Thiele, who has been his assistant for the past year. Jimmy Hilliard, who reported that his resignation was offered last Monday . . ."

The story included a history of Thiele and lauded him for his leadership at Signature, which "developed some of the top names in the record business today." Among these stars were Mindy Carson, Toni Arden, Alan Dale, and Ray Bloch.

According to *Cash Box*, in 1952 Thiele concluded an agreement with Coral that brought all the Signature masters under the Coral label, and then, several months later Thiele joined the A&R department. He also brought with him talent including Alan Dale, Ray Bloch, and an up-and-coming singer Eydie Gormé (which was misspelled as Eddie Gorme).[16]

With "Till I Waltz Again with You" a major hit, Coral rushed a couple more Teresa Brewer songs into the market and they did moderately well. "Dancin' with Someone (Longin' for You)" went to #17 on the pop chart and "Into Each Life Some Rain Must Fall" came in at #23.

Brewer's next blockbuster record, also in 1953, came to her as a result of controversy elsewhere. Deep in the August 1, 1953, *Billboard* column "Music as Written" was a story about a dustup between between a major label and a minor record company. The story noted that Capitol Records A&R veep Alan Livingston nixed a request by Sheldon Music's Goldie Goldmark to hold up the release of Vicki Young's rendition of a song titled "Ricochet." Livingston claimed that Goldmark gave Capitol the tune without a release date restriction and it could release the song anytime it wanted. Goldmark also turned the tune over to Coral Records, which had passed the song to Teresa Brewer.[17]

The fuss died down three weeks later, *Billboard* reported: "When Coral Records decided to rush the release of Teresa Brewer's waxing of 'Ricochet,' the label also ended a saga of publisher release dates which had the tune ricocheting from Capital to Coral to Sheldon Music."[18] Vicki Young's version of the song was pitched as early as August 1, but it would soon be run over by Brewer. To emphasize that point, Coral Records took out a full-page ad in the August 29, 1953, issue of *Billboard* touting "Teresa Brewer's Ricochet."[19] The main difference between the two was in the chorus, where the performer had to quick-pace sing a clutter of words and there was no one who could do that better than Brewer. Just try singing these lines fast with a broad smile on your face: "I don't want a ricochet romance, I don't want a ricochet love / if you're careless with your kisses, find another turtle dove," and it went on. There was nothing wrong with Vicki Young's version, it's just that this kind of song was in Brewer's wheelhouse.

According to *RV-Radio Mirror*, between "Till I Waltz Again with You" and "Ricochet" Brewer went out to Hollywood, where she costarred with singer

Guy Mitchell and Rhonda Fleming in the lighthearted romp *Those Redheads from Seattle*.[20]

Bob Thiele reportedly found the song "Ricochet" for Brewer. In Teresa's recollection, the record was not supposed to be released, at least not the version that was first recorded. "I had a cold that day and I didn't particularly care for that take and I said, 'Don't release it.' So we recorded it at a later date. In the end Thiele released the first recording."

Looking back, Thiele remembers the "Ricochet" ordeal completely differently. According to Thiele's memory, Brewer recorded the tune in the few perfect takes needed and everyone went home. After the recording, during the ensuing days as Thiele listened to the result of the session, he became increasingly unhappy as to how Teresa's vocal was balanced against the orchestra and he wanted to re-record. Not everyone saw the logic in that request and, Thiele wrote in his autobiography, "I finally persuaded Teresa to participate in a second session." After listening to the second recording, Thiele realized the first recording was better, and without informing Teresa he released the first version. When Brewer found out, she wasn't at all pleased with Thiele, telling him, "I thought you guys knew what you were doing."[21]

On October 10, Brewer's "Ricochet" appeared for the first time on the *Billboard*'s "Best Selling Singles" chart, at #14. By November, "Ricochet" was on all three *Billboard* charts: "Best Selling Singles," "Most Played in Juke Boxes," and "Most Played by Jockeys." The song would climb to #2 on *Billboard*'s record chart and sell a million records. In a 1954 interview with *Hit Parader* magazine, Brewer told the press, "I had a feeling that my waxing of 'Ricochet' would be a good one because it went along the lines of the type of tune I like the best. But, I had no idea that it would be another million-record seller."[22]

When "Ricochet" appeared on the *Billboard* chart at #14, the song came in one slot ahead of Joni James's "My Love, My Love." The way 1953 worked out for female crooners was singular, million-seller hits by chart veterans Patti Page and Teresa Brewer, and very strong showings by two relative newcomers to the scene, Joni James and June Valli. Of the two latter singers, the one who had the stronger presence, even a better year than Page and Brewer, was Joni James, who had a #1 record, "Why Don't You Believe Me," in 1952; the song was on the charts so long it was a Top Thirty best-seller in 1953. The real newcomer was June Valli, although she, too, started attracting attention the year before.

Most of the female crooners who migrated to television started out as recording stars. For June Valli, the opposite was true. It was really the television exposure that gave her a successful career as a singer—not much different from what happened with Ricky Nelson later in the decade.

Stop the Music was a successful radio game show on the NBC network until the FCC banned game shows from the radio and it moved over the new medium, television. In its first season on the air (1950–51), one the young stars was singer June Valli. (Later on, another female crooner, Jaye P. Morgan, would get her start on this show.) The show ran for five seasons but with cast changes, because another radio show, *Your Hit Parade*, had also migrated to television and it poached talent from *Stop the Music*. *The Times* of San Mateo, California, posted this short notice under the headline "Hit Parade Renewed"; "Tonight Snooky Lanson, Dorothy Collins, everybody's girlfriend, Raymond Scott, and June Valli will do their inaugural show of *Lucky Strike Hit Parade* for the 1952–53 season. June Valli will be the new face for the show. She got her big TV break when she joined the ABC *Stop the Music* show last fall. The gal can really sing."[23]

Apparently others thought so, too, because RCA Victor signed her to a recording contract in 1951.

Valli was born in the Bronx, New York, in 1928. In 1950, when she was twenty-two years old, Valli, an only child, represented the family at a friend's wedding. During the festivities, a girlfriend pushed Valli to the microphone, where she did well enough to catch the attention of another guest, writer and radio host Abe Burrows. He was so impressed he arranged for Valli to appear on *Arthur Godfrey's Talent Scouts*, where she won first prize for her rendition of "Stormy Weather." That's a good break, right? The story gets better. Harry Salter, the orchestra leader for *Stop the Music*, saw her on *Arthur Godfrey* and invited her to serve as a replacement for Kay Armen, who was leaving his show.

Salter mentored Valli, and by May 1951 she started gigging in New York nightspots. By July she signed her first recording contract with RCA Victor, one the big recording companies at the time.[24] She started recording immediately but with little effect, so RCA duetted her with singer Tony Bavaar. That didn't work either, despite a January 19, 1952, RCA Victor promotion in *Billboard* listing the company's new releases including "What You Don't Know of Love"/"It's Raining" by Tony Bavaar and June Valli.[25] About the only singer happening for RCA Victor in 1952 was Tony Martin.

At that time, Valli, thinking her career was hanging by a thread, penned a letter to a *Billboard* columnist thanking him for mentioning her with Eddie Fisher and Al Martino. She wrote, "I was so happy to find that you remembered me, particularly because I haven't recorded since last October. However, we did make a couple of sides last week. Harry Salter furnished the brilliant orchestrations and Hugo Winterhalter conducted magnificently. This may, of course, have been my last time at RCA Victor, but if it doesn't hit I hope you will be patient with me just a little while longer."[26]

For a moment it looked like her fears were not unfounded. RCA Victor released "So Madly in Love" with "Strange Sensation" on the B-side. Unfortunately, Georgia Gibbs covered the A-side song as well and her version seemed destined to be the hit. Meanwhile, disk jockeys flipped Valli's record and took a liking to the dramatic tango number "Strange Sensation." *Billboard* caught the vibe and in a quick "Record Review" on June 21, 1952, observed: "The thrush does her best job on the label to date with this exciting new ballad based on a Latin oldie . . . She sings it with a lot of heart, while the Harry Salter ork [orchestra] backs the girl in lovely fashion. With proper exploitation this waxing could break out."[27]

By June 28, 1952, it was the sixth best-seller in retail across the country, outdoing her band leader Hugo Winterhalter at #7 and labelmate Tony Martin at #8. Its *Billboard* chart position settled down at #23 and her recording career was jump-started.

As with Joni James, 1953 was Valli's peak year. She boasted two Top Ten records, "Tell Me, Tell Me" and her biggest record, the surprising crossover song "Crying in the Chapel," a song worth a whole book in and of itself. Written as a country tune by Artie Glenn, the tune was rejected by the big song publishers of the day, including Hill and Range and Acuff-Rose. It went to the small Valley Publishers and the tune was released as a country single by Artie's son Darrell Glenn. Country singing star Rex Allen took a whack at it and turned it into a Top Ten country record. In the R&B world, the Orioles covered it and that group's version became the #1 R&B song of the year and the classic version of the tune, so revered by music people they wouldn't even include the Elvis Presley redo in the same sentence. However, the best-selling version in 1953 was by June Valli. It climbed to #4 on the pop best-seller chart, hanging on to the record charts for over four months. Not bad for what essentially was a quasi-religious, inspirational song: "You saw me crying in the chapel, the tears I shed were tears of joy / I know the meaning of contentment, I am happy with the Lord."

Valli had a few more minor hit records, including another cover, "Unchained Melody," in 1955 and was lucky enough to get back to television in 1957 with the *Andy Williams–June Valli Show*. Still recording past the 1950s, she had one more substantial hit in 1960, a song called "Apple Green," which went to #29 on the chart.

In 1975, a Chicago newspaper reporter asked her what happened to her and career. She responded, "I was getting calls from movies, television and record companies when I met Howard Miller [a well-known radio disk jockey in that city] here in Chicago and made my biggest mistake. I married him . . . the marriage was a short, unhappy one. In two years, the divorce was final, but by then my career had taken a beating."[28]

Miller, wanting to keep Valli close, persuaded her to turn down every job that would have taken her to New York or California. Valli bitterly recalled that whenever they needed to talk about offers, like a good radio deejay "he twisted words and talked so fast I never had a chance in any debate."

She summed it all up this way, "You have only about five years to hit the top in this business . . . the trouble is that during those few precious years, most of us are too inexperienced to know how to deal with success."

On November 1, 1952, *Billboard*'s gossip column "Music as Written" reported on many of the music industry's familiar female names caught, or about to be involved, in recent activities. June Valli was due in Chicago for a tour of disk jockeys and key dealers to plug her latest on Victor Records; Mindy Carson opened at the Hotel Plaza's Persian Room in New York; Georgia Gibbs did three days at the Meadowbrook in New York before heading to the Latin Quarter and then on to Philadelphia; and Joni James was to meet MGM's Harry Meyerson, who flew into Chicago to record "Joni James, who is riding high with her 'Why Don't You Believe Me.'"[29]

By mid-November 1952, it was getting to be a real catfight among female singers for the top song in the country. Still #1 after fourteen weeks was Jo Stafford's "You Belong to Me," which left the hard-charging "I Went to Your Wedding" by Patti Page at #2, and a second Jo Stafford tune, "Jambalaya," at #4. Sliding down the chart after twenty-four weeks was "Half as Much" by Rosemary Clooney at #10. Going in the opposite direction was rookie Joni James's "Why Don't You Believe Me," at #9, its first week in the Top Ten.

By the end of November, the usual potential-hit-song scrum had already started. Patti Page cut a version of "Why Don't You Believe Me" and Margaret Whiting piled on as well. Neither could stop the James recording. On November 29, it shared the #1 Best-seller slot in the country with Johnny Standley's "It's in the Book" and then reigned supreme for three more weeks. James's "Why Don't You Believe Me" would stay on the charts for six months and sell over two million records.

The song was written by a trio of songwriters, Lew Douglas, King Laney, and Roy Rodde. Of the three, the most well-known is Lew Douglas, who conducted and arranged "Why Don't You Believe Me" and the next year would write a second big hit for James, "Have You Heard."

Joni James had the Christopher Cross career. For about three years at the end of the 1970s and into the '80s, Cross could do no wrong. Everything he touched turned to gold, er . . . platinum. He had two #1 songs, "Sailing" and "Arthur's Theme (Best That You Can Do)" (and a #2 song, "Ride Like the Wind"); won Grammys and even an Oscar for writing and singing "Arthur's Theme" for the movie *Arthur*. And then he disappeared. Maybe we should say Cross suffered the Joni James career: for three years she could do no wrong and then, she didn't disappear immediately, but she faded away from recording success—and then disappeared! Joni James (Giovanna Carmella Babbo) was born September 22, 1930, in Chicago. At first it seemed she was destined for a dance career, taking ballet lessons, touring with a show through Canada and becoming a chorus girl at Chicago's Edgewater Beach Hotel. While recuperating from an appendectomy, she filled in for a friend at a roadhouse in nearby Northern Indiana. People liked what they heard and she decided to switch careers. In 1951, she entered a talent contest at the Copa in Pittsburgh. As a finalist she received $12.50 for her efforts, but she lost the ultimate contest and with it a week's worth of work that went to the winner. She went back to playing Chicago area clubs and caught the ears and eyes of recording executives when she performed in a television commercial.[30] Her first two records ("Let There Be Love"/"My Baby Just Cares for Me" and "You Belong to Me"/"Yes, Yes, Yes") were released on the Sharp label, which had a deal with the much bigger MGM Records that if any Sharp single sold 10,000 copies it would be released on MGM, reported Jim Andrews, a Joni James musicologist and creator of the Joni James fan club. Both records easily hit the 10,000 mark within about a week and slid over to the MGM label.[31]

Billboard's gossip column "Music as Written" on April 19, 1952, picked up on the Chicago singer noting, "Joni James, nitery chirp [nightclub singer], has cut her first sides for MGM, with the initial pairing due for release in about 10 days."[32] At the end of the month, MGM released "Let There Be Love" on its own label and *Billboard* was on board again with a quick "Music Popularity Charts" (April 16, 1952) review, where the comments were warm and encouraging: "Chirp [singer] James, a Chicago lass, makes her bow with this etching [record] and proves that she has an interesting sound and a way with a ballad." As to "My Baby Just Cares for Me," the B-side, the reviewer said, "Tackling the oldie at a bounce tempo is just a good performance by the gal. It may not create a commercial stir, but should help sell. The gal's got pipes."[33]

She was catching on. By the next month James opened a two-week stay at the Flame Showbar in Detroit and then was headed for another two-week gig at Leon & Eddie's in New York.[34]

Finally her MGM recordings were released. In the September 27, 1952, issue of *Billboard*, the first hint as to what was to come appeared in a quick review for "Why Don't You Believe Me," which observed, "Miss James continues to impress with her chanting. With enough exploitation she could break thru [through]. Her reading here, of a nice, new, hit is smooth."[35]

The December 20, 1952, issue of *Cash Box* slotted "Why Don't You Believe in Me" as the #1 record disk jockeys played that week before Christmas. The song even bested seasonal hit "I Saw Mommy Kissing Santa Claus."[36]

MGM knew what it had in James and on the same page as the "Top Ten Records Disk Jockeys Played" column, the record company ran a top-to-bottom-of-page advertisement with a picture of a determined looking James peering out to the magazine readers. The promotional copy was already pushing a new Joni James record "Have You Heard"/"Wishing Ring" with the verbiage at the top reading "Another Smash Hit from America's Newest Singing Sensation . . ."[37]

One piece of the puzzle concerning James's amazing rise to stardom had little to do with her. It began in Philadelphia in September 1952 when a local television executive, wondering how he was going to replace old movies in the afternoon time slot, called in a local disk jockey named Bob Horn for some suggestions. The executive was already leaning to something involving music when Horn came up with the idea of dancing teenagers as a visual part of the program. *Bandstand*, with Horn and Lee Stewart as the emcees, hit the Philly airwaves the very next month. It was heavily promoted, and for the first show over 1,000 kids arrived to dance on television. Dick Clark, who would famously take over as the emcee of *Bandstand*, wrote, "Horn . . . had a sense of what was happening that I don't think anyone else had. He knew he struck gold and now wanted to mine the vein." The show was so popular that guest stars such as Patti Page and Eddie Fisher would appear to lip-sync their current records. As Clark noted, "Joni James was probably the first pop music star created by *Bandstand*."

Joni James becoming a star in 1952 was not an accomplishment to be overlooked. On January 3, 1953, *Billboard* looked back at the prior year and didn't like what it saw in regard to new talent. The double-deck headline read "Many Called, but Few Chosen: Few New Diskery [record company] Artists Able to Hit Big Time in '52." Following the results of a magazine survey, the story complained, only a few of the new artists pushed forward by the record companies "cracked the big time," adding "on the whole, the older, established artists held their own." There was one exception: the rhythm & blues sector. Otherwise, *Billboard* noted, "pop-wise," only Joni James, Al Martino, and children's-song singer Jimmy Boyd ("I Saw Mommy Kissing Santa Claus") came through "stylishly."[38]

James rolled into 1953 already in the stratosphere and kept going all the way to the moon. MGM released eleven James records that year; all but one were Top Thirty tunes. Among the standouts were "You're Fooling Someone," which climbed to #11 on the chart; "Almost Always," #9; "Have You Heard," #4; and the Hank Williams song "Your Cheatin' Heart," #2. Somehow getting overlooked in the shuffle was a record, "I'll Never Stand in Your Way," that climbed to the #22 slot, but it made a big impression on an eighteen-year-old Memphis teenage named Elvis Presley. In 1954, the young man paid four dollars to the Memphis Recording Service to record two "gooey ballads," one of which was the Joni James hit "I'll Never Stand in Your Way."[39]

Then the air started to go out of the balloon. MGM released seven more Joni James songs in 1954. Again, all but one were Top Thirty hits, but none were big hits. The everything-but-the-kitchen-sink approach continued in 1955, with seven more James releases, this time with decidedly mixed results. While most of the songs did not chart, she also had two of her biggest hits. "How Important Can It Be" went all the way to #2 and "You Are My Love" did almost as well, rising as high as #6 on the chart. In the great burst of rock 'n' roll year of 1956, six more James records were unleashed to the public, with only one "How Lucky You Are," becoming a modest hit. She continued to record into the 1960s with spotty results. Her last hits were a remake of Kitty Kallen's 1954 #1 tune, "Little Things Mean a Lot" in 1960 and "My Last Date (With You)" in 1961.

A few years later, the music industry experienced a Joni James resurgence, except it wasn't by Joni James. The Duprees, the doo-wop group that had a big hit with Jo Stafford's "You Belong to Me," redid two James songs, "Why Don't You Believe Me" (#37, 1963) and "Have You Heard" (#18, 1963).

"'Have You Heard' broke my heart," remembered Tom Bialoglow, an original member of The Duprees. "I got married in January 1963 and my wife quickly got pregnant. There wasn't enough money coming in so I had to leave the group. I was working part-time as a day-laborer loading tires. I had a new car at the time and the mechanic at the truck operation was adjusting the lights for me. The radio was on and the deejay said, 'Here's a new release by the Duprees.' It was 'Have You Heard.' The mechanic looked at me and said, 'What the fuck are you doing here?' Tears started rolling down my face. The song was beautiful and I wasn't part of it."[40]

It's not as if Joni James didn't give it her all. During her heyday she toured 250 days a year. By one account, she recorded forty-two albums and 125 singles.

"James's success was truly her own, as she picked all the material she chose to sing (that did not happen in the 1950s) and even retained her master tapes—which was simply unheard in the tale of the 1950s and early '60s. Joni James maintains an ageless purity and wholesomeness that practically defines pre-rock & roll music," wrote AllMusic reviewer Lindsay Planer.[41]

Most all modern singers have a period of time where they are popular and then the next generation pushes them aside. After her comeback in 1955, the rock 'n' roll year of 1956 knocked her career for a loop. However, in James's case it wasn't only about the change in music style. In the mid-1950s, during a recording session, she met a moderately successful composer and conductor named Anthony (Tony) Acquaviva. They fell in love and in 1956 were married at St. Patrick's Cathedral in New York. As in the timeless story of an average guy who marries a successful female performer, Acquaviva became her manager.

As a struggling musician in New York, he had roomed with singer Guy Mitchell, who was also looking to catch a break. Mitchell became a star, but it didn't appear that Acquaviva had caught on anywhere. In 1955, he released an album on the MGM label under the name Acquaviva and His Orchestra. It was called "Music for Your Midnight Mood," so he might have been under contract at MGM. Years later, he would dip into the mood music category once again with "The Exciting Sound of Acquaviva," this time on Decca Records. He was also a founder of the New York Pops Symphony Orchestra, not to be confused with the more notable (and still in existence) New York Pops, founded by Skitch Henderson. Otherwise his was a career adrift. It wasn't as if he quit a job to become James's manager. Even though he was a veteran of the music world, her career did not jump when he moved into the management of her business. In the end that all needs to be ignored, because this is a love story. When her husband's health first began to wane in 1964, James retired from the music world to care for him. She did equally as good a job as a nursemaid as she did as a singer; they were married for thirty years before he passed away in 1986. A *New York Daily News* columnist wrote in a 1996 interview with James that the two were so close "they were each other's shadows."

Her disappearance from the music scene was so complete that commentators referred to her as "The Garbo of Song."

In that *Daily News* interview, she commented about her career: "I didn't think of it as giving up. He needed me. And if truth be told, we won the battles but lost the war. People think of it as something special, and that embarrasses me. If you do something, you don't expect medals. After all, he was my husband, and we loved each other deeply. I didn't disappear. I just stopped singing and making public appearances. But it is true that I didn't realize how many people missed me."[42]

James did come back intermittently in later years. On her sixty-fifth birthday, at an affair for high-rollers, she appeared at Trump's Castle in Atlantic City. Donald Trump came onstage and cut a slice of birthday cake for her.

CHAPTER FIVE

LITTLE THINGS MEAN A LOT (1954)

BILL HALEY—THE CHORDS—THE CREW CUTS—KITTY KALLEN— TERESA BREWER—JOAN WEBER—BOB THIELE

In 1953, after a high school gig, Bill Haley and his band were loading instruments into their cars when a group of teenage hepcats wandered up to chat. When Bill asked one of them if they liked the show, the boy answered in teenage vernacular, "crazy, man, crazy." Haley took note and soon afterward constructed a song around the words, also dropping in a few more snippets of teen lingo such as "man, that music's gone."

His label, Essex Records, released the song in the spring of 1953 and it was quickly "gone, daddy, gone," selling 750,000 records in a matter of weeks. That caught the attention of Decca's Milt Gabler, who, by the next year, lured Bill Haley and His Comets to the bigger label. Gabler didn't waste time bringing Haley and band into the studio in April 1954. They recorded "Thirteen Women" and needed another tune for the B-side. Former bandleader and now independent record man James Myers had acquired a song called "Rock around the Clock" for his Philadelphia-based Myers Music from a songwriter named Max Freedman, and since he now owned it, he put his name on it as the songwriter, thereby making sure he would get all the royalties if he could find someone to sing it. He pitched it to Haley when he was still at Essex, but couldn't make a deal, so he got another band, Sonny Dae & His Knights to record it. Nothing happened, so when Haley went to Decca he pitched it again for the B-side. This time a deal was struck. While "Thirteen Women" was a moderate hit, some Haley fans and disk jockeys liked the B-side and Haley made it a regular song in the band's repertoire.[1]

Billboard's "Reviews of New Pop Records" on May 15, 1954, caught up with the disk, calling the performing group "Bill Haley Ork [Orchestra]." As for the A-side, "Thirteen Women," the reviewer noted: "Ops [juke box operators] could

84

make good use of a rhythm and blue-ish item about a guy in a town where he's the only man. The beat is strong and Haley sells the lyrics smartly." For the B-side, "(We're Gonna) Rock around the Clock," the review tried to place it in the context of the prevailing youth culture: "Big beat and repetitive blues lyric makes this a good attempt at 'cat [hepcat] music' and one which should grab coin in the right locations."[2]

For the June 5, 1954, issue of *Billboard*, Decca bought a whole page to promote its hitmakers. At the top was Kitty Kallen for her prodigious record "Little Things Mean a Lot." One of the groups just underneath was Bill Haley and His Comets with "(We're Gonna) Rock around the Clock" and the now B-side song "Thirteen Women." Decca realized the original B-side, now A-side, might have some legs.[3]

Haley and his band entered the recording studio once again in June 1954. This time Haley was determined to record a favorite song of his, Big Joe Turner's "Shake Rattle and Roll," which had been released by Atlantic Records in February that year and was still on the R&B charts.

The Comets added an instrumental chorus, hand claps and a "Go" cheer to make their version standout, writes Peter Benjaminson in his biography of him, *Crazy, Man, Crazy: The Bill Haley Story*. Haley also toned down the prurient lyrics to make it more palatable to pop disk jockeys and the record-buying public.[4] Gone were such lines "Way you wear those dresses, the sun come shining through; I can't believe my eyes, all that mess belongs to you," which became in Haley's version, "Wearing those dresses, your hair done up so nice; You look so warm, But your heart is cold as ice." Haley's record took off, rising into the Top Ten by August and still on the charts in November. According to *Billboard*, the tune was the twenty-sixth most popular song of 1954 and the first "rock 'n' roll" record to make the chart. As to that other song, "(We're Gonna) Rock around the Clock," that most people believe was the first true rock 'n' roll record to make a dent in the record charts, it would get there—in 1955.

In the 1950s, teenage rebellion was a hot topic in America that the media was anxious to exploit. The cinema made impact first with *The Wild One*, a 1953 opus where a Marlon Brando–led motorcycle gang took over a small town in California, a tale that was based on a real incident. In 1954, the book world chipped in with Evan Hunter's novel *The Blackboard Jungle*, about uncontrollable teenagers at an urban high school. The book sold more than a million copies and Hollywood bought the rights. An up-and-coming director named Richard Brooks was given the directing chores, perhaps due to the success of his prior movie *The Last Time I Saw Paris*, which was based on another literary property, F. Scott Fitzgerald's short story "Babylon Revisited."

The star of *Blackboard Jungle* was Glenn Ford, and Brooks would occasionally roll over to the Ford residence to discuss upcoming scenes. Early in the production Brooks still had not found the music he wanted for a movie about tough teenagers. Ford had a preteen son who was really into the current music at that time, especially R&B, and had a stack of records. Brooks and Ford worked their way through the platters, taking three back to the studio with them, including Big Joe Turner's "Shake, Rattle and Roll" and Bill Haley's "Rock around the Clock." He chose the latter. *Blackboard Jungle* was released in 1955 and the rest is history.

Before looking at the pop charts of 1954, it's important to turn to the R&B charts first, because when we look at what classic and enduring records were released that year, none would be found on the pop charts. All earth-shattering songs would be found on the R&B charts, the most prominent being Joe Turner's "Shake, Rattle and Roll."

The difference in the rock 'n' roll and rhythm & blues versions, besides the blanching of the original song, was the racial divide. Music writer Ed Ward strongly puts it this way: "Haley's band, which originally played western swing, was quite incapable of reproducing the sound of Turner's big band of jazz veterans, assembled by Ahmet Ertegun. They relied instead on guitars and a more swing-oriented rhythm section."[5]

For emphasis, Ward added, Haley, who was twenty-nine and soft-looking, was an unlikely teen hero, but "his face was clean and white, unlike the gigantic leering visage of Joe Turner, a man given to pronouncements like 'All I want to do is drink and sing the blues.'"

Haley did a credible job making a blues number into rock 'n' roll, but it's the original that endures for its gritty, hard rhythmic structure. It was an important root song for the genre of music that would take over the world beginning in 1955 and 1956.

"Shake, Rattle and Roll" was part of a group of four important songs at the top of the R&B charts that year. Two of the others were "Hearts of Stone" by the Charms and "Work with Me, Annie" by the Midnighters. Each of these would be covered by white female singers the next year. The last song in this group was "Sh-Boom" by the Chords.

The weird part of the "Sh-Boom" story is that this unique success tale and ultimate market betrayal would not have come about without a couple of female crooners. The story begins back in 1951 when a small clique of boys at P.S. 99 in the Bronx, New York, formed a singing group called the Keynotes. Personnel shifted around a bit over the next few years necessitating a name change, and by the time it was a quintet the new name for the group was the Chords. In 1954, they managed to wangle an audition with Atlantic Records' Jerry Wexler, who headed A&R. For that tryout, they sang an *a cappella* version of Patti Page's hit song that year "Cross Over the Bridge." Wexler liked the boys and decided to cut a record with them on Cat, an Atlantic subsidiary label. For the B-side tune, the boys wanted their own song, "Sh-Boom." Boom was another word popular in teenage jargon.[6]

According to writer Ward, the boys also sang "Sh-Boom" to Wexler, who liked it because "the song did have a nice skipping rhythm to it, as well as silly, optimistic lyrics and a tricky chorus, all delivered with tight, almost barbershop-style harmonies." The song was released in May 1954 and began to climb the R&B charts immediately. Then, to the industry's surprise it also jumped over to the pop charts—a very rare phenomenon.[7]

Meanwhile, further to the north, in Toronto, Canada, four boys who had been members of the St. Michael's Boys Choir, caught the doo-wop bug and formed a singing group that after numerous name changes would end up as the Crew Cuts. In March 1953, they were on a bill with local sensation Gisele MacKenzie, who was so impressed with the quartet she tried to get her record label interested. It didn't work out, but Bill Randle, an influential disk jockey in the States, liked them as well. He got them an audition with Mercury Records, which signed the quartet and put them in the recording studio to cut "Sh-Boom."[8] That version went to #1 on the pop chart, where it reigned for seven weeks, and ended up as the fourth best-selling record of 1954. The Crew Cuts would lie eternally in R&B-cover heaven, homogenizing every form of doo-wop: from girl group Shirley Gunther & the Queens' "Oop-Shoop"; to the Penguins' classic, "Earth Angel"; to duo, Gene & Eunice's "Ko Ko Mo"; to storytelling, the Nutmegs' "Story Untold." Everything they sang was turned to varying shades of milky opaqueness and thusly placed in heavy rotation on the pop charts.

While singers such as Joni James had been covering other genres, reinterpreting, for example, country & western into pop, what was different with "Sh-Boom" was that Mercury used the same arrangement, vocal and instrumental, as the original R&B song. "With 'Sh-Boom,' the pop establishment had found itself a potent weapon to use against R&B records—whiten them up and use the corporate might of a major label to get them to places a hapless indie caught with a hit on its hands could never reach," wrote Ward.

The crossover recording and surprise success of "Sh-Boom" by the Crew Cuts, while not unprecedented, amplified a new trend in the music world, which was good for pop music, a genre starving for inspiration, but was done at the expense of R&B musicians.

Music historian Phillip Ennis, while noting the success of the Chords' version of "Sh-Boom," educated the music world to "the power of the new R&B material." He added that the song also "illuminated the safest way for the ever-nervous broadcasting industry to accommodate such material, that is, to produce a cover record by a white performer." Ennis concluded, "This episode was another founding incident of 'rocknroll,' the beginning of many episodes in which fresh young, amateur energy [i.e., the Chords]" met the wily old practices [i.e., Mercury releasing the Crew Cuts' version of the song] of the prevailing broadcast industry."[9]

Obviously, the big news in 1954 on the pop charts was the incursion of rhythm & blues and rock 'n' roll, and not in such obvious ways as a new performer like Bill Haley or a cover record such as "Sh-Boom." The dominance of the male vocalist was also under attack. In the late 1940s, R&B blossomed because small, tight, jump-blues bands transformed the genre. In the 1950s came the harmonizing sound of the doo-wop singers. Mimicking the Black doo-wop groups were a flood tide of white, mostly quartets, some of which did quite well in 1954, including the Crew Cuts ("Sh-Boom," #4 for the year); the Four Aces ("Three Coins in the Fountain," #8, and "Stranger in Paradise," #29); and the Gaylords ("The Little Shoemaker," #15).

The older, white male singers hung on and the big names boasted one or two of their most well-known (not necessarily best songs!): Eddie Fisher with "Oh! My Pa-Pa" (#6 for the year), Frank Sinatra with "Young at Heart" (#11), Dean Martin with "That's Amore" (#16), and Perry Como with "Papa Loves Mambo" (#25). While "Stranger in Paradise" (#19) isn't an iconic tune, it was a classic for the still-peaking Tony Bennett.

Even with all that manly noise from so many different directions, 1954 was an amazing year for the veteran female crooners. In the top thirty songs of the year there were no breakthrough singers, but the key women in the genre were almost dominating. Of the top five songs for the year as tabulated by *Billboard*, three were by women: "Little Things Mean a Lot" by Kitty Kallen at #1, "Hey There" by Rosemary Clooney at #3, and "Make Love to Me" by Jo Stafford at #5. Also near the top were Doris Day with "Secret Love" at #9 and again Rosemary Clooney with "This Ole House" at #12. Other ladies in the Top Thirty were Kay Starr with "If You Love Me (Really Love Me)" at #21, Doris Day and Kitty Kallen with second big hits, respectively, "If I Give My Heart to You" (Doris Day at #20) and "In the Chapel in the Moonlight" (Kallen at #28), and the redoubtable Patti Page with two songs, "Cross Over the Bridge" at #14 and "Changing Partners" at #24.

The ladies held the #1 slot on the *Billboard* chart for twenty-five weeks out of the year in 1954. Although the song came too late in the year to make it into the Top Thirty, the Chordettes' "Mr. Sandman" was the #1 song for the last four weeks of the year. The Chordettes were a bridge group between traditional pop and rock 'n' roll. The quartet from Sheboygan, Wisconsin, were the rare white girl group in the mid-1950s that didn't consist solely of sisters, thus helping to clear the way for the girl groups of the rock 'n' roll era. They had come out of the barbershop quartet world and won the *Arthur Godfrey's Talent Scouts* competition in 1949. When they moved to Cadence Records, founder Archie

Bleyer pushed the group into the pop mainstream, continuing to update their sound to nascent rock 'n' roll. As music historian Larry Birnbaum noted, "The Chordettes had a more traditional background than most of the pop vocal groups of the 1950s, yet they adapted unusually well to the rise of rock 'n' roll."[10]

Even with the sudden appearance of a group like the Chordettes, the real female star of 1954 was vocalist Kitty Kallen, who would have one of the strangest careers of any of the female crooners.

On May 13, 1950, the *Billboard* magazine column "Record Review" highlighted four new songs all by female singers, Rosemary Clooney, Andrews Sisters, Evelyn Knight, and at the top Kitty Kallen, who had jumped into a couple of rumbles with songs already in rotation by other singers, Eddie Miller's "Juke Box Annie" and Teresa Brewer's "Choo'n Gum." The reviewer liked Kallen's renditions, especially the A-side song, "Juke Box Annie," which the listener noted: "The doodle-oodle-oo nonsense piece has one of its top renditions in this driving spirited slicing." As for the B-side, the even more novelty-esque "Choo'n Gum," the review stated: "Highly competent on this growing novelty by Miss Kallen with a neat assist from the two-beast Geller [Harry Geller orchestra] backing."[11]

"Juke Box Annie" proved a solid sender for Kallen, climbing into the Top Twenty in 1950, her best showing since the end of the war years, when she was the toast of the town as a big band vocalist.

Like so many of the female crooners, Kitty Kallen's (Katie Kallen, born in 1921) career started early. Her mother died when she was a child and her father, a barber, had difficulty feeding his brood of seven children. According to liner notes for her 1956 album *A Lonesome Old Town*, at the age of eight Kallen won her first amateur contest, after which she appeared on the original *Horn & Hardart Children's Hour* on radio station WCAU. Soon afterward, she had her own program with Jan Savitt's Orchestra on the same station.[12]

At fifteen years old, Kallen joined legendary jazz musician Jack Teagarden when he put together his own swing band comprised of sixteen men and one female (Kitty Kallen). Three years later while sharing an apartment with another fine singer, Dinah Shore, she got an offer to join Jimmy Dorsey's band, where she recorded five straight Top Five tunes including her first #1, "Besame Mucho" in 1944. According to *Washington Post* writer Adam Bernstein, Kallen, who was Jewish, split from Dorsey because of his anti-Semitism. She then joined the Harry James band, where she was an even bigger star. In 1945, eight Kitty Kallen/Harry James tunes hit the market and every one was a big hit, including two #1 tunes, "I'm Beginning to See the Light" and "It's Been a Long, Long Time."

In all the hullaballoo, she missed some very important gigs. Bing Crosby offered her the role of female singing star in his Kraft Music Hall radio show, but she stayed with Dorsey. Then Frank Sinatra asked her to join him in the cast of *Your Hit Parade*, but that show was broadcast from Hollywood, and Kitty, who at that time was getting married to Teagarden clarinetist Clint Garvin in New York, decided to stay east. The Garvin marriage was short and in 1948, she married Budd Granoff, a Broadway press agent, who, no surprise here, became her manager.[13]

Like other big band vocalists, in the late 1940s Kallen decided to make it on her own as an independent vocalist, but it wasn't easy. She was a recognized name so she pulled in the crowds at nightclub gigs. Still, she went a couple of years without recording.

The *Billboard* "Night Club Reviews" columnist dedicated a headline story about Kallen at the Versailles Club in New York for the July 16, 1949, issue: "Kitty Kallen pulled a showbiz and newspaperman crowd with her opening night, all of whom gave her some hefty mitting [wild applause]. She looked as lovely as ever and showed her vocal skill as she hopped from one song to another with blithe ability."[14]

At the start of the new decade, Kallen made her first appearance on the West Coast at the famed Mocambo in Los Angeles. From there she headed to Las Vegas' New Frontier hotel. A United Press International reporter named Jack Gaver caught up with Kallen for a syndicated story: He wrote: "Miss Kallen, who sings popular songs with style and pleasing voice . . . has blossomed out as a solo star this season. The change came . . . after disrupting her career a couple of times for essential matters as marriage and motherhood. . . . she now scarcely has breather between engagement from year's beginning to year's end."[15]

Also in 1949, the trades reported that Kallen signed a contract with RKO to star in a series of musical films, the first to be shot that summer. However, it wouldn't be until 1955 when Kallen debuted in a movie, Universal-International's flick *The Second Greatest Sex*, which also starred Jeanne Crain and Mamie Van Doren.[16]

Even with all that adulation and steady gigs, it wasn't until 1949 that she nabbed her first hit under her own name, "Kiss Me Sweet," which she recorded for Mitch Miller at Mercury Records. The next year, Mercury used the scattershot approach (which was popular during the early 1950s) to restart Kallen's career, dumping six new songs onto the turntables of disk jockeys around the country.[17] Only two songs hit: "Juke Box Annie" and, in a completely different mode, "Our Lady of Fatima," a #10 song. Mercury tempered the Kallen-dump strategy to just four songs in 1951, one of which, "Aba Daba Honeymoon," went all the way to #9 on the chart, but was outdone by the duo Debbie Reynolds and Carleton Carpenter, who sang the song in the 1950 movie *Two Weeks in Love*.

Kallen's husband Budd Granoff would eventually have a successful career as TV game show producer, often working with game show host Chuck Barris. However, that was in the future. As a syndicated *New York Times* story noted, "although Kallen had been an established singer when they met, she gave her husband full credit for building her into one of the leading singers of the 1950s. He managed every facet of her career, becoming a music publisher along the way [where did we see that before], and picked all of her songs."[18]

Although things would eventually turn out well for Kallen, from 1948 at the time of her marriage through the next six years, despite a huge name from the World War II era, her career as a recording star was underwhelming. Musical historian J. C. Marion writes that after "Aba Daba Honeymoon" things were looking up for Kitty Kallen. However, she all but disappeared from the music scene, and there were many reports that she had lost her voice, or was tired of the business. In any event Kitty Kallen was absent from the music scene for more than two years."[19]

Through 1952 and 1953, Mercury and then Decca released only three Kallen songs, only one of which, "Are You Looking for a Sweetheart," was a moderate hit. Granoff was supposed to be a top-notch press agent, but as manager of Kallen, nothing was working out.

In between all that came an entertainment industry squabble that didn't turn out well for Kallen. She was good friends with Frank Sinatra's first wife, Nancy Barbato Sinatra, who the singer had married in 1939. In 1951, Sinatra wanted to dump Nancy to marry actress Ava Gardner. Loyal to Nancy, Kallen recommended the lawyer Gregson Bautzer, who took Nancy on as client and made life very difficult for Sinatra, because Nancy didn't want to go through with a divorce. At the time, Kallen and Nancy were best friends, and Kallen was staying with her while appearing at the Mocambo. Nancy didn't know any divorce lawyers, so Kallen called Bautzer, who was so tough in representing Nancy that Sinatra held a grudge for years.

As Kallen recalled, "When Frank found out I was the one who brought in Greg [Bautzer] that did it! I was on his list." Not a good thing, because Sinatra was like the "godfather" in the entertainment industry—you did not want to cross him. Kallen continued, "He kept me from doing Jackie Gleason's television show and I didn't work Vegas for a long time. In fact, I didn't work for almost five years because of Frank's anger at me over that business. He didn't speak to me again for ten years, and then only because I was a friend of someone closely associated with the [Kennedy] White House."[20]

Then came 1954 and Kallen had a measure of revenge. Frank Sinatra's "Young at Heart" was the #11 song of the year. Kallen not only had the #1 song of the year with "Little Things Mean a Lot" but also the #28 song, "In the Chapel in the Moonlight."

Trying to divine the attraction of "Little Things Mean a Lot" decades after the song is not difficult. Certainly, there is Kallen's voice, a little deeper than most of the female singers of her time, and a profound believability in the emotive messages of her songs. Then there is the terrific arrangement. Many 1950s pop songs began with an elaborate orchestration. Not "Little Things Mean a Lot": Kallen's voice is heard almost immediately with a talk-sing introduction that ropes the listener in: "Blow me a kiss from across the room / Say I look nice when I'm not / Touch my hair as you pass my chair [great interior rhyme] / Little things mean a lot."

The distinctly feminine perspective of the song comes from one of the songwriters, Edith Lindeman Calisch (cowriter Carl Stutz), who was also the film and theater critic for the *Richmond Times-Dispatch* for over thirty years. She said she took up songwriting while driving through Kentucky and listening to the radio. Lindeman-Calisch said to her husband, "Oh Lord, I could write better lyrics than that." He responded, "Well, why don't you?"

As for the inspiration of the song, she said, "My father—and later, my husband—went by the philosophy that it's the little things that mean so much."[21]

Most of the established songwriters from the 1930s to early 1950s were men; this song, cowritten by a woman, touched the hearts of young females.

Kallen's other big hit from 1954, "In the Chapel in the Moonlight," was a traditional romantic pop song, with the usual lush orchestration by the Jack Pleis Orchestra. The matchup of Pleis with veteran Tin Pan Alley songwriter Billy Hill, was like a relationship consummated in a chapel. Hill, who had his first hit song in 1933, was an excellent craftsman in the traditional pop style. He also wrote "The Glory of Love," which the Five Keys turned into an early doo-wop standard back in 1951.

Decca released six Kallen records in 1954; one more made the chart, "I Want You All to Myself (Just You)." It was her year and if Granoff chose her songs, he could also claim some redemption as well.

That joyfulness was short-lived because Kallen's career went off the track again the very next year. Trying to cash in on Kallen's success in 1954, Decca, her record company since 1953, released eight new singles in 1955, all of which bombed despite some good reviews from the industry trades.[22]

The year started on a good note—literally!—as Kallen teamed up with Julius LaRosa for a New Year's Eve show at the Chicago Theater in New York. The columnist for the *Cash Box* gossip column "Round the Wax Circle" on January 8, 1955, wrote, "as the hour struck midnite, Kitty and 'Julie,' currently sharing billing at this 'thitter,' really singing up a storm. Kitty dropped up to the office to tell us how pleased she was that her 'Little Things Mean a Lot' was voted the top record for '53–'54 in our annual poll."

In February, crosstown rival publication *Billboard*, on February 5, 1955, gave thumbs up to a new Kallen release, "I'd Never Forgive Myself": "The stylized thrush should be able to stay on top again with this fine rendition of a lovely new ballad. She sells it winningly and is backed gracefully by the ork [orchestra]. It could be a big one." It wasn't.[23]

By mid-year, the incident that really set her career back occurred. The first indicator of a new adventure can be found in a *Cash Box* column called the "London Lowdown" on May 21, 1955, when the columnist reported, "Pretty Kitty Kallen told me how excited she was to be in England and Budd Granoff was busy soothing a few scratches which Kitty got from another kitty [gift of a cat] in a basket."[24]

Kallen was in England headlining a big show at the London Palladium. In the middle of her performance, she lost her voice and left the stage. The oft-told story claims she didn't again sing before an audience for four years. The press later reported vocal cord paralysis, a common voice disorder that occurs when the vocal cords do not open and close appropriately. More likely she suffered a recurring bout of nerves, which could have been the reality considering a similar career disappearance happened a few years before.

The whole London Palladium incident is fuzzy at best. In the liner notes to her album *A Lonesome Old Town*, a reference to the show reads that Kallen "achieved international acclaim with her tremendous success at the Palladium in London," which certainly doesn't seem as if the gig had to be halted due to frozen vocal cords. In addition, another "London Lowdown" column, this time from June 4, 1955, reported Kitty Kallen recorded two songs at the Decca studios in London with the Roland Shaw Orchestra for British release only.[25]

One month later, the *Cash Box* issue of July 16, 1955, reported this curious item: Kitty Kallen, opening at the Salisbury Beach Frolics, is having her latest platter, "'Let's Make the Most of Tonight,' promoted in the Hub through Ruth Shapiro Record Promotions." Then in September, Kallen's latest release "Come Spring"/"Only Forever," got the nod as *Cash Box*'s coveted "Sleeper of the Week," the reviewer noting: "Two excellent pieces of tune stuff are presented by Kitty Kallen on her latest Decca disk, and if they get a fair shake on the air waves, the thrush could hit the charts in a big way."[26] She didn't.

So after the London Palladium show, there was a British recording, live show, and new releases in the United States all when she was supposedly out of action for four years due to vocal cord paralysis.

She was late to unleash her version of "Go On with the Wedding." It came out in 1956, rising only as far as #39. It might have performed better if Patti Page's rendition of the song, which came out the year before, wasn't such a big hit, climbing to #11 on the pop chart.

As with the other female crooners, the coming of rock 'n' roll did not treat Kallen kindly. She scraped the bottom of the record charts with "Sweet Kentucky Rose" in 1955, had a minor hit with "Go On with the Wedding" in 1956, disappeared from the charts in 1957 and '58, came back with another minor hit in 1959, "If I Give My Heart to You," and then inexplicably had one more strong record, "My Coloring Book," which shot to #18 on the *Billboard* chart in 1962, before it all ended for her in the pop world.

She lived into her nineties contending with health issues and being plagued with phony Kitty Kallens, who seemed to pop out of nowhere. *Washington Post* writer Bernstein related this bizarre tale. In 1978, when one of the imposters, a Genevieve Agostinello, signed into a Los Angeles hospital, she did so as Kitty Kallen. Agostinello subsequently passed away while in the hospital and the press reported the death of singer Kitty Kallen. Then when an Associated Press reporter reached out to the real Kitty Kallen, she had to sing "Little Things Mean a Lot" to convince people she was still very much alive.[27]

Oddities and eccentricity abounded that occurred in later years but had roots in 1954. For example, in 1958, Bill Haley, who by this time saw his own career taking a dim-dim-the-lights turn, offered up one of his last hits, a song called "Skinny Minnie" with lyrics such as this couplet, "My skinny Minnie is a crazy chick / six foot tall and one foot thick."

In 1954, Teresa Brewer boasted a record that went to #22 on the record chart, her own "Skinnie Minnie." The full title was "Skinnie Minnie (Fish Tail)," a song so wacky and Brewer-idiosyncratic it's hard to understand what it's about, except that it has nothing to do with the Haley song of the same name. This one begins with Brewer and chorus chanting "cotch-a-me, cotch-a-me, cotch-a-me" in purposefully bad Italian. She then launches into one of her patented rapid lyric runs before settling into a kind oom-pah groove. Obviously, her fans enjoyed it.

At the end of the year 1954, Brewer entered into a real dogfight that would play out in 1955 with one of the best records of the year—except it wasn't by her.

It all began on November 15, when the television show *Studio One*, which in the early 1950s aired some of the best dramatic presentations, such as *Twelve Angry Men*, seen on any media, presented the screenplay, er, television-play *Let Me Go, Lover*. This was a murder mystery involving a disk jockey and what the presentation did extremely well was to integrate the music with the drama, in particular a song from Columbia Records, "Let Me Go, Lover!" as sung by a completely unknown Joan Weber. The show was only an hour long and the song was heard six times. It was all done so well that by the next day, retailers were reporting requests for that particular record. In addition, CBS, the show's network, was swamped with phone calls asking where the record could be purchased and disk jockeys around the country were getting requests for the song. Bob Thiele, the Coral A&R chief who rushed out a Teresa Brewer version of the song to compete with Joan Weber, claimed Columbia Records had issued the Weber record and presciently stocked record stores weeks before the *Studio One* show would be broadcast.[28] That statement made no sense because television was so new no one had even the slightest concept that a song heard on a particular TV show would attract such interest. According to the trade magazines, Columbia was caught completely by surprise; it had no clue that a television show could have such an impact on the sales of a record and had to put its Connecticut record-pressing plant on round-the-clock time to meet the demand.[29]

The story began in 1953, when a New Jersey teenager, Joan Weber, was taken by her manager Eddie Joy into New York to make the rounds at the Brill Building. Her audition song was "Marionette" and she was impressive enough that RCA producer Charles Grean decided to bring Weber in for demo recording session. He then sent the demo over to Mitch Miller at Columbia, who quickly offered her a contract.

Miller, always on the lookout for new talent and new songs for his talent, had heard a 1952 recording by Georgie Shaw called "Let Me Go Devil," which was a message song about the evils of alcohol. The inherent, if not over-the-top drama of the song, caught Miller's fancy, who thought it could be redone as a ballad. The song became "Let Me Go, Lover!" and Weber recorded it for Columbia with "Marionette" on the B-side.[30]

It might have gone unnoticed if it wasn't for the television show. It certainly caught Weber by surprise; she suddenly had a hit record at probably the worst time—when she was very, very pregnant. On November 23, 1954, Weber, who was married to her band leader George Verfaillie, gave birth to a girl.[31]

The other major thing that happened was the not unexpected pileup of singers rushing to make their own recordings of the song. This led to the unusual situation of the December 4, 1954, *Cash Box*, when choosing its "Disk of the Week," having to list four new records by female singers, all of which were "Let Me Go, Lover!" Patti Page's version was the B-side to a song called "Hocus Pocus," which was the same approach taken by Sunny Gale, who had the song on the B-side of "Unsuspecting Heart." For the Page rendition, the reviewer quickly observed, "Flip is the thrush's brilliant delivery of 'Let Me Go, Lover!' the 'Studio One' tune that set the music biz abuzzin.'" Sunny Gale received a mixed review: "Although Sunny Gale dishes up a tremendous job on the Victor version of 'Let Me Go, Lover!' with Hugo Winterhalter, we feel that the great performance Sunny offers on the flip [A-side] will win out in the long run."[32]

That left the heavyweight bout between veteran Teresa Brewer and rookie Joan Weber. Brewer got a thumbs up with these comments: "Coral comes up with a tremendous version of the tune that sent the music business into an uproar. It features the fascinating voice of Teresa Brewer accompanied by a stirring backdrop by the Lancers. A brilliant side that will cash in."

The Weber review included a brief prelude about the historic moment when a television show created a hit record: "Joan Weber offers the original version of 'Let Me Go, Lover!' as it was performed on the *Studio One* show. The disk has been out for a few weeks now and has a jump on other versions. Although it is the most exposed version of the song, the thrush will have to stave off some great opposition to hold the lead. It's a tremendous, sincere reading by the newcomer."

One of the people watching *Studio One* the night CBS aired "Let Me Go, Lover," was Teresa Brewer, who said, "I flipped over the song, just watching the show." Coral Records execs were also watching and they immediately called Brewer, telling her, "You've got to come in and do that song." Within twenty-four hours Brewer was in the recording studio.[33]

"An unknown Mitch Miller protégé named Joan Weber had recorded the soundtrack version, and every major label producer had their star female vocalist in the studio to cover the tune within hours after the program went off the air," Bob Thiele recalled. The Coral Records producer had Brewer in the recording booth at 2 a.m. the next morning. The arrangement was written right there on the spot.

The "Let Me Go, Lover!" atmosphere was white hot—and that wasn't just from the song. Mitch Miller claimed the Coral record made with Teresa Brewer copied the Joan Weber arrangement. In return, Bob Thiele exclaimed to the trade press his defense of Coral demanded to be heard. Miller did have a good point; there was not much difference between Weber's and Brewer's takes on the song. The arrangements are very close. The big difference is in the tonality, with Weber's deeper voice giving the song more resonance. Brewer plays it straight with no tricks, and sounding a little bit country.[34]

Weber's head start and strong performance gave her an insurmountable lead in sales and play going into the key holiday season.[35] On December 15, 1954, of the ten most played records by disk jockeys, six were by women: "Mambo Italiano" (#10, Rosemary Clooney), "If I Give My Heart to You" (#9, Denise Lor and Connee Boswell), "Make Yourself Comfortable" (#6, Sarah Vaughan), "Teach Me Tonight" (#3, DeCastro Sisters), "Mr. Sandman" (#1, Chordettes), and sneaking in at #2, "Let Me Go, Lover!" by Joan Weber.

Even after just giving birth to a baby girl, Weber was pushed out on the road. The "Round the Wax Circle" gossip column in *Cash Box* on December 18, 1954, reported, "Joan Weber, whose 'Let Me Go, Lover!' is reported to be the number one tune here in Chicago, arrives in the Windy City on Friday to meet and greet for the very first time dee-jays who have helped this disk soar to the top in such a short span of time."[36] That article was prescient, because the very next *Cash Box* issue, dated Christmas Day 1954, ran down a regional report as submitted by disk jockeys around the country, and Weber's "Let Me Go, Lover!" was #1 on stations in Chicago; Pittsburgh; Rhode Island; Mobile, Alabama; West Palm Beach; Fresno, California; New Haven, Connecticut; Denver; Cleveland; Massachusetts; and Milwaukee.[37]

Arriving in stores and on deejay turntables at the end of the year meant the big impact would come in 1955, and for two weeks in January it was the #1 song in the country. It would be the #18 best-seller for the year. This is not to say that Teresa Brewer's version didn't do well. It climbed to #6 on the record chart and would remain her best-selling record until 1956.

"As it turned out, all four recordings went Top 20 within the same month, each one selling a million copies," Thiele inaccurately remarked (the Sunny Gale and Patti Page versions fell short).[38] As for Brewer, she observed, "It sold a million copies for me, for Joan Weber, and probably for Patti Page, who also had a record of it. If only one girl had recorded that song, she would have sold three or four million!"[39]

What could possibly go wrong for a performer with that kind of career start? In short, everything! First, Weber was a new mother, which, except for a few out-of-town engagements, limited her ability to get in front of the public. Then the worst thing happened: her husband became her manager. Mitch Miller said in an Archive of American Television interview that when that happened, it "deprived Weber of experienced career guidance."[40] Finally, she was slotted for gigs in some of the biggest venues in the country such as the Copacabana in New York. Being a mother, under her husband's inexperienced guidance, and still a teenager, she admitted three years later in a United Press International interview, "When the record caught on I was caught without an act. I didn't even know how to take a bow. And there I was playing the Copa. I had no time to get my bearings. I just wasn't ready."

And she wasn't. Not one follow-up record charted and the big bookings evaporated quicker than a morning fog. Her record company dropped her and Weber pretty much was out of work before attempting a comeback in 1957.

She later was reported singing in bars and even working as a library clerk. Then all traces of her disappeared. In 1981, the press finally found her. In May of that year she died of heart failure at her place of residence, the Ancora Psychiatric Hospital in Ancora, New Jersey. She was just forty-six years old.

Mid-year 1954, before all the noise about "Let Me Go, Lover!" and before anyone heard of Joan Weber, *Song Hits* magazine polled its readers as to "Favorite Gal Singers," and the winner was Teresa Brewer in a narrow victory over Patti Page, Joni James, and Doris Day. Others in the Top Ten were Rosemary Clooney, Eartha Kitt, Dinah Shore, Jo Stafford, Kay Starr, and Sunny Gale.[41]

It was also around mid-1954 that Brewer released her other big hit of the year, "Jilted," which rose to #6 on the pop chart. Another version by country singer Red Foley almost matched it at #7. The same song sung by two different singers, both going in different directions. The Red Foley tune intros with a classic fiddle riff. Under the baton of the never-changing Jack Pleis, Teresa Brewer begins with a feint to "Music! Music! Music!" and then the usual over-orchestrated reliance on a Dixieland backbeat. Thankfully, Brewer, a little lower on the scale—and even a bit country-ish—takes control of the song.

The songwriters of "Jilted" were Robert Colby and Dick Manning. The latter was one of the masters of pop songwriting in the pre–rock 'n' roll days of the 1950s, having also cowritten such popular numbers as "Allegheny Moon," "Hot Diggity," "Secretly," and "Papa Loves Mambo."

Besides "Jilted" just being a good song, Brewer was still a very popular singer, as judged by the magazine poll, and there was some pent-up demand for a Teresa Brewer record. As early as March, the trades were reporting jukebox operators had a high interest in the new record. One jukebox exec told *Billboard*, "Dealers are asking for Teresa Brewer's new Coral platter, 'Jilted.'"

With that kind of preview, *Billboard* rushed out a commentary. In its "Reviews of New Pop Records" column of April 3, 1954, *Billboard* tackled "Jilted," implying a weariness of the Jack Pleis orchestration: "The petite thrush could have another smash with this zingy new effort . . . the thrush sings it with the vitality that has become her trade-mark, over wild hokey backing."[42] By the end of the month, the song was in the Top Twenty of record sales and most played tunes by disk jockeys.

"Jilted" was by no means a career-turning record for Brewer, but it was prescient in regard to her personal life. All was still honeymoon bliss and babies for the Brewer-Monahan marriage in 1954. The happiness would last a long time—just not long enough. One could say that Brewer "jilted" Monahan and then moved on with her life by marrying Bob Thiele. This would all happen way in the future, yet the roots of marital discord, as explained, were set within the espousal of a nice guy, a blue collar soul, an average Joe, with an ambitious, hard-working celebrity wife. There was also something insidious about Brewer's relationship with Bob Thiele, the Coral Records A&R chief who oversaw her career.

Thiele was a wunderkind at Coral, not only guiding female pop recording acts such as Teresa Brewer, the McGuire Sisters, and Debbie Reynolds, but also discovering rock 'n' rollers Buddy Holly & the Crickets and Jackie Wilson. (He also gets credit for cowriting Louis Armstrong's late career hit "What a Wonderful World.") Thiele's personal life was not so vaunted. He first married at twenty-one. That union lasted less than a year. In the 1950s, he was married to vocalist Jane Harvey, the mother of his only child, Bob Jr. That marriage lasted five years. When it was over he married again; that one fell apart after a year.

Meanwhile, there was always Teresa Brewer. In his memoirs, Thiele confessed, "With Teresa, I remember being in love with this warmly charming, exquisite woman from the time of our initial meeting in the early 1950s when I was a young producer at Coral Records and assigned to record her."

This is where the story gets unusual. In June 1956, *TV Star Parade* magazine published a profile of Brewer titled "Too Young, Too Young." One revealing paragraph commented, "For Teresa and Bill, home is the center of their life. Bill's brother lives in Scarsdale [where the Brewer family lived]." Brewer added, "Our best friends are Bob Thiele and Jane Harvey. He's the recording executive and she's the singer, and they live near us."[43]

Three years later, *TV-Radio Mirror* ran a feature on the Brewer's wonderful family-oriented life, starting with an almost full-page picture of Teresa, Bill, and their four girls in domestic bliss. Again, this tidbit of information is revealed: "Their best friends in show business live only about a mile down the road—Bob Thiele . . . his wife [singer Jane Harvey] and their little boy. They get together and eat pizza and discuss the music business, the cute things the kids say, the high cost of shopping and whether or not to put out as many bulbs next spring as they did last."[44]

Bob Thiele, married but with a desperate yearning for Brewer, not only sees her at business, but somehow manages to live near enough to the Brewer/Monahan family that the two households are rarely separated. Thiele came to Coral Records in 1953, worked there for nine years, and for that whole time he was in close contact with Brewer. In the early 1960s, he left Coral and moved on to another record company, and his spate of marriages were over for the time being. Munroe says he also left New Rochelle, taking an apartment in Manhattan.

In his memoirs, Thiele wrote, "I was intensely in love with Teresa, but could not say a word about my feelings. We were both married, and Teresa was a rigorously proper Catholic lady with four daughters and a large, decent family for whom any hint of scandal or the thought of divorce would have been profoundly abhorrent." The question is, was that an assumption or was it an ongoing conversation between two people who worked together closely and had feelings for each other?

Meanwhile, Brewer's perfect marriage, endlessly portrayed in fan magazines, was slowly coming undone. Jack Paquette, who wrote a book called *Small Town Girl* with a chapter about Brewer, commented, "her [Teresa Brewer's] marriage hit the skids in the late 1960s." Bill and Teresa divorced in 1972.

A year after Brewer's divorce and second marriage to Thiele, a journalist from Brewer's hometown of Toledo caught up with her for a feature in the local newspaper. In 1973, he wrote, for a period of about two years before her divorce Teresa was relatively inactive, spending most of her time at home with her daughters. The journalist added, "The marriage already had lasted far longer than many show business people thought it should. Teresa hesitated [to divorce] for a number of reasons including her religion and the probability it would hurt her parents [not her kids?]."[45]

Another Toledo *Blade* journalist in 1980 also got an exclusive with Teresa. The journalist put a parallel but affirmative spin on the Brewer's life at the end of the 1960s: "a whole new generation was growing up without being tuned into Teresa Brewer . . . live audiences, however, continued to discover or rediscover her . . . But Teresa had those lovely daughters at home. She also had marital problems."[46]

"I have no idea in the least why Teresa's and Bill's marriage eventually failed," Munroe hesitated. "Teresa rarely spoke of him in my presence, but when she did, there was never a negative word said. In fact, just the opposite . . . he was her first love and therefore he seemed to have a special place in her heart."

Marital problems and divorces are not unusual, especially among people who marry young, and is as normal as can be in the entertainment world. The Bob Thiele business was dicey. He wrote in his memoir, "I didn't comprehend it would be necessary for another decade to pass before Teresa and I would be free to act on our personal feelings toward each other."

Notice the phrasing, "our personal feelings toward each other," from which one can infer that not only did Thiele have an infatuation for Brewer but she had ardor for him as well. Notice also that he said "for another decade to pass." That would refer back to 1962, because they were married in 1972. If that's true, Brewer's affection for her husband would have been waning for a very long time.

Thiele's comments could be innocent. But again, from the pen of Thiele, his comment "after her husband had died, we began to date and soon decided to marry," is suspiciously misleading. The timeline runs this way: in 1972, Bill and Teresa divorced and Teresa and Bob married soon afterward. Bill Monahan died on May 6, 1974, reported Bill and Teresa's daughter Kathleen Monahan.

"I know for certain that in 1972 Teresa divorced Bill, and then married Bob later on that year," said Munroe. "Teresa and Bob married in Bridgeport, Connecticut. A friend of his, who was a judge in that municipality, officiated. When Bob died in 1996, as a favor for Teresa I went to the Hall of Records there and picked up a certified copy of his marriage certificate for probate purposes. On the certificate was the date in 1972 that they were married."

Teresa and Bob wasted no time dating. The wedding happened so quickly Teresa didn't tell her parents until it was done. Parents of even an adult child are not fools about their children. Her mother knew for quite some time her daughter had affection for her old coworker, Thiele, and that her daughter's existing marriage was rocky. As Thiele remembered it, when Teresa telephoned her mother back home to announce she was "in love and about to be married," her mother promptly said, "I'll bet it's that nice Bob Thiele you used to record with."[47]

Brewer would tell reporters a different story. Some months later when she called her mother to say that she'd just run off and married Bob Thiele in Bridgeport, Connecticut, her mom replied, "I hope you'll be very happy—and if you're not, maybe this time you won't wait so long."

In 1980, a journalist referred to Thiele as Brewer's agent and manager. Brewer took umbrage and responded, "He's not my manager; he's not my agent. He's my lover."[48]

"I knew Bob Thiele, and quite well, too," Munroe said. "I'd meet him and Teresa for extended lunches in Manhattan two or three times a year, and Jane [Munroe's partner] and I were guests in their home in upper Westchester County—Bedford—a number of times. Bob invited me to recording sessions, which I enjoyed immensely. . . . When he died, Jane and I attended his funeral."[49]

Teresa Brewer and Bob Thiele were married from 1972 to his death in 1996.

CHAPTER SIX

DANCE WITH ME HENRY (WALLFLOWER) (1955)

ETTA JAMES—HANK BALLARD—GEORGIA GIBBS— LAVERN BAKER—DECASTRO SISTERS—FONTANE SISTERS— DON ROBEY—JOHNNY ACE—TERESA BREWER

When Etta James (Jamesetta Hawkins) was growing up in the Watts section of Los Angeles in the 1940s and early 1950s, that part of the city was a hotbed of rhythm & blues music. The boys she hung with would go on to write songs such as "Earth Angel" and "Louie Louie" or form groups such as the Platters or just were stars on their own terms like Jesse Belvin.

She was born in 1938 to Dorothy Hawkins, who was fourteen years old (father unknown). James spent much of her early years moving around from relatives to foster parents. At the age of fourteen she began to hang with another fourteen-year-old teenager named Jean Mitchell, who also had aspirations to be a singer. The two began work as a duet before Jean's sister Abysinia, known as Abye, joined them. Since the Mitchells were light-skinned and Creole-looking, they called themselves the Creolettes. Basically, the group worked a tight three-way harmony made popular by the doo-wop groups. There weren't a lot of female vocal groups singing doo-wop at the time, and the Creolettes received a good deal of local attention, or as Etta James observed, "We were getting to be a pretty popular girl group around town. We were winning amateur shows and drawing good crowds." The girls even figured out a few choreographed moves, creating an entertaining set for their fans.

The Creolettes were singing at a local record shop when who should walk in but the popular Hank Ballard and his group the Midnighters. This was in 1955, and the year before Hank Ballard and the Midnighters chewed up the R&B charts with hits like "Work with Me, Annie," "Sexy Ways," and "Annie

Had a Baby." After hearing the Creolettes sing, the Midnighters were very complimentary, raising confidence levels through the roof of the record store of the three girl singers. The Midnighters had arrived at the retailer to do a promotion, and when they launched into their ever-popular "Work with Me, Annie," the place erupted.

The next day, still feeling the glow from the Creolettes' encounter with what James called the "superfine" Midnighters, it occurred to her to write an answer song to "Work with Me, Annie," a not unusual concept since answer songs were always popular.

"So I wrote 'Roll with Me, Henry,' a pushy little jive-ass reply to Hank," recalled James. The Creolettes worked it up and put it into their repertoire, not thinking it was anything special until about a week later when working a sock hop, Hank Ballard and The Midnighters showed up once again. The girls couldn't wait to sing their answer song right in the faces of the guys. "What did ya think of it," James and girls asked Ballard, who responded with one word, "Cool!"

It was a very cool song and soon it would become white hot in terms of the ongoing controversy about white singers covering songs written or originally sung by female Black performers.

While Jean Mitchell and James were just fourteen years old, Abye was twenty-three years old and on the prowl. One night she slipped into the Primaline Ballroom to catch the Johnny Otis show, particularly to hook up with Otis's drummer Kansas City Bell. Abye also wanted to do a bit of promotion for her group, telling Otis about the wonderful Creolettes. Otis took the bait and said he would like to hear them sing. So the three girls went to Otis's hotel room, but James suffered a panic attack and couldn't sing. To make herself more comfortable, she stood in the john near the sink while the two girls positioned themselves close to the bathroom door. Otis loved the group, in particular the strange girl who sang from the bathroom. He invited the three to cut a record, renaming Jamesetta as Etta James and the Creolettes as the Peaches.

In her memoir, *Rage to Survive: The Etta James Story*, James wrote, "Thanksgiving Eve, 1953, was unusually foggy. Me, Johnny Otis and the Peaches were at the studio in Hollywood, cutting 'Roll with Me, Henry' for Modern Records." Hank Ballard's "Work with Me, Annie" was a big hit in 1954, so James probably got confused and this recording session was actually Thanksgiving Eve 1954. James's friend Richard Berry (who would write "Louie Louie," the big hit for the Kingsmen in 1963) was in the studio and was given the job of doing the deep bass song-talk, "Hey Baby, what do I have to do, to make you love me too?" The James response: "You got to roll with me Henry." The word "roll" was also slang for having sex. This was James's first time in a recording studio and it all went down peachy.

Then everything would get complicated. First, Otis decided to put the song out credited to Etta James and the Peaches and not just by the Peaches. The song sold locally and King Records out of Cincinnati wanted to buy the rights and take over distribution, which was okay except some stations wouldn't play the song, thinking it was too risqué. Nevertheless, it was a solid recording, so Modern and King decided to just change the name to "The Wallflower" and accentuate the dance theme.

The title change didn't bother James much because the record took off like lindyhoppers flinging their bodies to a jive beat. "The Peaches were pissed because I was getting the glory," James said. "But I was even more pissed than the Peaches because suddenly Georgia Gibbs came out with her Suzy Creamcheese version."

"Work with Me, Annie" was purely sexual, with lines such as "Annie, please don't cheat / Give me all my meat, ooo!" James's response song became a dance-theme song, but a bit sexual as it still hung strongly on the word "roll" as in the title "The Wallflower (Roll with Me, Henry)." When Georgia Gibbs covered the record, the word "roll" was dropped and replaced by "dance" so that the song was now "Dance With Me Henry (Wallflower)."

"Georgia's cutesy-pie do-over went over big," James wrote. "My version went underground and continued to sell while Georgia's whitewash went through the roof. Her 'Henry' became a million-seller. I was happy to have any success, but I was enraged to see Georgia singing the song on *The Ed Sullivan Show* while I was singing it in some funky dive in Watts."[1]

James was not the only female R&B singer unhappy at being covered by Georgia Gibbs. Teenage LaVern Baker (Delores Evans) had been performing in Chicago blues clubs since the late 1940s, mostly under the moniker Little Miss Sharecropper, even though she was born in Chicago. In 1953, she signed with Atlantic Records, which should have been a contractual relationship made in heaven. It wasn't; Baker's first two years with Atlantic were fallow. Then all hell broke loose in 1955 with the recording of a sexy novelty song, "Tweedle Dee," which became Top Five record on the R&B chart and then quickly jumped to the pop chart, climbing rapidly up the success ladder until it reached #14 and momentum stalled. What happened? Georgia Gibbs's cover version of the song took over the pop chart, rolling over almost everything in sight before landing at #2.

"Georgia Gibbs moved in with a cover version so close to the original of Baker's song that it seemed she'd actually been able to record a new voice over the old backing track," wrote music historian Ed Ward. He also claimed Tom Dowd, Atlantic's recording engineer, was contacted by personnel at Mercury Records after engineering "Tweedle Dee" for Baker. He said Mercury was going to cut the song with Georgia Gibbs and they already had the same musicians, the same arranger, and wanted the same engineer. Dowd turned down Mercury.

Baker figured Gibbs cost her $15,000 in royalties (about $150,000 in 2020 dollars), which was a lot of money to an R&B singer at the time. She was so irate she tried to get her congressman to do something to help singers in a similar situation. "She wrote her congressman to see whether he could spark some legislation," Ward wrote. "All she got back was an envelope full of reelection materials."[2]

R&B singers not only didn't make as much money as headlining pop singers, they also didn't have the same opportunities to headline big clubs such as the Copa in New York or hosting radio or television shows. So, when the historical moment arrived that R&B was mainstreaming in the music world of radio and records, it was financially and emotionally painful for R&B performers to see their efforts blunted by white performers stealing their thunder—and potential income.

It shouldn't, however, have been a surprise because of existing trends such as a host of singers—from all programmable types—piling in when a potential hit song came to market. Also, good songs moved across genres all the time. Pop singers sang country songs, country singers adopted pop songs, R&B singers doo-wop-ized pop songs and sometimes even country songs. Dinah Washington does a nifty version of Hank Williams's "Cold, Cold Heart." "Crying in the Chapel" began as a country song. By 1955, some songs such as "Most of All" were successfully pop as sung by Don Cornell, successfully R&B as sung by the Moonglows, and successfully country as sung by Hank Thompson.

Behind all this was a number of evolutionary changes in the music industry. In the 1940s, national network radio shows, under the tutelage of popular singer-hosts, were the bee's knees. Many of these shows had their own orchestras. By the 1950s, the local deejay sitting alone in the studio supplanted the big radio productions. While it was far cheaper to hire one man than a whole orchestra, it also gave the deejay the independence to make decisions as to what songs would be played. He could do that because he didn't need to do live performances when so much recorded music in the form of recordings was available. Country and R&B records were just as likely to arrive at the radio station as a pop record, because there were so many more independent labels producing these kinds of sounds, while traditional pop music was dominated by a handful of majors.

In 1954, record sales jumped to $213 million and then just kept climbing exponentially through the remainder of the decade, hitting $603 million in 1959. There was plenty of room for independents, although even in 1955 the big hits were still maneuvered to the top of the charts by the majors. That year, four-fifths of the Top Ten hits were by the major record producers, according to music writer Charlie Gillett, who added, "but during the years of hard fighting among the independents who constituted the rhythm & blues market, the companies that had survived had acquired ambitions for growth that were no longer restricted to a section of the music market. Then, once they realized the possibilities of rock 'n' roll, they were prepared to record almost anybody singing almost anything . . . The independents doubled their Top Ten hits from 1955 to 1956, then doubled them again in 1957."[3]

Under the coming storm of rock 'n' roll, the lunch table was cleared for more R&B music, whether it was doo-wop, blues, or ballad, although imitations still dominated the baskets of goodies. As Ward wrote, "Cover versions were definitely the ants at the increasingly sumptuous rhythm & blues picnic."

Mercury, which was printing money with cover versions of R&B hits, according to Ward, suddenly in March 1955 announced that it would do no more covers after Georgia Gibbs's "Wallflower," thinking the trend had reached the end of the line. It definitely did not and by 1956 Gibbs was back covering R&B with her version of "Tra La La," a LaVern Baker song.[4]

When looking at *Billboard*'s Top Thirty songs of 1955, the clear winner as to the most important tune of that year is "(We're Gonna) Rock around the Clock," the song that ushered in the rock 'n' roll era. If there is a #2, it would be Tennessee Ernie Ford's "Sixteen Tons," which adroitly crossed many music genres from country to folk to pop, and still feels fresh today because its sentiments are broad and empathetic. Even now one can identify with the key lyrics, "You load sixteen tons, what do you get? / Another day older and deeper in debt."

The power of the R&B charts in 1955 illustrates the real transcendence of the genre, as the classics come spilling out one after another after another: Chuck Berry's "Maybellene," Fats Domino's "Ain't It a Shame," the Penguins' "Earth Angel," Johnny Ace's "Pledging My Love," Ray Charles's "I Got a Woman," and the Moonglows' "Sincerely." And that's leaving out such songs as the Platters' "The Great Pretender," the Cadillacs' "Speedo," and Bo Diddley's "Bo Diddley."

As for the ladies, except for Georgia Gibbs, the stalwart, veteran crooners Patti Page, Rosemary Clooney, Jo Stafford, and Teresa Brewer didn't have the major songs that year. Instead the market made way for a number of new voices, including the McGuire Sisters ("Sincerely," #8), the Chordettes ("Mr. Sandman," #18), Gisele MacKenzie ("Hard to Get," #26), and Jaye P. Morgan ("That's All I Want from You," #28).

Despite Bill Haley and the Comets, Chuck Berry, and the advent of rock 'n' roll, the most apparently controversial story in the music world at that moment in 1955 was the cover song. Of the Top Thirty songs that year, almost a quarter of the tunes were R&B covers: "Sincerely" by the McGuire Sisters, "Dance with Me Henry (Wallflower)" by Georgia Gibbs, "Ain't That a Shame" by Pat Boone,

"Hearts of Stone" by the Fontane Sisters, "Tweedle Dee" by Georgia Gibbs, and "Ko Ko Mo" by Perry Como.

Most R&B singers felt the pain of the covers, but the animus was very strong among the R&B ladies. Etta James and LaVern Baker had their say—and so did Ruth Brown, who hit the charts earlier than her contemporaries. Her first #1 on the R&B chart was "Teardrops from My Eyes" in 1950, but she saw no teardrops as success rolled in; she notched ten more Top Ten hits on the R&B charts over the next four years, including four more #1 R&B tunes. She seemed immune to the cover record folly until 1954 when her #1 R&B hit, "Oh, What a Dream," a song written specifically for her by Chuck Willis, was covered by Patti Page. Later that same year she scored another R&B #1, "Mambo Baby." As Brown noted, "Mercury, not to be outdone, hit back with a Georgia Gibbs duplicate . . . same result, the bulk of sales creamed off."

Brown didn't think the term "covered" was appropriate because what Mercury and Georgia Gibbs were doing was duplicating. "My gripe would never be with legitimate covers, or subsequent version but with bare-faced duplicates, with no artistic merit whatsoever," she said. "Everybody in the business accepted covers as fair game. I covered songs myself, but they were never by any stretch of the imagination mere duplicates."[5]

Due to Mercury Records' craven, but effective strategy to maintain its percentage of the pop record hegemony, Georgia Gibbs had become the scapegoat for repressing original Black voices via cover songs. It was a taint she could never get out from under, although it wasn't necessarily her fault because she had little say over the tunes she was assigned to record.

Georgia Gibbs was known for remaking records by Black artists and was criticized for it. But Gibbs didn't decide what to record; she sang what the record companies delegated her to sing. Noted Mark Sendoff, an attorney who helped her gain back unpaid royalties: "Yes, most of her hits were earlier performed by a Black artist and she wound up with a hit and that was a cause of resentment in the Black community. LaVern Baker was very vocal about it."

The most repeated LaVern Baker quip about Georgia Gibbs is that Baker took out a life insurance policy on herself before an overseas flight naming Gibbs as the beneficiary and then writing to her, "You need this more than I do, because if anything happens to me you're out of business."

Sendoff reiterates, "Gibbs wasn't in control of that and it wasn't her idea. The record company figured it could make money if it had a white singer who was well-known, could take this great music and put their own spin on it."[6]

Rosemary Clooney noted that, after signing with Columbia, "I couldn't pick and choose the songs I recorded."[7]

When asked how, in the 1950s, songs were selected for her to record, Teresa Brewer, who had more control at Coral than she had at her original record company, said, "demonstration records of songs were submitted to her to see which ones she liked, while at the same time the record company would say which ones it preferred, and then there would be a compromise. Usually, four songs were picked for each recording session."[8]

Years later, Gibbs told a reporter: "It was a tragic thing that happened to Black artists in the '50s, but I don't think I should be personally held responsible for it, because I had nothing to do with it. At that time, artists had no right to pick their own songs. I came into the studio and had no say at all about the background or the arrangement."

To writer Karen Schoemer, she added, "A&R just came in, gave me the songs, and I did them. I had no say about what I recorded. My arrangements were made up before I came in. All the Black artists have come down on me. Ruth Brown was putting me down. Sarah Vaughan was putting me down. 'Georgia Gibbs did this and that.' I think it's quite unjust."[9]

Brewer and Gibbs had a number of things in common. They were short in height, started their careers young, dropped out of school, and were road warriors as teenagers. Whereas Brewer came out of the Midwest, Gibbs was a New Englander.

Gibbs (Frieda Lipschitz) was born in 1918 (some biographies say 1919) in Worcester, Massachusetts, the youngest of four children. She was just six months old when her father died and her mother, having to go to work, put all the children in a local Jewish orphanage. She was reunited with her mother at seven but, left to herself very often, found solace in listening to music on the family radio. Her talent was recognized early and she was often given the lead at the orphanage's annual variety show. As a preteen she would make appearances on the local Worcester radio stations. Her big break came at the age of thirteen, when the manager of a Boston vaudeville house heard her on the radio and hired her. She did such a good job at the Plymouth Theater that a bigger vaudeville house, Raymoor Ballroom, lured her away with a better salary, $20 a week—a good deal of money for a teenager in the heart of the Depression. She never finished high school because by seventeen years of age she began barnstorming across the country with the Hudson-DeLange Orchestra.[10]

Songwriter/arranger Will Hudson put together his first big band in Detroit in the early 1930s. In 1935, he got together with songwriter/vocalist Eddie DeLange to the form the swing band known as the Hudson-DeLange Orchestra. The following year they added Gibbs, then known as Fredda Gibson, to the band. Hudson-DeLange were a band on the run; between 1936 and 1938, the group played over 200 gigs, principally eastern colleges, ballrooms, and hotels. Gibbs was with the group about six months and, as she later told an interviewer, "It was the most unbelievably hard work in my life . . . we didn't have a bus, it was broken-down car with the shift between my legs."[11]

Despite the long hours on the road, the Hudson-DeLange Orchestra recorded more than fifty songs for Brunswick Records between 1935 and 1939, which encompasses Gibbs's time with the band. Reportedly, this was her first time in the recording studio. After she left Hudson-DeLange, she freelanced with other big bands including Tommy Dorsey and Artie Shaw. When Gibbs moved from Mercury to RCA Victor in 1957, a *Billboard* story noted when she was working Frankie Trumbauer's big band at the end of 1930s, she recorded "The Loneliest Gal in Town," also on Brunswick. In 1942, while singing with Artie Shaw, Gibbs finally charted with a song called "Absent Minded Moon."[12]

Gibbs spent much of 1940s appearing on radio shows before signing with Majestic Records in 1946. She was a step ahead of Teresa Brewer, coming to Coral Records in 1950, which was unsure as to what to do with her. The label first teamed her with Bob Crosby. When she appeared on Garry Moore's radio show in the mid-1940s, he jokingly referred to her as "Her Nibs, Miss Georgia Gibbs." The word "nibs" cuts two ways: a shortened form of the word nibble, which would have referred to Gibb's height; and a reference to the main focus of something, which would have been a compliment. In either case, the convoluted nickname stuck with her and Coral in 1950 released "I Still Feel the Same about You" with singing credits going to "'Her Nibs' Singing with Georgia Gibbs and vocal with Owen Bradley Sextet." Coral was trying everything and threw Gibbs into the scrum for "If I Knew You Were Comin' I'd've Baked a Cake." The song didn't outperform Eileen Barton's stellar version, but it did make it to #5 on the record chart, and suddenly Gibbs was a star. Her next song was part of a Crosby family brouhaha. Bing and Gary Crosby recorded the 1917 Irving Berlin tune "Play a Simple Melody," a #2 hit in 1950, so, of course, Coral released its version, simplified to "Simple Melody," under Gibbs's name. But, in reality, it was a duet with Bob Crosby. That song became a middling hit.[13]

Mercury quickly lured Gibbs away from Coral, and in 1951 released six Gibbs records, five of which charted, including "While You Danced, Danced, Danced," which was a Top Ten record. The most interesting record in the lot was Gibbs's cover of Johnnie Ray's "Cry." Sung without Ray's dramatic flourishes, it was done straightforward with Gibbs at the low range of her register. Nicely done, it was a mid-tier hit for her.

Then came her signature hit, "Kiss of Fire," a tango adapted from an Argentine recording "El Choclo." The song had heat: "I touch your lips and all at once the sparks go flying / Those devil lips that know so well the art of lying / And though I see the danger, still the flame grows higher / I know I must surrender to your kiss of fire."

Over the next two years her career cooled. She boasted a number of mid-tier hits with one real standout, "Seven Lonely Days," which went #5 in 1953. After Rosemary Clooney scored with "Come On-A My House," the pop charts were treated to a smorgasbord of ethnic-sounding tunes, all of which for some reason found an audience. Clooney came back in 1952 with "Botch-a-Me," which vaulted to #2 on the record chart. Georgia Gibbs got her shot two years later with "Somebody Bad Stole De Wedding Bell," which was unbelievably subtitled "Who's Got the Ding Dong." It was a more innocent time. But some people got the joke, because it became a Top Twenty record for Gibbs.

Gibbs's career was essentially moving sideways until Mercury had her cover Ruth Brown's "Mambo Baby." It didn't chart in the United States, but did in Canada; so the following year, Mercury had Gibbs cover LaVern Baker's "Tweedle Dee" and it was pop magic, shooting all the way to #2 on *Billboard*.

Later in life, Gibbs was interviewed by Karen Schoemer and told her, "To this day I've never heard her [LaVern Baker's] record. Because it was all segregated . . . they had the R&B for blacks, they had pop, which was white, and they had country-and-western, which didn't sell above the Mason-Dixon Line. I never heard of any of those black singers. You never heard them on the radio. If you wanted to buy a black record you went to Harlem. I didn't know about LaVern Baker."

Gibbs didn't have time to gasp the clean air near the apex of the music world because her next song, a cover of Etta James's "Wallflower," went all the way to #1, and Gibbs needed an oxygen tank at that height of success. Mercury pushed out seven Gibbs singles in 1955, six of which charted in various positions up and down the charts from #1 to #74.

That was the last year of kindness to most traditional pop singers because in 1956 Elvis arrived and with him came rock 'n' roll and the mainstreaming of rhythm & blues. Gibbs gave rock 'n' roll her best shot, a song called "Rock Right," which charted. She also came back with another cover, "Tra La La," but her best effort was a bouncy traditional pop tune called "Happiness Street," that was summed up in the opening line "Why am I happy, Why am I gay?" It was a Top Twenty tune.

It was pretty much all over for Gibbs as a recording star. She barely made the charts in 1957 covering Ernest Tubbs's country hit "I'm Walking the Floor Over You" and then she bravely entered the novelty song world singing "The Hula Hoop Song," to a Latin beat in 1958. Catching the hula-hoop craze, the song rose to #38 on the record chart. While it was Gibbs's last major charting tune, it was enough to catch the attention of NBC, which gave her a summer replacement slot with a show called *Georgia Gibbs and Her Million Record Show*. Around 1960, she married Frank Gervasi, later the official biographer of Israeli prime minister Menachem Begin. They were married for thirty years until his death in 1990. She passed away in 2006 at the age of eighty-eight.

"The Review Spotlight," about upcoming records, in the February 26, 1955, issue of *Billboard* highlighted "Dance with Me Henry (Wallflower)" by Georgia

Gibbs. It was, as it turned out, a good choice, considering how popular the song became. In a list of about twenty other songs introduced at the same time were three others that didn't fare so well: "It May Sound Silly"/"Doesn't Anybody Love Me?" by the McGuire Sisters; "Mama—He Treats Your Daughter Mean"/"Goofus" by the Dinning Sisters; and "Shtiggy Boom"/"Johnny, My Love" by the Dooley Sisters.[14]

Outside of the occasionally gathering of extended family members to record folk tunes, female singers uniting to form a singing group were very rare across the genres of early twentieth century music. From R&B to pop, it just didn't happen except for one spectacular oddity: sister acts. The first really important girl group recording act was the Boswell Sisters in the 1930s. They were followed by the immensely popular Andrews Sisters in the 1940s.

In the R&B world, the success of small jump blues bands in the 1940s accelerated the demise of the big bands. Then in 1950, the harmonizing sound of doo-wop groups, consisting of two, three, or as many as five unrelated men became popular. Doo-wop would remain a male playground until 1954 when Shirley Gunter & the Queens out of California scored with "Oop Shoop" and the Hearts out of New York hit with "Lonely Nights." The ladies finally broke through in doo-wop and began laying the groundwork for the rise of the girl group sound at the end the decade. In the traditional pop world, the breakthrough group was the Chordettes, with their big hit "Mr. Sandman" in 1955.

Most of the female crooners of the early 1950s began their careers as vocalist with big bands in the 1940s. Jo Stafford was one of the rare success stories of a solo singer coming from a vocal group. She sang with the Pied Pipers, a popular singing group consisting of all men and one lady, Stafford. That type of roster would appear again in the doo-wop world when Zola Taylor joined the Platters, heretofore an all-male group.

While the Andrews Sisters continued to have hit records going into the 1950s, their time in the white-hot spotlight of hit records was closing, especially as Patty Andrews began edging to a solo career. She broke away from her sisters in the early 1950s only to return again a few years later. With the slow retreat of the Andrews Sisters from the radio station playlists, America was looking for next great sister act, which would arrive via the McGuire Sisters.

Gillian Gaar, in *She's a Rebel: The History of Women in Rock & Roll*, nicely summed up the mid-1950s pop music scene in regard to women this way: "The white female vocal groups of the '50s tended to be more oriented toward pop than the bluesier strains of doo-wop. The barbershop vocal stylings of the Chordettes . . . gave them a series of hits, including 'Mr. Sandman' and 'Lollipop.' There were also innumerable 'Sister' combos that appeared in the Top 40, such as the Fontane Sisters, the Shepherd Sisters, the Lennon Sisters, the DeJohn Sisters, the DeCastro Sisters, and the McGuire Sisters."[15]

Plucking from Garr's list, between the Andrews Sisters and the McGuire Sisters there were two sister acts in the mid-1950s that were of interest. One did well over a short period of the time and the other just missed being great.

The first was the DeCastro Sisters, Peggy, Cherie, and Babette, who were born 1921 through 1925. Their mother was a Ziegfeld Follies performer and their father a wealthy Cuban who owned sugar plantations. After being raised in Cuba, they migrated to Miami in 1942, where the DeCastro Sisters entered show business. Their first recording was a single with Tito Puente in 1952. Two years later, they had a huge hit with "Teach Me Tonight," which went all the way to #2 on the record chart. The next year, their song "Boom, Boom Boomerang" was a Top Twenty hit. Thereafter, the DeCastro Sisters' bloom was over and Babette retired in 1958 to be replaced by a cousin.

The more famous and successful of the sister acts were the Fontane Sisters. Like Georgia Gibbs, their career would peak in 1955 covering R&B songs, although they would also have surprising success by being the first female act to successfully cover a rock 'n' roll song, which might be why historically they escaped the opprobrium that targeted Gibbs—and also might be why most music historians skip over the Fontane Sisters: they were a speed bump in the rise of rock 'n' roll machismo.

Like many other female crooners, the Fontane (Rosse) Sisters were not youngsters when the 1950s rolled in. Bea, the oldest of the girls, turned thirty-five at the end of that year; Marge, the second oldest, was two years younger; only Geri, born in 1921, was still—barely—in her twenties at the start of the 1950s.

They were all born in New Milford, New Jersey, where their mother led the choir and was a contralto soloist at the St. Joseph's Church. Bea and Marge began singing as duet, first at local functions and then further afield. Eventually, the two were joined by brother Frank, which made the group a trio. An audition with the National Broadcasting Company in New York proved successful, although they were farmed out to Cleveland for radio shows and to season the act. In 1944, Frank was drafted and his place was taken by the youngest sister, Geri. (Frank never came back from the World War II; he was killed while serving in Europe.)[16]

According to Geri, her plan was to be a secretary but her mother was determined that she join the act. Her sisters made her audition and then audition again, until they said, "Well, maybe she'll make it." Geri would warm up by singing along with records by the Boswell Sisters, who she says were the inspiration for the Fontane Sisters.[17]

As an all-female trio, the girls adopted the name Fontane Sisters; Fontane was a shortened version of their great-grandmother's name Fontaine. The girls began recording as early as 1946 with a small label called Musicraft, which didn't quite catch the subtle alteration of the surname, so they were credited as being the Fontaine Sisters.

It was also about this time that the girls kept crossing paths with an up-and-coming singer named Perry Como. By 1948, the Fontane Sisters started working regularly with Como, first appearing as part of his supper club troupe; then they replaced the Satisfiers as Como's backup group on his radio show, *The Chesterfield Supper Club*. By the next year, the ladies signed with RCA Victor, cutting records under their own name but often paired with Como.

In 1950, RCA Victor pulled out all the stops for the Fontane Sisters, although clearly without direction, trying everything at once. The ladies recorded eight singles that year, including a children's song, a holiday song, ballads, another Perry Como duet, and a couple of scrum shots, "If I Knew You Were Comin' I'd've Baked a Cake" and "Tennessee Waltz," the latter of which was the group's first hit.

Their luck finally changed in 1951. At the bottom of page 2 in *Billboard's* Television-Radio section of the January 6, 1951, issue, a small story noted that Ken Murray and Perry Como were going to cover for Milton Berle, as the star vacationed for two weeks away from his very successful television show. The magazine noted, "With Como the second week will be platter partners the Fontane Sisters, Lorraine Rognan, Mindy Carson, Louis Jordan and perhaps Bert Lahr." (Como would become one of the most successful singers-turned-television emcees in the history of broadcasting. For almost twenty years, he hosted four different versions of *The Perry Como Show* on different networks.)[18]

With the Fontane Sisters getting regular television exposure, RCA Victor doubled down on the group, recording a dozen singles in 1951. Again, the strategy was to try a little bit of everything from children's songs to holiday tunes to Perry Como duets. On February 17, 1951, *Billboard's* "Going Strong" column, which rated songs by actual sales, slotted "You're Just in Love" by Perry Como and the Fontane Sisters at #4 in the country.[19] They would do a couple more duets that year, although RCA Victor found success with the Fontane Sisters in a far different universe, country music. That week when "You're Just in Love" was in the "Going Strong" column, coming in right behind it was country singer Hank Snow's "The Rhumba Boogie." The Fontane Sisters would also record that tune, pairing it as the B-side to "Moon, June, Spoon." The *Cash Box* review of the record, starting with the A-side, on June 23, 1951, reads: "A very cute novelty is offered on the top deck by the Fontane Sisters. With lots of dubbing that makes this interesting to hear, the girls play with the lyrics in a light manner. Second half is a current western hit with a steady, fast pace. Ops will want to hear these sides."[20]

In 1951, the girls would also tackle such country songs as Hank Williams's "Cold, Cold Heart" and Red Foley's "Alabama Jubilee." They even joined with the Sons of the Pioneers for "Handsome Stranger"/"Grasshopper Heart." The girls' most successful record of the year came about when they were teamed up with veteran western singer Texas Jim Robertson for the country-polka novelty

song "Let Me In." On March 17, *Cash Box*, in its "Record Reviews" column
of twenty or so new records, it was Red Ingle versus the Fontane Sisters in
dueling versions of "Let Me In." Both got thumbs up. Red Ingle's notice read:
"Needless to say it's wild. Red pours everything into it and with a lot of other
interpretations around this one could easily spurt through." As for the Fontane
Sisters, the review gave them a nod: "The Fontane Sisters team up with Texas
Jim Robertson to come through on a tune which always sounds like a great
big party. The girls and Jim make this one extremely appealing and it should
get a lot of play."[21]

The Fontane Sisters did well enough in 1951 that they came in fourth in
Billboard's mid-year 1951 survey of the "Top Small Singing Groups of the Year,"
one behind the Andrews Sisters but four ahead of the Dinning Sisters.[22]

None of the 1951 releases were major hits, so RCA Victor came back again
with nine more singles in 1952, none of which were very successful, although
the Fontane Sisters did team up once again with Perry Como for "Noodlin'
Rag," which rose as high as #23 on *Billboard*. Good for the Fontane Sisters, just
okay for Como, who charted ten records that year, including the #1 hit "Don't
Let the Stars Get in Your Eyes."

With 1953 pretty much a washout at RCA Victor, the label appeared to
give up on the gals, so the sisters moved on to Dot Records in April 1954.
The company was excited to get the Fontane Sisters and planned to promote
them heavily. They also got them into the studio quickly to record enough
songs for an album. The one thing Dot was not going to do was end the ladies'
relationship with Perry Como.[23]

The Fontane Sisters first release from Dot was a remake of an old Ruth Etting
song from 1928 called "Happy Days and Lonely Nights." Indeed, the timbre of
the tune was right out of the Boswell Sisters' playbook with styled three-part
harmony. Not quite the Andrews Sisters but light enough to attract a modern
audience. The song shot to #18 on the pop chart.

At the end of 1954, the Fontane Sisters were back in the studio, this time to
cover what was the #1 R&B hit of the year, the Charms' version of "Hearts of
Stone." Good or bad, this was the trend. In 1954, there were about twenty-five
crossover R&B and pop records. One year later, forty-nine crossover records
blossomed in the magic dust of radio stations. These were divided between
those that crossed directly from the R&B market to pop and those that were
covers, close imitations by pop artists.[24]

In an interview, years after the Fontane Sisters stopped recording, Geri
recalled how record producers would keep tabs on the other genres, including
country & western, and then would put together an arrangement of the same
song for the pop field. "Everyone was doing that then and it was very hectic,"
said Geri, adding that sometimes the Fontane Sisters would only have a few
hours to learn and rehearse a song before it was recorded.

The year 1955 began with women ruling the pop charts. For the first three weeks of the year, the Chordettes' "Mr. Sandman" held the #1 slot, to be replaced by Joan Weber's "Let Me Go, Lover," which sat at #1 for two weeks. Then came "Hearts of Stone" by the Fontane Sisters for one week, which was followed by "Sincerely" (another cover) by the McGuire Sisters for six weeks. But as the record market pushed closer and closer to the rock 'n' roll world, the time of the ladies faded and there were no more #1 records by women for the remainder of the year.

Music historian Larry Birnbaum is a reluctant fan of the Fontane Sisters, although he goes out of his way to include an opposing point of view in his book *Before Elvis: The Prehistory of Rock 'n' Roll*. He included an extensive quote by musicologist Brian Ward, who compared the Charms and the Fontane versions of the song: "While basic arrangements had much in common, the King [the Charms' label] record showcased Otis Williams' expressive lead tenor, which peeled away from the strict melody-line and toyed with the basic rhythm . . . By contrast, the Fontane Sisters abandoned the vocal and rhythm fluidity of the original in favor of a rigid adherence to the melody and a more explicit statement of the dominant beat."[25]

Birnbaum's view was that the Fontane Sisters' "Hearts of Stone" had enough rock 'n' roll feeling that its "omission from the usual lists of first rock records is baffling."

The key difference between the two versions was that Otis Williams was the standout lead in the Charms version, whereas the Fontane Sisters led with three-part harmony against a male chorus singing the doo-wop background.

Although the oldest sister, Bea, was forty years old in 1955, she courageously dived into the rock 'n' roll zeitgeist of teenagers at the time. The act covered "Rollin' Stone," originally sung by the Marigolds, and "Most of All," a hit for the Moonglows. The ladies went all in to the new sounds of America when they took on R&B singer Lula Reed's "Rock Love." More the country side of rock 'n' roll than the R&B side, it was still a full-throated success. The Fontane Sisters were charting new territory because in 1955 all there was, was new territory. In 1955, Bonnie Lou became the first successful female rock 'n' roll singer with a rousing song called "Daddy-O," which rose to #14 on the *Billboard* chart. Sure, it was more a novelty song, but it worked—and it was covered by the Fontane Sisters that same year.

Charlie Gillett, writing about the early independent record producers that had segued into rock 'n' roll, looked at King Records out of Cincinnati. Ignoring the success of Bonnie Lou (perhaps because she was a woman), who recorded for King, he wrote: "Except for the rough arrangement of 'Seventeen' by Boyd Bennett and the Rockets, which made the top ten in 1955 (as did the Fontane Sisters with their cover version for Dot), King's country rock records had relatively little success."[26]

"Seventeen" was rough, but this was in the pre-Elvis days and rock 'n' roll hadn't been taken over by the major record producers. Boyd Bennett captured the feel of young America with a country-tinged rocker: "Now, sloppy shirt, old blue jeans, dirty shoes, by all means; Patch of blonde, peroxide hair, jukebox baby, ain't no square." The Fontane Sisters were able to make a big hit of this cover because it copied the Boyd Bennett arrangement down to a rockin' sax introduction. The key here is once again that the Fontane Sisters were successfully singing rock 'n' roll by covering rock 'n' roll tunes in three-part harmony.

They continued to cover almost everything in sight throughout 1956 (LaVern Baker's "Still," Fats Domino's "I'm in Love Again," the Teen Queens' "Eddie My Love") before going completely bonkers, remaking the Andrews Sisters' wonderful 1945 hit "Rum and Coca Cola" into (as lame as it sounds!) "Dancin' to the Rock n Rolla."

The real rock 'n' roll finally won out and Fontane Sisters recordings tapered off in 1957 and 1958. When Geri became pregnant in 1961, the Fontane Sisters retired from the grind. They had done alright for themselves accommodating to early rock 'n' roll, keeping the seat warm until the men took over.

When it came to cover records, not everyone gets a pass. Georgia Gibbs didn't and neither did Teresa Brewer, who managed to get herself involved in the most squeamish cover in a music trend that had an uncomfortable reflection of Jim Crow America. Brewer may have entered into the cover game innocently, but the optics were not good and that has not changed over time.

This story begins around 1949 in Memphis, Tennessee, when a musician soon to be known as B.B. King (Riley B. King) hooked up with a singer soon to be known as Johnny Ace (John Marshall Alexander Jr.) and a few other musicians to form a popular but ad hoc aggregation of musicians called the Beale Streeters. King also worked as deejay at WDIA, a station that would move to an all R&B format. By 1951, WDIA would be run by David James Mattis, who established his own recording label, Duke Records, in the studio. One the first people he brought in to record was Johnny Ace, who sang a slow romantic ballad, "My Song." It would become a huge hit and everything Ace sang afterward became Top Ten, if not #1 or #2 on the R&B charts. In that interregnum between Frank Sinatra and Elvis Presley, when guys like Johnnie Ray and Eddie Fisher tried to fill the teen idol slot, the real action was in the R&B world where Johnny Ace became America's unknown teen-idol because the media ignored him. Johnny Ace was Black and the young ladies who bought his records and stormed his concerts were Black because it was a segregated, Jim Crow world at the start of the 1950s.

However, someone was paying attention: a Black entrepreneur named Don Robey, who operated out of Houston. He began his entertainment empire by running the most popular Houston club for Blacks. For most of the early to mid-twentieth century outside of New York or Los Angeles, the concert world was almost totally segregated. The Black loops of venues, from major halls such as the Apollo in New York City to juke joints across the South, were called the chitlin circuits and Robey controlled the piece of the circuit that ran through the mid-South, stretching from Texas up the Mississippi River to Memphis. In addition to all that, he owned a record label, Peacock Records, which began recording blues and gospel singers. Even with all that, Robey had bigger aspirations. When he saw that tiny Duke Records in Memphis was sitting on a hotbed talent, he bought the label from David James Mattis, bringing Johnny Ace under his stewardship.

Robey was one of the few successful Black music entrepreneurs of his time, but he gets little credit today because his operations were considered a bit shady and gangsterish—not that the mafia hadn't penetrated the nightclub and record world in the country's big cities during the 1940s and 1950s.

This all brings us to the closing days of 1954, when Johnny Ace went into the studio to record "Pledging My Love" and then on the road to support what looked like a tremendous hit for the heartfelt-ballad singer. On December 25, 1954, Ace was in his dressing room at the Houston Auditorium, where he and Big Mama Thornton of "Hound Dog" fame were headlining a big concert. Playing with a handgun, Ace accidentally shot himself (or was he playing Russian roulette?) and died instantly. Ace was so popular that by one account 5,000 mourners showed up for his memorial service in Memphis. Meanwhile, "Pledging My Love," which looked like it was going to be big hit for Johnny Ace, launched into the stratosphere.

On January 15, 1955, when the Charms' "Hearts of Stone" was the top-selling R&B record in the country, followed by "Sincerely" by the Moonglows, *Billboard* introduced "Pledging My Love" under the column "This Week's Best Buys" with this observation: "The recent death of Ace gave added impetus to what would probably have been heavy first week sales in any case. It is spiraling upwards at dazzling speed, and is almost as popular with pop customers, as with R&B."[27]

One person seemed to have missed that review. Don Robey, who had decided to hedge his bets with "Pledging My Love," struck a revenue-sharing deal with a company called Wemar Music. He took half the songwriter credits to "Pledging My Love" and was desperate to have the song cross over to the pop charts. He agreed to share half of publishing revenue with Wemar if it could convince a well-known white pop singer to record the song. Robey made the deal before it became apparent that Johnny Ace's recording was itself crossing over to the pop charts. Barely waiting for the ink to dry on its contract with Robey's Peacock Records, Wemar arranged for Teresa Brewer at Coral Records to cover the song.[28]

On February 12, 1955, Coral took out a full-page ad in *Billboard* to promote two new Teresa Brewer songs under the strange headline "Brewer = Business." The two songs were "I Gotta Go Get My Baby" and "Pledging My Love."

This is how crazy the pop market became. On February 26, 1955, *Billboard* reported four of the five best-selling records in the stores were crossovers: "Sincerely" by the McGuire Sisters at #1, "Hearts of Stone" by Fontane Sisters at #2, "Ko Ko Mo" by Perry Como at #4, and "Tweedle Dee" by Georgia Gibbs at #5. In addition, one of the key songs reviewed in the column "This Week's Best Buys," which was about up-and-coming tunes, was "Pledging My Love" by Teresa Brewer.[29]

The review was prescient: "This is shaping up as the most important pop-stylized version of Johnny Ace's great R&B hit. With the exception of those territories where the Ace record is firmly entrenched and pop customers will have no substitute, the Brewer disk is doing extremely well. Good markets for Brewer included Los Angeles, Nashville, Detroit, Pittsburgh . . ."

Johnny Ace's version of the song sat ten weeks in the #1 slot on the R&B chart, and was the year's top R&B leader in sales, radio plays, and on jukeboxes. The song crossed over to the pop charts, eventually climbing #17. Despite other singers and groups also recording "Pledging My Love," the Brewer recording was the most visible and ironically, it also rose to #17 on the pop chart.

A very popular young African American singer died and having a white female singer such as Teresa Brewer crashing the memorial left a bad impression. Cover records were de rigueur for the female crooners, but coming to market so soon after Johnny Ace's death smacked of exploitation. Bob Thiele in his memoirs doesn't even mention the song in his book. He elucidates such Coral hits with Brewer as "Till I Waltz Again with You," "Ricochet," "Jilted," "Let Me Go, Lover," "A Tear Fell," "Sweet Old Fashioned Girl," "You Send Me," even "I Love Mickey"—but no "Pledging My Love," so whatever arrangement Coral made with Wemar is unknown to this day.

Years later, Bill Munroe asked Brewer about covering R&B songs. Brewer answered, "I don't think the white artists, the pop singers, even realized that such things were going on. I know I didn't. I wasn't aware that I was covering a black record. I thought I was just covering a song that was out. I also covered country songs and other pop songs." However, she did add in response to another question: "At that time, rhythm and blues artists couldn't break through in the pop field. Every pop artist was covering the R&B record. In retrospect, I feel that it was unfair, especially since they usually had better versions of the songs than we did. But, the songs were so great that the pop artists did them."[30]

As Johnny Ace (and Teresa Brewer!) sang in "Pledging My Love": "Just promise me darling your love in return / May this fire in my soul, dear, forever burn."

CHAPTER SEVEN

A SWEET OLD FASHIONED GIRL (1956)

THE TEEN QUEENS—TERESA BREWER—BOB MERRILL— MICKEY MANTLE—THE CHORDETTES—ARCHIE BLEYER— PATIENCE & PRUDENCE—THE DINNING SISTERS— CATHY CARR—GOGI GRANT—KAY STARR

Record charts, oh record charts: "Don't Be Cruel" to the traditional pop singers. Yes, 1956 was the year rock 'n' roll took charge in record sales, in deejay play, on jukeboxes, and statistically on *Billboard*'s listing of top records of the year. This was the moment of Elvis Presley, who had seven of the top fifteen records of the year, including the top two, "Heartbreak Hotel" and "Don't Be Cruel." This kind of dominance would not be seen again until the Beatles came ashore in America eight years later. So if one seeks the transcendent song for the year, don't bother because the only item of transcendence was not a song but a performer, Elvis Presley.

Other rock 'n' rollers crashed the party as well. Looking at an expanded *Billboard* listing of the Top Fifty songs, rockers such as Carl Perkins with "Blue Suede Shoes," Gene Vincent with "Be-Bop-A-Lula," Sanford Clark with "The Fool," and Little Richard with "Long Tall Sally" also charted. As did New Orleans R&B singer Fats Domino and doo-wop group extraordinaire the Platters.

None of this meant the kind of music that dominated the pop record charts for the first five years of the decade disappeared. The year 1956 was a big-tent fest. Crooners such as Dean Martin, Guy Mitchell, Don Cherry, and Perry Como had big years. Plus there was plenty of room for straight-up novelty songs, such as "The Flying Saucer" by Buchanan & Goodman and "Transfusion" by Nervous Norvus, and crossover folk tunes like Tennessee Ernie Ford's "Sixteen Tons" and Lonnie Donegan's "Rock Island Line."

The big surprise in 1956 was the strength of instrumentals, mostly in the form of orchestral works, some of which were motion picture theme songs.

Orchestra leaders including Nelson Riddle, Les Baxter, Morris Stoloff, Hugo Winterhalter, and George Cates boasted amazing years.

Billboard worked on a national scale, but the all-important radio stations had local playlists, and by 1956 most stations either tried to hold the line on traditional pop or just completely moved over to rock 'n' roll. One of the bigger stations in the country's biggest market, New York (probably WABC but source uncertain), created its own Top Forty record chart for 1956 and it didn't much look like *Billboard*'s because it was one of the stations that went all in for the teen market. Its #1 song for the year was the most-cherished doo-wop song of its day, "In the Still of the Night" by the Five Satins, with "Don't Be Cruel" as the #2 song. Doo-wop, rock 'n' roll, and rhythm & blues took at least thirty of the top forty slots. The only traditional pop song on the list was Dean Martin's "Memories Are Made of This" and the singular orchestral number was Morris Stoloff's "Moonglow," which was the theme song from the movie *Picnic*.

Not only did rock 'n' roll crash the pop charts; it also pushed onto the R&B charts as well. Elvis Presley, Pat Boone, and even traditional pop singer Guy Mitchell with his "Singing the Blues" all made the Top Ten R&B list for 1956.

Rock 'n' roll from the start was a male provenance, and to some extent the same was true for R&B. So let's look at how all these different top record charts treated the female side of the industry—a quick hint here, not very well.

Working backward, we'll start with the Top R&B songs of the year as compiled by playback.fm. Of the top forty R&B songs for the year, only two women singers as a solo act made the list, LaVern Baker for "Jim Dandy" and Ruth Brown for "I Want to Do More."

New Orleans singer Shirley Mae Goodman made the list as part of the singing duo Shirley & Lee for their rousing R&B record "Let the Good Times Roll." The real news for the ladies was the success of an all-female doo-wop group, another break in the glass ceiling of that particular genre of music. If you were a teenager in the mid-1950s who went to record hops, school dances and basement parties, you slow danced to "In the Still of the Night" by the Five Satins, "Tonight, Tonight" by the Mello-Kings, and "Eddie My Love" by the Teen Queens.

What's interesting about the Teen Queens is that it was actually a sister act, Betty and Rosie Collins. The word "sisters" was important in the white pop music world but carried little weight in R&B, so the girls took on a completely different name, one that accentuated their teenage-ness. Their brother was Aaron Collins, who sang with such doo-wop groups as the Jacks and the Cadets; the latter had a big hit with the novelty doo-wop song "Stranded in the Jungle." Brother Aaron wrote "Eddie My Love" for his sisters, but as was the practice in the day, he was forced to share credits, in this case with Maxwell Davis, the arranger, and Sam Ling, a pseudonym for Saul Bihari, one of the record company owners. Part of what made the record click with listeners was the key line, "Please, Eddie, don't make me wait too long," which Betty and Rosie adroitly and rhythmically strung out: "don't make me wai-ai-t too lonnnnnnnnnng." The record was easily transferrable to the pop market, and both the Chordettes and Fontane Sisters charted with their versions of the song.

How did all this translate to that New York radio station on its Top Forty chart? First of all, the radio chart exhibited the same dearth of female singers. The Teen Queens and Shirley & Lee both made the Top Twenty cutoff. Only two more females made that list: Doris Day with "Que Sera, Sera (Whatever Will be Will Be)" and Gogi Grant with "The Wayward Wind."

Now, let's swing over to the more official *Billboard* list of the Top Fifty songs of 1956 to see how the women did. And the answer is not all that well. Only nine songs by females made the expanded chart. Starting from the bottom, at #19 and #46, respectively, were Teresa Brewer's cuts of "A Sweet Old Fashioned Girl" and "A Tear Fell." Brewer was in a category by herself. As for everyone else, there were two girl groups, the Chordettes with #37 "Born to Be with You" and Patience and Prudence with #26 "Tonight You Belong to Me." Then came three traditional ballads: Cathy Carr's #32 "Ivory Tower," Patti Page's #24 "Allegheny Moon," and Gogi Grant's #5 "The Wayward Wind." Finally, two singers in their own category, Doris Day with a #7 song "Que Sera, Sera" from her movie *The Man Who Knew Too Much* and at #10 a wild swing at rock 'n' roll with Kay Starr singing "Rock and Roll Waltz."

The big tent of 1956 included a wide variety of female voices and song types, and oddly enough, one of the big songs by a lady that year, really summed up, in a kind of musical metaphor, the changing scene of pop music, from traditional to rock 'n' roll. That song was Teresa Brewer's "A Sweet Old Fashioned Girl." For a song that was a #7 hit record it has been very underappreciated.

On the 45 to be played on phonographs, songwriting credit goes to Bob Merrill (Henry Robert Merrill Levan), one of the more agile and prolific songwriters of the 1950s and 1960s. However, there is a mystery here. Few summations of Bob Merrill songs include "A Sweet Old Fashioned Girl." It certainly was not that he had been embarrassed by writing of what was essentially a novelty song, because he was one of the best novelty songwriters in the business, having scribed two of the most popular novelty songs of the pre-rock era, "If I Knew You Were Comin' I'd've Baked a Cake" for Eileen Barton and "How Much Is That Doggie in the Window" for Patti Page. He was also just as proud of his other hit songs for the ladies, including "Mambo Italiano" for Rosemary Clooney, "Make Yourself Comfortable" for Sarah Vaughan, and from his Broadway years, the songs that Barbra Streisand made famous from the play *Funny Girl*, "People" and "Don't Rain on My Parade."

So why few listings for "A Sweet Old Fashioned Girl"? Is it an unloved song?

Teresa Brewer occasionally pooh-poohed the song. In the Bill Munroe interview sessions, she told him, "Really, at that time, I got a lot of songs with silly little lyrics . . . 'A Sweet Old Fashioned Girl' had 'scoob-el-ee-doo-bee-dum' . . . I was stuck with that type of song for many years."[1] Even as late as the 1980s, she was still critical of what had been a big hit for her, telling a reporter, "Come to think of it, 'Sweet Old Fashioned Girl' was another stupid, ootsie-poo song."[2]

In more optimistic moments, she realized why the song was so popular. The structure of the tune, in and of itself, proffered the listener a singular message concerning the musical duality of the times. "'A Sweet Old Fashioned Girl,' I must say, had a cute gimmick, with the transitions throughout it, back and forth from a sweet pop tune to an attempt at rock 'n' roll,"[3] she told an interviewer. In another encounter with the press, she carefully explained, the song was a transition between two styles and it was deliberate because "rock and roll was just coming in. The song was a clever idea, a cute little idea, and at the time it suited me just fine."[4] When she was an active performer, she always said it was a song her audiences would often request.

Brewer was right that it was a novelty with a cute idea. That didn't mean it was an easy song to pull off, because the singer had to use two voices to represent two different music styles. Again, this was a type of song that played to Brewer's unique vocal range and singing skills. The concept, as written by Bob Merrill, was—explained in rhythmic terms—exactly what was happening in the music world at that moment, the transition from traditional pop to rock 'n' roll. The title of the song referred to the old world of song, which Brewer sings coyly against a backdrop of strings. Then the tenor of the song abruptly and dramatically drops into a more beat-driven rhythm and Brewer sells the change ardently, singing with a rocking gusto. From "Doesn't anybody care to meet a sweet old-fashioned girl," the lyrics jump to "Who's a frantic little bopper in some sloppy socks / Just a crazy rock n' rollin' little goldilocks." What made the song work was Brewer, who, given the brief moments in the song to work a hard rhythm, sounds like she is that rock 'n' roller she is singing about.

One of the reasons she could effectively hit both nodes, the traditional and the now of rock 'n' roll, was that she was still young. In 1956, she was just twenty-five years old. She was even younger than all the Chordettes, who were doing very well in the new rock 'n' roll milieu.

In an interview that took place during that crucial year of 1956, a journalist asked her what at the time was a loaded set of questions, such as: What was her stand on rock 'n' roll and was it wrecking young America?

Despite being a veteran of the music industry, married, and mother of three girls at the time, she was still so young she viewed herself as part of America's new rock 'n' roll generation and took umbrage at the question. "Wrecking *us*?"

she exclaimed. "How could it do that? *We're* just the same as always and we're not half as easy to wreck as people seem to think."

The journalist duly took note, ending the story with this line, "That 'we' is the key to Teresa."[5]

The year before, a *Song Hits* magazine survey of readers asked who their favorite female performer was and found the answer to be Teresa Brewer, even though it had not been her best year in terms of record sales. Still, she charted five songs, three of which were Top Twenty, so she rolled into 1956 with a lot of momentum.[6] What had worked for the female crooners over the past two years, including for Teresa Brewer, were the cover records, so Coral kept her on the R&B track, covering Fats Domino's "Bo Weevil" (not to be confused with the Brook Benton hit tune, "The Boll Weevil Song," from 1961) as a countrified knee slapper.

Mellow bluesman Ivory Joe Hunter had been churning out R&B records since 1945, scoring his biggest hit in 1950 with the classic "I Almost Lost My Mind." In 1956, he was back on top of the charts with a soft-touch blues song, "Since I Met You Baby" and what looked like it was going to be another big hit, "A Tear Fell." Unfortunately, the latter song fell into Coral Records' sweep of potential hits, and Teresa Brewer came into the studio for a cover. "A Tear Fell" by Hunter even stalled in the R&B market as Brewer's version swept the radio stations.

Years later, when asked about "A Tear Fell," Brewer said, "I loved that song; it was really taken from the rhythm and blues record. At that time, The R&B artist just couldn't break out in the pop music world so everybody, every pop artist, was covering the R&B records. I felt very guilty about it because they had better records out than we made."[7]

In 1956, Ivory Joe Hunter's "Since I Met You Baby" crossed over to the pop charts, rising as high #12 on *Billboard*. His "A Tear Fell" experienced no crossover. Brewer's version of the song climbed all the way to #5, making it her biggest song of 1956, doing even better than "A Sweet Old Fashioned Girl."

In retrospect, it's easy to empathize with Brewer's frustration with the material that was often given to her at Coral; much of it leaning toward the "bouncy" or the "ootsie-pootsie." "A Tear Fell" was a pure ballad and exceptionally performed by Brewer with all the apparent pathos it deserved. It was not her best "grown-up" record of the year. That was "A Good Man Is Hard to Find," another tune where Brewer was able to switch tone from soft and jazzy to hardcore and bluesy. Structurally, the pace of the song moved around too much and the record didn't chart. It was a good if disappointing effort.

Much more fun was a song, "I Love Mickey," that charted, but only because of the dominant New York City market; otherwise it was probably reeeeeeeeeally hated everywhere else in the country. In 1956, the New York Yankees, led by centerfielder Mickey Mantle, were the dominant baseball team in the country, winner of seven straight pennants and six World Series. There was even, at the time, a Broadway play about the team, *Damn Yankees*, headlined by Gwen Verdon. It ran for over 1,000 performances and was made into a movie starring Tab Hunter and Gwen Verdon.

After attending one of those famous New York Yankees versus Brooklyn Dodgers World Series game in which Mantle smacked a home run, upon returning home Brewer enthusiastically began describing the game to a friend, often repeating the phrase, "I love that Mickey." Being a singer, the words, trimmed down, began to form in her brain as a refrain in a song, "I Love Mickey." She picked up the phone and sang what was just cerebral ramblings to an associate who wrote it all down, resulting in the song "I Love Mickey." The lyrics are seriously "ootsie-pootsie": "Oh, I Love Mickey (Mickey who) / You know who, the one who drives me batty every spring" or "I wish that I could catch him and pitch a little woo."[8]

Daughter Kathleen remembered Mickey Mantle coming to the Brewer house for a luau; the event was covered by the *New York Daily News*.[9]

For Yankee fan Brewer, the thrill was getting Mickey Mantle to come into the studio to play straight man against her double entendre lyrics. Treating it all as lark, Mantle afterward joked, "Why, I didn't know I could sing."[10]

Brewer did well in 1956 but she wasn't part of the female crooner story for the year; she was more a sidebar or sandbar, depending on point of view, to a newly flowing musical drift. In 1956, in regard to women singers, three different crosscurrents hit all at once: the sudden importance of girl groups, a last hurrah of traditional female pop but by new voices, and the survivalist strategies of the veteran crooners.

As with the arrival of rock 'n' roll, the coming of the girl groups really began in 1955 and found confirmation the following year. The Fontane Sisters, McGuire Sisters, and the unique Chordettes all had big songs in 1955. One year later, the Chordettes were back again, this time to be joined by newbies Patience & Prudence.

The most important difference between the Chordettes and the McGuire and Fontane Sisters was that the group was not a sister act but a quartet of ladies, some of whom were related and some not. Due to circumstances, the lineup was fluid, with either Janet Ertel, Carol Buschman, Margie Needham, Lynn Evans, Jinny Lockard, or Nancy Overton.

The group was organized in Sheboygan, Wisconsin, primarily to sing barbershop harmony, sometimes called "close harmony." In 1949, they competed on *Arthur Godfrey's Talent Scouts*, winning first prize and then becoming regulars on his show. The highly successful television program started to unravel in 1953 when both Godfrey and spotlighted vocalist Julius LaRosa went to war, resulting in the departure of the popular LaRosa. Godfrey's bandleader, Archie Bleyer, left and formed his own company, Cadence Records, and the Chordettes went with him. Their second recording at Cadence under Bleyer's stewardship was a little number called "Mr. Sandman."

"We were in Las Vegas performing and Archie would call Janet [Ertel] saying to her, 'I think we have a hit.' By the time we got back to New York, you couldn't turn on the radio without hearing it," Evans recalled.[11]

At the time, no matter how one diced up the talent slipping in and out of the Chordettes, they were no longer youngsters, average age in the late twenties to early thirties, so their ability to make that connection with teenagers was amazing—and it had a lot to do with the genius of Archie Bleyer. He would produce major hits for a wide range of artists from the Everly Brothers to Andy Williams to Lenny Welch to Johnny Tillotson to Link Wray.

Under Bleyer's sway, music historian Birnbaum wrote, "the group [Chordettes] turned from barbershop to mainstream pop, although Bleyer's arrangements did make use of barbershop motifs such as the charming arpeggios on . . . 'Mr. Sandman.'"[12]

By coming over to Cadence, the Chordettes put themselves in Bleyer's hands, trusting him to make the right choices for their singing style. "We would go into the studio and he [Bleyer] would choose the material we would sing," said Evans, including discovering the song "Mr. Sandman," which was the very obscure B-side to Vaughn Monroe's Top Ten hit of 1954, "They Were Doin' the Mambo." Someone was flipping records over and listening to what were supposedly the secondary songs.

Bleyer would ask the Chordettes if they cared for a chosen song. If there were no vocal objections, he would do the arrangement and orchestrations, leaning to the group's barbershop voicing, which was the tenor on top, then the leader, alto, and contralto. Bleyer was something of a perfectionist, and it wasn't unusual for the Chordettes to still be in the recording studio at three in the morning—and in those days the four singers were sharing just one microphone.[13]

While they didn't have another skyrocket-to-the-moon hit like "Mr. Sandman," the Chordettes boasted a strong year in 1956 with four records hitting the charts, three of which became Top Ten songs: "Lay Down Your Arms," "Born to Be with You," and a cover of "Eddie My Love." Trying to nail down their acceptance among the young adults of America, the Chordettes also in '56 released "Teenage Goodnight," with opening lyrics that began "the school dance is over." It wasn't their best effort.

Nevertheless, they were still on good terms with teenage listeners and could frequently be seen on Dick Clark's *American Bandstand*. They managed another

Top Ten record in 1957 with "Just Between You and Me." The group's last major zinger was the rollicking "Lollipop," which zoomed to #2 on the chart.

Not quite as obscure a choice as "Mr. Sandman," the song "Lollipop" has an interesting history. It was written by a teenage songwriter named Beverly Ross, who toiled at the Brill Building in New York. She first teamed with Jeff Barry, who would write a bunch of big hits with Ellie Greenwich. Later, working with Black songwriter Julius Dixson, she wrote "Lollipop" after seeing Dixson's daughter get a sucker tangled in her hair. Dixson's neighbor, Ronald Gumm, a Black teenager, was recruited to record a demo with Beverly, which was so good it was released as a single with credits to the duo Ronald and Ruby. It quickly rose up the charts. When it got to #20, things stalled. First, since Ronald and Ruby were an interracial singing group, bookings and television appearances evaporated. Secondly, the better-known Chordettes covered their efforts.[14]

The Chordettes continued to record sporadically into the 1960s with occasional success. The group's last big hit was a vocal rendition of "Never on Sunday," the Academy Award–winning theme song to the movie of the same name. The instrumental by Don Costa reached #19 on the pop chart in 1960. A year later, the Chordettes took their version to #13. It was the group's last Top Forty hit.

From a female singer perspective, the real teenage story in 1956 was the appearance of the newly minted duo Patience & Prudence on the pop charts. If there is any importance to this story, it's because the two sisters who made up this duo were actual teenagers—barely. Patience Ann McIntyre turned fourteen years old in 1956 while her sister Prudence Ann McIntyre would turn eleven that year. Their age, their success, and the nepotism that gave them a start has galled writers for years. Their sound has sometimes been diminutively referred to as bubblegum pop, which as a sub-genre of rock 'n' roll didn't exist back then. What Patience & Prudence accomplished were two songs that helped create the proto–girl group sound.

Yes, they wouldn't have done what they did had their father Mark McIntyre not been a music industry veteran who had worked with Frank Sinatra in the 1940s. The family lived in Los Angeles and Mark McIntyre fostered his daughters' interest in music. Like many suburban girls of their day, they learned piano. Except they were better than that and could read music as well. Dad liked what he saw and heard with his gals, especially a song they learned while at camp the summer before. It was called "Tonight You Belong to Me." The tune bugged dad until he realized it was the Billy Rose tune from the 1920s that became a hit for a singer named Gene Austin. In 1951, Peggy Lee recorded the song as the B-side to her one big hit of the year, "(When I Dance with You) I Get Ideas," which treated the song in a languid, big-band style. That got someone in the Frankie Laine orbit interested in the cut and he brought it back from obscurity the following year with an overly dramatic, masculine sound—but still a big-band rendition. It is probably that version of the song the girls learned at camp. Thinking it could be a hit again, dad recorded an arrangement for cabaret singer Lisa Kirk, and because he had the time and the opportunity, he decided to record a version of the song with his two girls. This cut started out as just a personal effort but he passed the demo to his friend, songwriter Ross Bagdasarian, who moved it up the line to Liberty Records. The cut by the McIntyre girls boasted wonderful two- part harmony played against a piano-led background. There was nothing tricky about it, just an innocence that was attractive. Liberty jumped at the chance to record the song, mostly adding overdubs to the original version.[15]

"Tonight You Belong to Me" soared to #4 on the record chart. The sisters came back later in the year with "Gonna Get Along Without Ya Now," a cover of Teresa Brewer's hit from 1952, and took that to #11 on the chart. Then it was over. They recorded a handful of other tunes, but their moment in the sun was brief and slightly impactful. It's hard to find any reference to Patience & Prudence, but in 1970 Len Brown and Gary Friedrich put together paperback *Encyclopedia of Rock & Roll* for teenagers. The authors decided to include the Patience & Prudence story and wrote an entry using a pen dripping with the black ink of sarcasm and wonder:

> A freaky recording act of 1956, Patience and Prudence were two pre-teen girls who got a chance at releasing a record because their father was one of the owners of Liberty Records. What's really got to frustrate some aspiring singer of today, the girls even hit a couple of times during their brief career. Their first hit sold a million and the second one didn't miss by too much. Remember "Tonight You Belong to Me"? It was the top of the charts the week before "Heartbreak Hotel" by Elvis took over. The girls' sweet, whispery vocals found an ear with the record buyers. While everyone in the record business were writing the duo off as one-shot wonders, Patience and Prudence were climbing into the Top Ten again with a second hit, "Gonna Get Along Without You Now."[16] Go figure.

The strength of the female crooner sound in the early 1950s was the tour-de-force, take-no-prisoners power ballad as represented by songs such as "Let Me Go, Lover!" by Joan Weber. These were not the soft, wispy, dew-eyed ballads sung by waifs trying to come across as innocents in a world swirling with fickle lovers. These were in-your-face songs about a woman confronting her man in a convoluted entanglement of yearning and need for independence. The apotheosis of this sound came in 1956 with tunes by two pop chart novitiates, Gogi Grant and Cathy Carr, who respectively sang "The Wayward Wind" and

"Ivory Tower." While these two songs may not be eternal classics that live forever in America's songbook, they are exemplary representations of this particular genre of music.

The genesis of "Ivory Tower," goes back to 1953 when veteran jazz musician and songwriter Jack Fulton teamed up with Lois Steele to write a song called "Keep Your Promise, Willie Thomas," which was recorded by The Dinning Sisters.

Originally, the Dinning singing group consisted of three girls Ella (Lou), Jean, and Virginia (Ginger) Dinning from farm country (born in Kansas and raised in Oklahoma). Lou left the group in 1946 and was replaced by Jayne Bunderson without a group name-change. The girls first sang in the style of the Boswell Sisters and then by the 1940s like the Andrews Sisters. They did well enough to travel to Chicago where they auditioned for NBC radio, where they remained for seven years. They had a few minor hits in the 1940s and hung on into the 1950s, when in 1952 Jayne Bundesen left and was replaced by Tootsie Dinning. Whatever heat the group had in the 1940s had dissipated, and, although the Dinning gals kept trying, their sound never carried into the 1950s. In 1953 they recorded "Keep Your Promise, Willie Thomas," a pleasant ballad with a bit of a nod to country.[17] In the recording studio, the ladies were backed by Teresa Brewer's favorite bandleader Jack Pleis, although the Dinning sound was somnambulant compared to anything by Brewer.

The song would eventually be recorded by Hank Snow and Anita Carter, but the Dinning version didn't get much action. Nevertheless, the team of Fulton with Steele worked so well they went at it again, writing "Wanted," which was a big hit for Perry Como in 1954. The writing team returned to the piano once again, scribbling a song called "Ivory Tower," which Jack Fulton introduced in 1955.

Although Fulton's version of the song disappeared quickly, there was something very potent in the tune, and A&R men around the country grabbed for the rights, creating the usual melee. In March 1956 alone, four different recording acts released a take on the song: Gale Storm, Cathy Carr, the Four Hues (from Coral Records), and Otis Williams and His Charms.

"Ivory Tower" became a melody puissant, reaching #6 on the R&B chart for Otis Williams and crossing over to pop, where that version climbed to #11; for the popular TV actress Gale Storm, who took the song to #6 on the pop chart; but the clear winner in terms of performance, sales, and everything else was Cathy Carr. On *Billboard*'s pop charts, the song peaked at #2. So the question is, besides boasting a fabulously heartfelt rendition of "Ivory Tower," how did she sneak past a couple of well-known names to climb near to the pinnacle of the pop charts?

Carr (Angelina Helen Catherine Cordovano), who was born in 1936, was still a teenager when she signed in 1953 with Coral Records,[18] which at the time was gathering a bloc of female voices, including Teresa Brewer. With so much competition from the likes of Brewer, the McGuire Sisters, and Debbie Reynolds, Carr got lost in the shuffle. She left Coral and ended up at a smaller label, Cincinnati-based Fraternity Records. It was her saving grace.

For the pop market, most records come out of the big cities of New York or Los Angeles. Fraternity Records, a Midwestern company, broke Carr in its home territory. A March 10, 1956, *Billboard* story out of Cincinnati noted Carr was in town for several days plugging "Ivory Tower" with the local deejays: "promotion included a guest shot on Paul Dixon's television show over at WLW-T. Miss Carr is currently playing Midwestern clubs for General Artists Corporation."[19]

Sensing a longer story about the emerging Carr, *Billboard* kept up with her rise. The magazine at the end of same month reported that Carr put in a "whirlwind weekend that darn near had her bumping into herself." Carr appeared as guest of Detroit deejay Ed McKenzie for a Saturday afternoon and then hopped a private plane to go back to Cincinnati to appear on the WCPO Bob Braun's Coca-Cola Show for teenagers. That evening it was back to Detroit where she appeared on Mickey Shorr's *Teen Dance* show on WJBK. The next day it was Toledo as guest of deejay Freddie Mitchell. From there her schedule would take her to Buffalo, Pittsburgh, and then the big eastern cities of Philly, New York, and Boston.[20]

On March 31, *Billboard* placed Carr's "Ivory Tower" in "This Week's Best Buys," which was based on sales in key markets: "Middle Western markets agog with the surprising take-off of the disk. Cincinnati, Cleveland, Chicago, Milwaukee and St. Louis all indicated unusually heavy sales. This week the record began hitting in Eastern cities like Baltimore, Buffalo and Providence, and seems certain to spread quickly to others."[21]

Most importantly, Carr got a jump on Gale Storm, who would be her main competition in the pop world. The next week *Billboard* reviewed Storm's version with this notation: "Miss Storm has the hit look about her again with the fine waxing of the haunting tune. The Carr version has already hit the charts, but Storm has the power in this heartfelt effort to catch up fast."[22] It didn't.

Unlike Storm, Carr was only a singer, not an actress. Before "Ivory Tower" hit, her calendar was completely empty for the important summer season. Then it was nonstop because her record company had control of her time. It was *The Perry Como Show* on June 2, 1956, followed by live shows at the Coney Island in Cincinnati, Vermillion on the Lake in Cleveland, and then the *Canadian Hit Parade* in Toronto, as her record was #1 in that country.[23] From there the road led to Folly Pier in Charleston, West Virginia, the Eddy Arnold TV show, and the Amphitheater in Evansville. Finally, and this was important because she was a teenager, she was given a place in a traveling omnibus of teen acts, the type of multi-act show that was a staple of rock 'n' roll concerts into the mid-1960s. On the bill with her were Carl Perkins, Al Hibbler, the Teenagers, and others for a six-week tour of one-nighters. In November, she was booked on an "all-star rock 'n' roll review in Buffalo, which included Carl Perkins, Eileen Rogers, the G-Clefs, The Drifters and Big Maybelle."[24]

Then it was all over. Neither she nor her record company was able to reproduce the magic of "Ivory Tower." She moved to more youth-oriented labels such as Roulette and Laurie without success, sporadically recording into the 1960s.

If there ever was a stronger incarnation of the female power ballad than "Ivory Tower," it was surely "The Wayward Wind," which arrived in stores and on the desks of deejays the same year as Cathy Carr's big hit.

The singer was Gogi Grant and the song was the result of cosmic convergence. Stanley Lebowsky, who later became famous as a Broadway music director, and Herb Newman, the co-owner of Era Records in Hollywood, met while at UCLA. They both had an interest in music and decided to try to write songs together. It appears they didn't get too deep into the process, and the only known song to come out of that collaboration was a tune about an erratic zephyr, which was put into an envelope and stashed away with other college papers saved by Newman. Flash forward many years to 1955, and Newman along with Lou Bedell decide to create a new record company to record pop, country & western, and jazz performers. They called it Era Records, eventually signing a recently orphaned singer from a larger record label who went by the name Gogi Grant. (In 1958, Bedell and Newman formed Doré Records; its first big hit was "To Know Him Is to Love Him.")

Born in Philadelphia in 1924, Gogi Grant (Myrtle Audrey Arinsberg) moved with her family to Los Angeles at the age of twelve. Although Grant was a natural singer, she never considered becoming a performer until friends convinced her to enter a weekly talent contest at the popular Los Angeles nightspot the Mocambo. Then the stars aligned in a weirdly coincidental way. The Mocambo orchestra leader thought Grant had talent but did not yet know how to use it, so he suggested she work with a voice coach. Three months later she made a demo at Gold Star recording studio, which was left on a turntable. The head of MCA's talent agency comes to Gold Star, discovers an abandoned record, the Gogi Grant demo, and plays it—a song called "I'm Yours." The MCA man undergoes a "wow" moment and issues an all-points bulletin for the woman whose name, Gogi Grant, is on the demo. The powerful MCA group signed Grant and quickly got her a contract with RCA Victor. For a while, Myrtle Audrey became Audrey Brown, a pseudonym she used while singing in the Catskills.

Dave Kapp, who headed A&R at RCA, didn't like that name either, so he decided on Gogi Grant, which, in popular legend, was because Kapp used to lunch at a New York restaurant called Gogi's La Rue.[25] There is another version to this story. According to Grant, "My face fell when Mr. Kapp told me I was going to be billed as Gogi. I thought it sounded frilly and nonsensical. Kapp thought the name was right for me and I guess it was—but I couldn't resist asking 'What's a Gogi?' His answer was, 'Darned if I know, I dreamed it last night.'"[26] Grant didn't really have a say in the decision, because in the 1950s the A&R head of a major record company was so autocratic that he (and it was always a he in the 1950s) not only told the singers, especially the new signees, what to sing, but under what professional name they now would be singing.

Kapp gave Grant a rhythmic appellation; he just couldn't give her a singing career. RCA didn't know what to do her. From 1952 to 1953 she recorded just a couple of songs, which immediately went to the shelf, and that was it. Kapp left RCA to start his own label and Grant was gone from RCA as well. Like Cathy Carr, Grant eventually ended up at a much smaller label, and as with Carr, it saved her career.

Grant started recording with Era records in 1955. The company arranged for the songwriting team of Chuck Meyer and Biff Jones to meet with Grant to decide on songs for an upcoming recording session. The one tune she liked best was a number called "Suddenly There's a Valley," which was recorded, deemed salable, and immediately promoted. When it began getting airplay from deejays, Era sent Grant on a twenty-eight-city promotional tour. That turned out to be a brilliant move because, when "Suddenly There's a Valley" looked like a song with potential, a baseball team's worth of singers piled in.[27] But, the rookie held her own. Her version went to #14 on the *Billboard* chart, beating back established veterans such as Jo Stafford, whose version of the song got as high as #16, and Julius La Rosa, whose rendition only got as far as #29. Gogi Grant had her first hit record.

With Grant riding high, Era Records brought her back into the recording studio to put down a follow-up record, which was going to be "Who Are We." The studio was booked for three hours and the "Who We Are" session took most of that time. Before Grant got in front of the microphone, however, she needed to work through the arrangement. On break, Newman asked her to come into his office. As Grant recalled, he pulled out a manuscript that was so old it was brown with age. It turned out to be the song he had written in college with Stan Lebowsky.

Speaking with a Salt Lake City reporter in 1956, Lebowsky said, "Herb Newman wrote the lyrics for 'Wayward Wind.' I liked them so I composed the music. We played around with it for six years before a recording was made that we really liked."[28]

As written by Newman and Lebowsky, the voice of the song was to be male, but Grant took a liking to the tune and rewrote some of the lyrics to make it from a woman's perspective. Even so, it probably still wouldn't have gotten studio time except that the recording of "Who We Are" only took two hours and forty-five minutes to complete. Studio time didn't come cheap and the extra fifteen minutes wasn't going to be wasted, so Grant hastily returned to the mic and recorded "The Wayward Wind."

Elvis Presley began his domination of the music world on April 21, 1956, when "Heartbreak Hotel" hit #1 on the record chart and stayed there for eight weeks. He would be dethroned on June 16 for six weeks and then come back with another #1 song, "I Want You, I Need You, I Love You," on July 28.

In the middle of "Heartbreak Hotel's" dominance of America's record and radio industry, the ladies were having a moment. On page 26 of the *Cash Box* issue of May 19, 1956, the regional record report took up a half page and the magazine filled the rest of the sheet with its usual mix of short articles and small-one column ads. The top photo was about the McGuire Sisters. Below it, the first article concerned Teresa Brewer introducing new songs including "Sweet Old Fashioned Girl" on *The Ed Sullivan Show*. The second article was about film star Monique Van Vooren signing with Request Records. The first ad promoted Gale Storm singing "Ivory Tower," while the second advertised new singer Connie Francis with a song called "Forgetting."[29]

Meanwhile, the regional record report showed most markets had been conquered by either "Heartbreak Hotel" or the instrumental hit "Moonglow and Theme from *Picnic*." Yet another battle was brewing underneath in the remainder of the top ten songs of each city, where "Ivory Tower" was slipping and "The Wayward Wind" was ascending. In Milwaukee, for example, the top four songs were "Heartbreak Hotel," "The Wayward Wind," "Moonglow and Theme from *Picnic*," and "Ivory Tower." In Kansas City, "Moonglow and Theme from *Picnic*" and "Heartbreak Hotel" were #1 and #2, while "Ivory Tower" was #7 and "The Wayward Wind" #8.

A young teenage girl, sitting in class, longingly staring at the dark-haired boy with the high pompadour and an odd curl hanging on the forehead, wearing slim trousers cut above the ankle and black shoes with Cuban heels, didn't have to understand the meaning of, or even know the word *metaphor* to accept the opening lines—"The wayward wind is a restless wind / a restless wind that yearns to wander"—to understand this song was about a fellow. The kind of guy the Shangri-Las would sing about years later: "Yeah, well I hear he's bad / Mm, he's good bad, but he's not evil." Or as Gogi Grant sang in her hit song, "and he was born the next of kin / the next of kin to the wayward wind."

On June 16, 1956, "The Wayward Wind" booted "Heartbreak Hotel" from the #1 slot and ruled for six straight weeks. On July 7, *Billboard* reported the song was tops in record sales, in deejay plays, and with jukebox dealers. The next week Grant told reporters, "The song tops every poll in popularity now. We've passed the millionth mark, for which I received a gold pressing of the record."[30]

Such good news for such a good song—and then it was over. Grant's recording career was sidetracked by brief encounters with Hollywood and she rarely cut any more singles. In 1958 and 1959 Grant recorded a sheath of albums for RCA Victor, none of which even came close to creating the kind of stir that a "cool" wind brings to an arid place.

The question is, why were the careers of Carr and Grant so short? Part of the reason was the changing music scene. The female power ballad peaked in 1956 just as the genre was becoming too old school, especially as compared to the more beat-oriented rock 'n' roll.

All the latter-day crooners of the 1950s, male or female, tried to figure a way to come to terms with rock 'n' roll. The key issue they had to answer for themselves was whether they would stick to what had been successful for them in the past, or if was there some kind of compromise they could perpetrate that would make them attractive to the teenager crowd, which overwhelmingly was now the audience for radio and the buyers of records. Many of the female singers flirted with some sort of rock 'n' roll-ish type of song, sometimes with modest triumph.

The most successful of these songs was also the most unlikely. It was called "Rock and Roll Waltz," which, in and of itself, was an astounding slice of hubris, an oxymoron so apparent it should have set off warning signals with deejays all over the country. In the end it was neither much of a waltz nor a rock 'n' roll tune, it was novelty song in the same limited, very 1956 vernacular as "Sweet Old Fashioned Girl" in that the understated meaning of the song was really about the tenor of the times: rock 'n' roll had arrived and the music of mom and dad was being retired. These two songs offered a lightweight zeitgeist that appealed to older teenagers, who might have just started junior high school (seventh grade) in 1950 or 1951 and were now on the verge of high school graduation. They enjoyed rock 'n' roll but still held an affection for the songs of the early 1950s. They were at a crossroads in life and "Rock and Roll Waltz" as well as "Sweet Old Fashioned Girl" showed them they were not alone.

The lyrics to "Rock and Roll Waltz" were written by veteran songwriter Roy Alfred working with composer Shorty Allen. Alfred's tunes began getting picked up by pop singers in the mid-1940s and he was able to maintain a busy career deep into the 1960s. His most well-known song from forties was "The Hucklebuck" by Roy Milton and the Solid Senders. Nat King Cole's early group The King Cole Trio turned a couple of his songs into big hits. He continued his streak of sporadic successes until 1956, when everything he planted came a cropper: "Who Can Explain" by Frankie Lymon & the Teenagers, "My First

Formal Gown" by Patti Page, and "Wisdom of a Fool" by the Five Keys. "Rock and Roll Waltz" was recorded near the end of 1955, not becoming a #1 hit until February '56.

The latter song was written in story form. A girl comes home from a date, hears the sound of a "jump" tune, and discovers her mother and father dancing to one of her rock 'n' roll records. Only they were getting it all wrong because they were trying to waltz to the jump (already an outdated term for beat-driven rock 'n' roll) music. Alfred wrote the humorous chorus: "A-one, two, and then rock / A-one, two, and then roll / they did the rock and roll waltz." The pop-country tune benefited from having the versatile bandleader Hugo Winterhalter and his orchestra in the recording studio.

Despite the lyrics, again the metaphor was not in any singular line but in the motif. This kind of song was not only tricky to write but just as difficult to master in voice due to the abrupt changes in tonal expression. The singer had to be able to sell nice as well as be a hard rock 'n' roller (which was akin to being a delinquent in 1956). It took a couple of capable singers to make these kinds of songs approachable to what was then the current radio audience. Teresa Brewer had done it with "Sweet Old Fashioned Girl" and the veteran Kay Starr accomplished the feat with "Rock and Roll Waltz."

Kay Starr (Catherine Laverne Starks) was born July 21, 1922, on an Oklahoma reservation. Her mother was of mixed parentage, white and Native American, while her father was Iroquois, making Starr one of the earliest (Mildred Bailey preceded her) Native Americans to become a pop recording star. As with so many other female singers of her time, her career began when she was just a child. An aunt arranged for her to appear on a Dallas radio station talent contest. She was already such a good singer that by the age of ten she was earning $3 a night, which was good money during the Depression years. When her family moved to Memphis, she got a lucky break when the orchestra at the city's grand Peabody Hotel didn't have a girl singer and needed one quickly. They hired the fifteen-year-old Starr. By the end of the thirties, she was singing with big bands, making her recording debut with the Glenn Miller band. During the war years, Starr moved to Los Angeles and sang with Charlie Barnet's jazz band, replacing Lena Horne. In 1947, she signed with a major label, Capitol Records, which had been gathering female vocalists (Peggy Lee, Ella Mae Morse, Jo Stafford, and Margaret Whiting) as if it was going to field a woman's baseball team. Starr scored a few hits for Capitol in the late 1940s, most importantly a cover of Russ Morgan's "So Tired," which became her first Top Ten hit in January 1949.[31]

The next year started slowly for Starr as her first releases failed to chart, but then her version of "Hoop-Dee-Doo" began to climb out of the mosh pit. The silly polka song was taken on by everyone under the sun, including Perry Como and the Fontane Sisters. Crooner Como took the song all the way to #2 on the pop record chart. Starr's version did well, rising as high as #14 on the chart. Then came her real breakout song, "Bonaparte's Retreat." She would have two more hits with Tennessee Ernie Ford in 1950 and a couple of more in 1951.

The following year was the year of Kay Starr. Her "Wheel of Fortune" was the second best-selling record of 1952, somehow coming in behind the instrumental "Blue Tango," a now-forgotten song. This is the way music historian Larry Birnbaum writes about the phenomenon:

> "Wheel of Fortune" . . . had been recorded by the jazz singer Johnny Hartman, the doo-wop group The Cardinals, The Billy Williams Quartet, Dinah Washington, and the white singer Sunny Gale with the Black Eddie Wilcox orchestra by the time Starr covered it. . . . but Starr's version, a #1 pop smash, outsold them all. Washington's delivery may be more poignant and world-weary, but Starr makes the song wholly her own, belting the lyrics with stirring conviction. Although it's a ballad without a backbeat or boogie-woogie bass line, part of it, especially the bridge, where Starr overdubs her own backing harmonies, have a slow-motion rock 'n' roll feel.[32]

Starr boasted five more hits in 1952. A March article in *Billboard* that discussed the coming of R&B had this notation: "The influence of r&b discs on the pop market tunes and artists has been of great import over the past year. Johnnie Ray with a singing style closest to r&b vocalists, sells just as well in both fields. The same can be said of Kay Starr."[33]

In 1953 and 1954, Starr boasted ten more Top Thirty hits. Her output severely slowed in 1955 with just five new releases, of which only one charted. Just when it appeared her career was on the skids, she toasted the new year of 1956 with "Rock and Roll Waltz."

Billboard's first notice of the song was on December 10, 1955, when the magazine placed it and three other records in its "Review Spotlight." Along with a Nat King Cole song were new records by Doris Day, the McGuire Sisters, and at the top of the heap, Kay Starr. The reviewer for "Rock and Roll Waltz" liked what he heard: "Miss Starr sells it all the way in the very best offering in a long time. Gal rocks and rolls in great style thru the decidedly good lyrics, and there's a powerful assist from the gal's first Winterhalter ork and chorus backing. This one could break out fast."[34]

The song initially appeared on *Billboard*'s record chart the first week in January. By the last week in the month, the song was the fifth best in national record sales, juke box plays, and deejay spins.[35] By April, "Rock and Roll Waltz" was the #1 record in the UK.[36] In May, it was still in the Top Twenty of *Billboard*, eighteen weeks on the chart.

In 1956, *Billboard* desegregated its charts. Little Richard, Fats Domino, Clyde McPhatter, and Ray Charles regularly appeared on the Best Selling Records list and on the Honor Roll of Hits, wrote music historian Preston Lauterbach, "mixing with Elvis Presley, Carl Perkins, Perry Como, and the unforgettable Kay Starr, whose 'Rock and Roll Waltz' outsold 'em all that year."

Starr had one more Top Ten record, "My Heart Reminds Me," in 1957 and was still recording into the 1970s. Nevertheless, she had made her mark, and Starr's influence on other female singers, particularly Patsy Cline, was strong. Owen Bradley, Patsy Cline's arranger, thought Cline was influenced by Starr and possibly Jo Stafford, adding, to those who might be confused by the lack of parallels in voice and career, "I don't think she sounded like those singers [Starr and Jo Stafford], but I think she listened to them."[37]

Dale Turner, who sang with Patsy Cline on *Town & Country Jamboree* in 1955 when Patsy's career was still in the chrysalis stage, was interviewed about those days and recalled: "She [Patsy] was wonderful. She could sing anything . . . It wasn't all country back then; we mixed the pop charts and the country charts. We might do 'Teach me Tonight' and then turn around do the Patti Page stuff, the Teresa Brewer stuff. Patsy back then reminded me a lot of Kay Starr. She had that quality to her voice."[38]

Since it wasn't really rock 'n' roll, "Rock and Roll Waltz" did not make any impact on the genre, but one unlikely song from that year did: Doris Day's "Que Sera, Sera."

Here's the unusual story.

Mike Palermo, as a teenager on Long Island, New York, lived next door to a classmate at Island Trees High School named Eddie Mahoney, who later would reinvent himself as rock 'n' roller Eddie Money. One day, teenage Palermo, who also became a singer/songwriter, while walking his dog passed the Mahoney house and heard Eddie's mother loudly singing "Que Sera, Sera"; she was a big fan of the song. Palermo never thought of that moment again for forty years until he hit a cultural convergence and the memory emerged. He had just watched the movie *The Man Who Knew Too Much*, where Doris Day introduced the tune. The most memorable lyric being: "Que sera, sera; Whatever will be, will be; The future's not ours to see." About the same time, Palermo hears on the radio Eddie Money's first big song, "Baby Hold On," which he wrote. The opening lyrics to Eddie Money's song reads: "Baby hold on to me / Whatever will be, will be / The future is ours to see."

"I saw Eddie Money several times after he made it big," Palermo said, "I never thought to ask him about the lyrics."[39]

About those lyrics!

The song was written by the songwriting team of Jay Livingston and Ray Evans at the behest of Alfred Hitchcock, the director of *The Man Who Knew*

Too Much. Livingston and Evans had never written a song for a particular scene in a movie and Hitchcock had to explain the importance of the tune in relation to the scene and arc of the film. The two got the concept and wrote "Que Sera, Sera" in a matter of hours, but waited several days before delivering it to the director because they didn't want him to know how easily it came to them. Biographer David Kaufman wrote, "it would become Day's theme song, forever identified with her."[40]

CHAPTER EIGHT

TAMMY (1957)

TERESA BREWER—PATTI PAGE—JACK RAEL— DICK MANNING—DEBBIE REYNOLDS—EDDIE FISHER— GALE STORM—BONNIE GUITAR—DORIS DAY

With the hegemony of rock 'n' roll, including an overlap with rhythm & blues, *Billboard* ended the segregation of its pop music charts, which meant that for every Elvis Presley listing there might be a Platters song and every Pat Boone tune could be calculated against a Frankie Lymon and the Teenagers melody. Since both rock 'n' roll and R&B were so male-dominated, the only real loser in all this were the ladies. Indeed, the wonderful era of the female crooner that began in 1950 came to a close in 1956. The following year, of the top fifty songs for 1957, only three were by female soloists—"Tammy" by Debbie Reynolds, "Dark Moon" by Gale Storm, and "Old Cape Cod" by Patti Page—and one other song, "Mr. Lee" by a female group, the Bobbettes, which turned out to be a foreshadowing of what the other side of rock 'n' roll would look like in the next decade.

Cultural trends don't just end sharply; more or less the threads continue on for months or few years gradually losing emphasis, which was what happened to the musical phenomenon of the white female crooners. Some of the singers would continue to have another decent year in 1957, 1958, or 1959.

The era of the female crooner began in 1950 with Teresa Brewer and Patti Page in ascendency, and these two veterans could boast some fine accomplishments in 1957; it just wasn't getting any easier for them to land space on the *Billboard* Hot 100.

Coral Records released eight Teresa Brewer singles in 1957; only three charted. One, "Teardrops in My Heart," never got higher than #64 on *Billboard*, and if an enterprising deejay was flipping the single over to seek an undiscovered gem on the B-side, he wouldn't have found it here. The B-side was the embarrassing "Lula Rock-A-Hula," a Hawaiian-beat condescension and descension into the ear canals of rock 'n' roll–infatuated teenagers with lyrics such as: "Lula Rock-A-Hula that's me / rockin' underneath the banyan tree / won't you share my hula, hula, hu."

Brewer's two big hits of the year were cover songs. The first was "Empty Arms," when Coral Records decided to pick over the Ivory Joe Hunter oeuvre once again. Never in public without his sincere, wide smile, Hunter was known by the nickname "The Happiest Man Alive." In 1957, while in Memphis, he was invited to visit Elvis, who spent the day with him singing some of Hunter's old songs—and there were a lot of them (literally, about a thousand with his name as songwriter).[1] One of his most successful was the slow ballad "Empty Arms," which he took to #2 on the R&B chart. It crossed over to the pop chart and looked like it was going to be a hit when it stalled at #43. According to Maury Dean, in his book *Rock 'n' Roll Gold Rush: A Singles Un-Encyclopedia*, "Teresa Brewer's cover version hit the pop charts the same month as Hunter's original crossed over. His version was dead in the water and Brewer's shot to #11 on the pop charts."[2] (Sonny James notched a #1 country & western hit with the song in 1971.)

Brewer would do better—and worse—with her next cover, "You Send Me," originally recorded by Sam Cooke. Although Brewer took the song to #8 on the pop chart, today the existence of that version is relatively unknown. That's because the Sam Cooke original was a behemoth of a tune: #1 on the R&B and pop charts, and the twentieth best-selling song of 1957. The esteem for Cooke's "You Send Me" has never diminished. The song ranked #115 on *Rolling Stone* magazine's "The 500 Greatest Songs of All Time."

The Teresa Brewer website summed up her middle years of the 1950s this way: "Toward the later 1950s . . . the industry began to realize the cover version of a recording was no longer necessarily the best seller. In Teresa's case, the results were mixed . . . she sold more copies of Ivory Joe Hunter's 'A Tear Fell' and 'Empty Arms,' Fats Domino's 'Bo Weevil,' and possibly Johnny Ace's 'Pledging My Love' than the original artists. However, her version of 'Rock Love,' 'Tweedle Dee' and 'You Send Me' were bigger hits for the original artists—Lula Reed, LaVern Baker and Sam Cooke, respectively."[3]

It was not quite time yet to feel bad for Teresa Brewer: a 1957 article in *Look* magazine suggested her income for records, shows, and television was $200,000 (just under $2 million in 2020 dollars), and that was when the average family income was just $5,000.[4] In addition, *Teen Magazine* readers, looking back a year, voted Teresa Brewer their favorite female recording star at the start of 1958.[5] Coming in fourth in that same vote was Patti Page.

If there was another singer who defined the female crooner era, it was Patti Page. From 1948 through 1958 there was not one year she didn't boast at least one Top Twenty hit. If anything, during the early years of rock 'n' roll, one could almost say Page's career peaked, not in terms output or #1 singles, but in terms of quality. Two of her best singles beyond "Tennessee Waltz" were released in 1956 and 1957 and were major hits. "Allegheny Moon," the #24 best-selling song of '56, and "Old Cape Cod," the #46 best-selling song of 1957, were also two of the finest tunes in the female crooner genre of the 1950s.

The difference between "Allegheny Moon" and "Old Cape Cod" in comparison to the great female crooner tunes of "The Wayward Wind" and "Let Me Go, Lover," was that the latter songs were power ballads, while the Patti Page's tunes were soft, seductive. Page never tried to conquer listeners; she preferred to lure them into her idylls: "Allegheny Moon it's up to you / Please see what you can do / For me and for my one and only love." Or the more well-known lyrics of "Old Cape Cod": "If you're fond of sand dunes and salty air / quaint little villages here and there / you're sure to fall in love with old Cape Cod."

One might attribute Page's long and successful career (over 100 million records sold) to stable, professional management that lasted fifty years—and that she had from the start.

Patti Page (Clara Ann Fowler) was born November 8, 1927, as the tenth of eleven children. The family lived in Claremore, Oklahoma, about thirty miles from Tulsa. Her father was a railroad worker who strummed guitar and sang, while her mother played organ in church. As a child she sang in a vocal trio with two of her sisters. Her big break came about by accident. Thinking she would become an artist, the summer after her freshman year in high school, she got a job making posters at radio station KTUL in Tulsa. As she recalled, "There wasn't much work for an artist in a radio station. So, I operated the telephone switchboard, did whatever typing there was and sometimes, whenever they needed a singer, I sang . . . I got five dollars for singing on the radio."

KTUL had a fifteen-minute program each weekday afternoon sponsored by the Page Milk Company. Clara Ann Fowler was dragged from posters and typing to act as a last-minute substitute on the show under the name Patti Page—obviously, a reflection of the sponsoring company. The gig worked out so well that the newly named Patti Page continued to sing at the station for the next three years, eventually picking up a second gig at a place called the Bengalair Supper Club. By this time, Page was a local celebrity in Tulsa.

In 1944, Jack Rael, who was the advance man for the Jimmy Joy Band, a swing troupe coming to Tulsa, took a room at the local Bliss Hotel. With nothing to do, Rael was lying on the bed listening to the radio when he heard the soothing voice of what sounded like a professional female singer. That was odd because he was in the business and thought he knew everyone on network radio. So, with nothing else to do, he telephoned KTUL and asked who was singing. When he was told it was a local gal, he insisted on talking with her. Rael explained to Page that he was passing through town for bandleader Jimmy Joy and when Page said she would be singing at Bengalair Club, he said would come see her. Afterward, Rael would bug Page to send him airchecks from her radio show. By December of that year, she flew to Chicago where she joined the Jimmy Joy Band. She was seventeen years old.

While in Chicago, agents began visiting her gigs wanting to talk, but Rael told Page that they should come talk to him instead because "I'm your manager." Page recalled: "That was news to me. We had never discussed such a thing. But as a single woman far from home, the idea of having a manager felt a bit comforting."[6]

Rael managed Page for almost fifty years. He asked, and was given 50 percent of what she earned, which seems exorbitant, but they had formed a production company of which each owned 50 percent. Song decisions were often left to be worked out between Rael and whoever the A&R guy was. Ditties were pitched directly to Page as well. She never was heard to say, "I hate that song and won't sing it." The end of the Rael relationship came with bitterness and it was left to the courts to unwind it all.

"Jack discovered her. They worked together for five decades, and when you end a relationship like that, there will always be controversy and hurt feelings," said Mike Glynn, who managed Page for seventeen years at the tail end of her career. "It had to go to court to be cleaned up. Rael worked his butt off to make her a star."[7]

Soon after joining the Jimmy Joy Band, Page received an entertainment business lesson about meeting your idols. The band was in Omaha, Nebraska, to back up a show by Connee Boswell, who was still on the road after the breakup of the Boswell Sisters in the late 1930s. Page had sung the opening number and gotten a warm response from the crowd. She was pleased with her performance until Jimmy Joy informed her she was to take the rest of the night off. Jimmy's excuse was that the set needed to be tightened when the reality was Connee Boswell didn't want Page singing on the same show—she felt threatened.

Rael didn't disappoint. In 1947, he severed her from the band and got her a contract with Mercury Records as a solo act. She was in the studio shortly thereafter. Her first singles (78 rpms) did not attract much attention. Then in 1948, she boasted two Top Twenty hits, "Confess" and "So in Love," and one more in 1949, "With My Eyes Wide Open, I'm Dreaming."

The last song was Page's first million-selling hit. "After this song every single she released would sell at least 300,000 copies, an unprecedented level at that time," wrote Skip Press. "It was not only the advancements in recording technology since 'Confess' that enabled the ambitious recording of a four-part harmony by one singer. It would never have been possible without Page's extraordinary vocal range, which spans bass, alto, soprano, tenor and low F."[8]

From "Eyes Wide Open," it was all uphill. Her first two #1 records "Tennessee Waltz" and "All My Love" arrived in 1950 and then came eight Top Twenty records in 1951. Corks popped for more #1 records: "I Went to Your Wedding" in 1952 and "How Much Is That Doggie in the Window" in 1953. Four more Top Ten records charted in 1954. Her first disappointing year came in 1955 with only two Top Twenty records, "Croce di Oro" and "Go On with the Wedding."

She was back again in 1956.

The prehistory of "Allegheny Moon" begins in the early 1940s, when Dick Manning (Samuel Medoff) and his band were regulars on a radio show called *Yiddish Melodies in Swing*. The vocalists on the show were Minnie and Clara Bagelman, who were originally known as the Bagelman Sisters, but for the show became the Barry Sisters. Arranging and writing women-voiced songs came easy, although the Barry Sisters, who continued into the 1940s and '50s, never made the big time.[9] Instead, Manning was the one who became successful, not as a bandleader but as a songwriter and composer, including numerous hits for women and crooners such as Teresa Brewer's "Jilted" (cowritten with Robert Colby).

It's unknown how Manning's cowritten song "Allegheny Moon" came to Page. Glynn said that during that time period Page and her manager Jack Rael kept an office in New York's Brill Building, which was where all the songwriters took offices as well. Songwriters would pitch songs on the run in the morning or during lunch hour. Every day another songwriter promoted another song. Glynn suspects that "Allegheny Moon" was pitched to Rael because it was known he had a lot of say about what songs Page would get to hear.[10]

If there was a peak year for Manning, it would have been 1956, when he was steadily working with another veteran songwriter Al Hoffman. Among their tunes that scored that year was "Mama, Teach Me to Dance," which would be a minor hit for Eydie Gormé.

The songwriting duo's biggest hit in 1956 came about by accident. Manning was riding home on the subway when he bumped into Mickey Glass, who managed Perry Como's music publishing company. After some initial chit-chat, Glass mentioned that Como was looking for a "happy novelty" song. Manning replied he and Al Hoffman just did a demo of one and no one had heard it yet. Glass followed up. The song was "Hot Diggity," which was the #16 best-seller in 1956, one behind Elvis Presley's "Love Me Tender" and eight ahead of another Manning/Hoffman song, "Allegheny Moon."

Looking past "Tennessee Waltz," some might say that, in the Patti Page canon, it would be hard to top "Allegheny Moon." But there is dedicated fondness for

Page's 1957 hit "Old Cape Cod," maybe because in certain sections of New England the song never goes out of style. It was one of Page's favorites, if not the favorite of all her songs. It's the same for Patti Page fans. Asked what the attraction is about the tune, Glynn said: "It's not offensive, not in your face, not complicated and not about relationship drama. 'Old Cape Cod' conjures up peacefulness and calmness regardless of where you grew up. Plus, in the early 1950s it was important to hear all the lyrics and Patti sings the tune crisply."

On the record, the songwriting credits for "Old Cape Cod" go to three people: Claire Rothrock, Milton Yakus, and Allan Jeffrey. The centrifugal force in all those names belongs to Yakus, although the original hard work of conceiving and lyric-writing goes to Rothrock, who scribbled the words as a kind of tone poem.[11]

Unlike the biblical Genesis stories, inception arrives in two competing tales. The first legend suggests Rothrock brought her poem to Milton Yakus, who with his brother founded Ace Recording Studios in Boston.[12] He wasn't just a technician, however. Yakus also dabbled in songwriting and had some success, having written "Go On with the Wedding" for none other than Patti Page. Yakus met with Rothrock, who thought her poem had potential, reworked the lyrics into song format, and called in his associate, Allan Jeffrey, to put it to music.[13]

Page has her own version of how the song came into being. On her eightieth birthday, she was interviewed by reporter Steve Desroches, who asked how she came to record the song. In her memory, Rothrock brought the song directly to her while she was playing at a Boston nightclub. At the time Page was looking for a B-side song to her for her next release, which was to be "Wondering."

"I just fell in love with it ['Old Cape Cod']," Page remembered—so much so that she took the train to New York to record the song and then rushed back in time for the evening performance in Boston.[14]

What happened to "Wondering"? We are still wondering. As for "Old Cape Cod," it zoomed to #3 on the pop chart. It would be her last Top Ten hit until 1964, when Page sang the theme song to the movie "Hush, Hush, Sweet Charlotte."

Page was never flashy, nor did she have that trick in her voice like Teresa Brewer, yet she remained the most reliable hit singer of the era. Writer Karen Schoemer encapsulated her appeal this way: "She [Page] was not an especially varied or inventive singer—she stuck to the melody line, hit her notes square on the head, held them with minimal vibrato, and rarely budged from the given tempo. Her tone was unwaveringly warm and tender. She sang like she cared, like she wanted to wipe your worries away. She mothered her listeners. She buffed the edges off emotions, kept them safe and unthreatening."[15]

Patti Page put the luster on the lusterless and transformed workaday crooning into something great, which was a tremendous accomplishment.

As good a year as it was for Teresa Brewer and Patti Page, the bigger story for female crooners was the success of singers who were primarily actresses in motion pictures and on television: Debbie Reynolds and Gale Storm, with "Tammy" and "Dark Moon," respectively.

Debbie Reynolds was not a frequent visitor to the record charts in the early 1950s, although she did boast a breakthrough song in 1951, "Aba Daba Honeymoon," from the movie *Two Weeks in Love,* a romantic comedy starring Jane Powell and Ricardo Montalban. "Aba Daba Honeymoon" was an old comic song from early in the twentieth century and revived for a musical interlude and quasi–dance number by the movie's teenagers, played by Debbie Reynolds and Carleton Carpenter. Released as a single, credited to the duo Reynolds and Carpenter, the song charted as #22 on the *Billboard*'s biggest-hits-of-the-year list. The duo's version of the classic sold over a million records. *Two Weeks in Love* was Reynolds second film. Soon to be in production was *Singin' in the Rain.*

The success of "Aba Dabba Honeymoon" was small potatoes compared to the song "Tammy," from the movie *Tammy and the Bachelor,* released in 1957.

Two years before, movie star Debbie Reynolds married the handsome pop-music idol Eddie Fisher, in one the most talked-about marriages of the 1950s. They had two children: Carrie (Princess Leia in *Star Wars*) arrived in 1956 and Todd in 1958. The year after the birth of Todd, the storybook marriage fell apart as Fisher admitted to having an affair with Elizabeth Taylor after the death of Taylor's husband Mike Todd. Just like the wedding, the divorce was a headline story that took years to fade away—if it ever did.

Here's a backstory worth considering. Eddie Fisher's career peaked around 1954 although he remained moderately successful for another year or two. By 1955, the music world was changing away from the post–big band crooners of the early 1950s. That year he aimed for the teenager crowd he was quickly outgrowing with a song called "Dungaree Doll." (Before blue jeans were blue jeans, they were dungarees.) The lyrics were all about the teen world: "I Want you to wear my orange sweater / the beat up sweater with the high school letter." The gamble worked and the not-quite-beat-driven tune shot to #7 on the *Billboard* chart.

By the next year, his career was definitely treading water. While he boasted two Top Twenty hits that year, these records were covers—and the original artists did better. So while Fisher rode "Cindy, Oh Cindy" to #10 on *Billboard,* the version by Vince Martin and the Tarriers, a folk group, went to #9. Fisher's cut of "On the Street Where You Live" dropped at #18, while Vic Damone's "Street" platter spun in at #4. For a competitive egoist like Fisher, the year didn't turn out great, except for the birth of Carrie.

Then 1957 rolls through with six new Eddie Fisher singles and no action whatsoever. To pour salt in his wounds, Coral Records releases "Tammy" by his wife and it shoots all the way to #1. Pop idol Eddie Fisher had to play second fiddle to Debbie Reynolds at his own game. It only got worse. In 1958, the music world hears barely a peep from Eddie Fisher while wife Debbie brags a Top Twenty hit with "A Very Special Love." The end of the marriage was written in the cold, wayward wind of the music business even before Fisher's hook-up with Elizabeth Taylor.

That's not even half the story of the "Tammy" record.

As noted, with the coming of rock 'n' roll, men rolled over the women singers to the extent that, of the fifty top songs of the year, only four were attributed to females. The market was so arid for women that, when "Tammy" hit #1, it was the only single by a lady to go to #1 between July 28, 1956, and December 1, 1958. Before "Tammy" arrived at the top of the charts, Elvis Presley's "Loving You" was #1 for seven weeks. "Tammy" came in first for two weeks to be overthrown for a week by Paul Anka's "Diana" and then "Tammy" was back for a week before being kicked out by "That'll Be the Day" by the Crickets. It would be more than two years before a woman singer would feel the glow of a #1 record again.

Debbie Reynolds (Mary Frances Reynolds) was born April 1, 1932, in El Paso, Texas. The family moved to California and at the age of sixteen she entered the Miss Burbank contest because she heard everyone who entered received a silk scarf, blouse, and free lunch. She won the contest and was quickly offered a screen test by Warner Brothers. She appeared in five movies before *Singin' in the Rain* made her a star. By the time she walked on the set of *Tammy and the Bachelor* she was already a veteran with seventeen movies under her belt. She was twenty-five years old but was short in height and looked younger than her years.[16]

The storyline for *Tammy* is pure hokum: young backwoods girl living with grandfather goes out to scavenge from a downed small plane and discovers the pilot is unconscious but alive. They nurse him to health and when he leaves he tells the grandfather if anything happens to him, Tammy could come to his house. Grandpa is arrested for making moonshine and Tammy goes off to find the pilot. She does and they eventually fall in love. Although it doesn't sound like much, the movie was very profitable and spawned three follow-ups. What worked is that it was a movie marketed to teen girls (Reynolds played a seventeen-year-old-girl) when the important teen movies of the early 1950s such as *The Wild One*, *Blackboard Jungle*, and *Rebel Without a Cause* were male-driven movies. The protagonist in *Tammy and the Bachelor* was the girl Tammy. No wider issues (teen rebellion, disaffection, delinquency, and the like) were at play here. It was a simple romance that worked because Debbie Reynolds was tremendously affecting.

The theme song was written by the veteran songwriting team of Jay Livingston and Ray Evans. They had first gotten together in 1945 and over time proved to be one of the most enduring and successful creators of songs in the second half of the twentieth century, writing such hallmarks as "Dear Heart," "Silver Bells," "Never Let Me Go," "Tammy," and their Oscar winners "Mona Lisa," "Buttons and Bows," and "Que Sera, Sera." Female singers performed wonders with his songs: Dinah Shore took "Buttons and Bows" to #1 in 1947, Doris Day rode "Que Sera, Sera" to #2 in 1956, and Debbie Reynolds scored a #1 with "Tammy" in 1957.

Oddly, the "Tammy" song that was sung over the main titles of *Tammy and the Bachelor* was not by Debbie Reynolds. Instead, the movie producers brought in the Ames Brothers, who did their usual resolute, manly take on what was a soft wisp of song. Their "Tammy" hit the market on the same day as the Debbie Reynolds version and they didn't do badly, riding the song all the way to #5 on the best-seller chart—although one wonders why. The Debbie Reynolds version clearly captures the yearning of a young woman on the cusp of first love. When Reynolds sang "Tammy," teen girls everywhere felt that ache of a love stranded by the unknown and unmet. The lyrics were clear: "Wish I knew if he knew, what I'm dreamin' of / Tammy, Tammy, Tammy's in love."

The Ames Brothers had been at Coral Records but had moved to RCA Victor by the time they recorded "Tammy." They were gone when wunderkind Bob Thiele arrived. Oddly, in his autobiography Thiele spends very little time discussing the great women singers he worked with during his tenure at the company. His longest comment on Debbie Reynolds was to note she had her only #1 record while at the company. His only remark about the song "Tammy" was that it was an "indestructible paean to pubescence."[17] Whew!

That phrase was written by an older Thiele, with Coral Records long in the rearview mirror. At the time of the "Tammy" record, when he was a young go-getter with fire in his belly, he absolutely knew what a hot record he had made with Reynolds and got Coral to push all the promotional buttons (not bows!) to get the song across to the public. Take this gossipy news clip from June 1957: "Bob Dupree, of FAB, reports his new juke box in front of the Joy Theater on Canal Street [New Orleans] is drawing plenty of attention from passersby. It is there to plug Debbie Reynolds' new picture *Tammy and the Bachelor* having its world premiere this week in New Orleans."[18] A month later, Coral took a whole page ad in *Billboard* to promote six singles it was pushing. The top song was "Tammy" by Debbie Reynolds, followed by another song that would be a huge hit, "I'm Gonna Sit Right Down and Write Myself a Letter" by Billy Williams. The next two promotions were weaker: "Teardrops in My Heart" by Teresa Brewer and "Around the World" by the McGuire Sisters. Then came the least fascinating cuts, songs by Don Cornell and Dick Jacobs. And to show where the market was going, even for Coral, at the bottom of the promotion, the label threw in, seemingly at the last minute, one more song from its Brunswick subsidiary: "That'll Be the Day" by the Crickets.[19]

Everything fell into place for "Tammy." Near the end of July, *Billboard* took notice of the "Tammy" record by Debbie Reynolds: "This is the strongest disk for the artist in some time. The Ames Brothers' platter was selected as a 'Best Buy' last week, and now this version has also built up considerable sales strength in all markets."[20]

On July 22, for the first time, the Reynolds record reached *Billboard* "The Nation's Top Tunes" chart, coming in at #13, behind "Old Cape Cod" at #5 and "Dark Moon" at #9. The other "Tammy" was nowhere in sight.[21] On November 11, *Billboard*'s "1957 Top Tunes" placed the combined versions of "Tammy" as the #1 song in the country.[22]

Thiele had a busy autumn. In New York, he presented a gold record to Billy Williams for "I'm Gonna Sit Right Down and Write Myself a Letter"; stopping in New Mexico, he gave a gold record to the Crickets for "That'll Be the Day"; and finally, on the West Coast he handed out gold records to Lawrence Welk for selling one million albums, and finally, to Debbie Reynolds for "Tammy."[23]

The year 1957 was a busy one for another actress, Gale Storm. In September of that year, the opening show for the second season of *The Gale Storm Show* featured Pat Boone. He was her teammate on Dot Records and a youthful, clean-cut lad, who was the pop charts' successful antidote to Elvis Presley, Little Richard, Chuck Berry, and the R&B side of rock 'n' roll. *The Gale Storm Show* was a comedy, not a variety show, where she played Susanna Pomeroy, a cruise director for a ship sailing around the world. This premier effort was scripted to showcase Storm's musical abilities and to promote her recording career. The plot involved Storm doing a duet with Boone plus various opportunities for each to sing a solo. As writer David Tucker observed, "the main plot, which largely took back seat to the music, concerned Susanna (Gale Storm's character) attempting to spotlight Boone in a musical show on board, threatened by his confinement to sick bay with a diagnosis of measles, Susanna is, of course, not so easily dissuaded, and fills in the for the downed singer."[24]

When "Tammy" first appeared on the *Billboard* chart of top songs in the country, actress Gale Storm's cut of "Dark Moon" had already been there for fourteen weeks and was still in the Top Ten.

Storm had a short and to some extent unlikely passage as a pop singer, since it all started so late in her career. Then again, even her years as a star had to wait for the advent of television.

Gale Storm (Josephine Owaissa Cottle) was born on April 5, 1922, in Bloomington, Texas. Her father died when she was an infant and eventually she, her mother, and four siblings moved to Houston. After excelling in drama club performances for her junior high and high schools, her teachers urged her to enter a radio contest called "Gateway to Hollywood," which she won. The prize was a one-year contract with a movie studio. She first appeared in film in 1940 and spent the rest of the decade as an actress in B-movies such as *Revenge of the Zombies*, *Freckles Comes Home*, and *Curtain Call at Cactus Creek*. As film historian Ephraim Katz summed up career: "Wholesome leading lady of minor Hollywood films of the 1940s."[25]

Television arrived in America at the end of the 1940s and in 1950, Storm made her television debut on a show called *Hollywood Premiere Theater*, an anthology series on ABC. Two years later, she was the star of *My Little Margie* and for the rest of the decade she was never away from the little screen. *My Little Margie* ran from 1952 to 1955. She served as hostess on the *NBC Comedy Hour* in the winter of 1956 before starring in *The Gale Storm Show*, which ran from 1956 to 1960. She continued to appear on a variety of television shows in the 1960s.

One fan of Gale Storm was Randy Wood, who was the president of Dot Records. After his daughter asked about Storm while watching her on television, Wood decided he was going to call her directly with the intent on signing her to a contract. The year was 1955.[26]

Dot Records was based in Gallatin, Tennessee, at the time and Wood was familiar with the singers and songwriters in the South, including New Orleans. The best singer/songwriter and arranger (and talent scout for Imperial Records) in the Big Easy was Dave Bartholomew. He penned a song called "I Hear You Knockin'" for Fats Domino, but instead gave it to an old neighborhood friend, Smiley Lewis, who took the song all the way to #2 on the R&B charts early in 1955. After signing Gale Storm, Wood brought her into the studio to record Bartholomew's tune and a number of other covers: Dean Martin's "Memories Are Made of This" and Gloria Mann's "Teen Age Prayer."

All were successful for Storm, but the one that hurt the original most was "I Hear You Knockin'" because of the discrepancies of opportunity and compensation available to Black singers at the time—but also because Storm's recording wasn't as good a record. Sounding like a country & western lounge singer, Storm almost turned the song into a novelty tune. It was nothing like the bluesy rendition by Smiley Lewis.

As music writer Jeff Hannusch scribbled: "[Lewis's song] Kicked off with Huey (Piano) Smith's characteristic piano intro. Smiley tells his woman in no uncertain terms '. . .you can't come in.'[27] But, once again, some of Smiley's thunder was stolen when Gale Storm's insipid cover version rose to #2 on *Billboard*'s Hot 100." Fats Domino biographer Rick Coleman added his own tart wording about Gale Storm and her cover: "Segregation was still the rule in pop music. Reflecting the song's lyric, black artists were knocking, but, for the most part, they couldn't come in."[28]

For white teenagers who had not yet completely bought into rock 'n' roll or rhythm and blues, Gale Storm was the 'tweener tonic. Her first five records, including "Why Do Fools Fall in Love" and "Ivory Tower" in 1956, were all covers. Then Storm lost her mojo. Her next five recordings didn't do much, not even making the Top Fifty. In 1957, Storm covered not an R&B tune, but the country & western song "Dark Moon."

When Fabor Robison at Dot Records picked up Ned Miller's tune "Dark Moon," he knew there was a hit record in there and he had already determined which of his recording artists he wanted to record it. When Bonne Guitar (Bonnie Buckingham) heard the song, she wanted it. Bonnie Guitar wasn't Robison's first choice of Dot artists, so they dickered. The resulting outcome was that Bonnie Guitar agreed to waive her royalty rights so that she would be allowed to record the tune, which was just another coercive, if not exploitative, move by record company management to cheat artists out of whatever income was due them.

As Bonnie Guitar told an interviewer later in life, "He [Robison] played 'Dark Moon' on the phone and I started to shake. My body just physically shook when I heard that song. I just knew that song was something that I wanted to do."[29]

The country song crossed over from country to the pop charts, rising as high as #6 on *Billboard*'s Hot 100. It was Bonnie Guitar's signature moment as a singer and it could have been even better except sleazy ol' Dot Records also gave the song to another of its recording artists, Gale Storm, who took the song to #4 on the Hot 100. Once again, it's hard to find congruity between the two songs, with Storm's version so much more pallid than the other.

As befitting someone who renamed herself Bonnie Guitar, her version begins with the soft plucking of the guitar strings, whereas Gale Storm gets a full male chorus introduction. Storm's version was featured on her popular television show. In one episode, when her character is alone with a date, she slips the record on a phonograph. The song begins and she asks the man, "Mind if I join the quartet?" and they dance while she lip-syncs "Dark Moon." The TV preview certainly helped her sales.

Although Storm remained a television star for the remainder of the decade, in the music world rock 'n' roll was wiping out the last vestiges of white female crooners, and in the end that included Storm. She never again charted another record. She recorded a couple of songs in 1958, nothing in 1959, and a couple more in 1960. By then that part of her storied career was over.

The real giant of motion-picture-to-pop-singer crossover was Doris Day, whose career arc was more like pop singer to motion picture star to pop singer.

She was so long in the public eye as a movie marquee name—for seven years the top female box office star in the United States and one Oscar nomination—the fact that she was an immensely successful singer gets washed over. Yet she began her career behind the microphone singing with big bands. As a lead vocalist for a big band and then as a solo artist, she recorded more than 650 individual songs on the Columbia label, and that included over seventy-five charted records and five #1 hits. To quote online researchers, "She was one of the most popular and acclaimed singers of the twentieth century."[30]

Doris Day (Doris Mary Anne Kappelhoff) was born April 3, 1922, in Cincinnati, Ohio, the youngest of three siblings. As a young girl Day took dance lessons, and after winning a dance contest where the first prize was lessons from a Hollywood choreographer in California, it looked like the world was going to get a new hoofer. That all ended with a violent accident, when a train hit a car in which she was a passenger. Day was diagnosed with a double compound fracture of her right leg and spent fourteen months in the hospital. With time on her hands she listened to the radio, sometimes singing aloud with Ella Fitzgerald on the air. A friend, overhearing the impromptu duets, suggested she take singing lessons, which she did. Her voice teacher recognized Day's talent and got her (at sixteen years old) a spot on a local radio station. The voice teacher's husband recommended her to sing at a local Chinese restaurant on Saturday evenings. The gig paid $5 a night, money that came in handy during the Depression. By the time she was eighteen years old, Day had joined Les Brown's band as a vocalist.[31]

In 1945, while still with the Les Brown, she recorded one of the best of the late–big band tunes, "Sentimental Journey." The languid musical joyride traversed a long instrumental introduction before Day eases in with the delightful lyrics: "Gonna take a sentimental journey, gonna set my heart at ease / gonna make a sentimental journey, to renew old memories." With World War II winding down and GIs coming home, the song captured the mood of the country. Day's first effort as a recorded vocalist shot to the top, becoming the #1 song in the country. The same thing happened with her second effort, "My Dreams Are Getting Better All the Time."

Amazingly, Day's first twelve recordings, all with Les Brown, were Top Twenty hits. In 1948, after leaving Les Brown, she recorded her third #1 record, "Love Somebody," as a duet with Buddy Clark.

With the new decade of the 1950s, Day barely slowed down, releasing four to eight new songs a year through 1953 with almost everything charting, often as a Top Twenty song. That would include her fourth #1 in 1952, "A Guy Is a Guy." In 1954, Columbia went all out on Doris Day, introducing nine new records, but the results were the most erratic of her career to that point. While some of the songs didn't chart, "If I Give My Heart to You" went to #3 on the chart and

"Secret Love" was her fifth and last #1 record. The song from the movie *Calamity Jane* won the Academy Award for film year 1953—not bad for a tune that was recorded in just one take. Ray Heindorf, who headed the music department at Warner Brothers, had worked with Day on many of her prior movies and knew well her recording habits. Day explained the one-take phenomenon this way: "He [Ray] just knew when I wanted to breathe, when I wanted to stop, when I wanted to slow down and when I wanted to pick up."

Over the next two years, with the coming of rock 'n' roll, Day's releases slowed and success was still erratic, although she just missed getting her sixth #1 when "Que Sera, Sera" ended its rapid climb up the chart at #2.

After that, Doris Day's days as a pop singer wound down fairly quickly, with just one or two new songs through the early 1960s. Not that it made much difference, at least at the start of the sixties when she was still the ruling queen of Hollywood box office. By the middle of that decade, the rebellious sixties would catch up to Day as with other older motion picture stars and a new order of young actors and actresses—Jack Nicholson, Dustin Hoffman, Faye Dunaway—would take over.

As far as the husband/manager paradox is concerned, Martin Melcher is still regarded as the nadir. After he died in 1968, Day discovered he had squandered all of her vast earnings and left her in debt. Getting back to work, she starred in *The Doris Day Show* which ran for five years.[32]

Columbia Records' Mitch Miller, who knew Melcher well, once said, "It was not hard to dislike Marty Melcher. I never had any respect for him."[33]

CHAPTER NINE

SUGARTIME (1958)

THE SHIRELLES—THE CHANTELS—THE PONI-TAILS— THE TEDDY BEARS—THE McGUIRE SISTERS—CONNIE FRANCIS— JAYE P. MORGAN—JANE MORGAN—DORIS DAY—PEGGY LEE— CHARLIE GRAEN—BETTY JOHNSON—GEORGIA GIBBS

Ninth grade in Passaic, New Jersey, wasn't very exciting for a few students like Shirley Owens, so she took her pen and began jabbing the girl sitting in front of her, whose name was Beverly Lee. The end result was a heated, whispery discussion between two girls who knew each other from a distance. Shirley lived next door to Beverly's aunt, and when Beverly visited her relations she would see Shirley. The jab was a crude way to start a friendship, but that's what happened. Soon the two girls would get together to sing along with the songs they heard on the radio. One fine day, Beverly's friend Addie "Micki" Harris came by and joined them. The girls thought they sounded pretty good, but to sing doo-wop they felt they needed one more person, so they invited Doris Cooley to join them. As Beverly recalled, "we were all about the same age, literally. Doris and I were born in August 1941 and Shirley in June 1941. Micki was slightly older, born in January 1940."

By their sophomore year they became the Pequellos and started getting more serious about the music, constantly practicing and even getting some gigs at local functions around Passaic; mostly they performed for free, although sometimes they were slipped a few dollars for their efforts. One day in high school gym class, the girls were singing, just fooling around, when their teacher caught them not exercising like everyone else. Their penalty for misbehaving was one of two options: they could fail P.E. or do a show for the school in the gym. "It was obvious the teacher wasn't trying to punish us," Lee said. "She knew we were a singing group and was doing us a kindness. Maybe she saw potential."

The trouble was, the Pequellos didn't have a big repertoire of songs. In the auditorium that day they sang "Walking Along" (by the Solitaires), "Little Darlin'" (by the Gladiolas), "A Sunday Kind of Love" (by the Harp-Tones), and a song called "I Met Him on a Sunday," which was written by all the girls while practicing in Beverly's apartment.

The next day, an older student, Mary Jane Greenberg, came to them and said, "my mother owns a record company. Let her hear that song." The girls were confused at first and said no, but Greenberg was relentless and eventually they came around.

"We were invited to Florence Greenberg's home and a few days later we went by there," Beverly remembered. "Passaic isn't that big, but she wasn't in our neighborhood, she lived in Saint Park, whereas we lived downtown. We walked to Passaic High School and we walked to her home. It was a lovely house on Minnow Springs Avenue. Florence had a piano. Her son, Stanley, was there. He played the piano and when we sang 'I Met Him on a Sunday' Stanley accompanied us by feeling his way along with what we were doing."

The song sold itself. It told a story. It was catchy enough that Florence Greenberg liked the song and wanted to record it. The girls were offered a contract with Florence's nascent effort, Tiara Records, which had to be signed by parents because the girls were underage. However, the first thing that had to be addressed was the name of the group. Florence didn't like the name Pequellos. She wanted the group to be called the Honeytones, but they didn't like that name. Instead, the girls made up a list of potential names for a singing group. At the time a lot of groups had the letter L sound somewhere in the name, such as the Orioles, Dells, Spaniels, Shells, Edsels, and Channels, so they made up names that had that final sound. Eventually, they came around to the name Shirelles.

In 1958, "I Met Him on a Sunday" was first introduced to the record-buying public on Florence's fledgling label Tiara and she ardently hustled it to disc jockeys in the New York area. It began to get airplay and local demand increased. The song was the first record Florence ever produced and suddenly when record stores wanted it Tiara wasn't big enough to handle the demand. Decca Records picked up on the buzz and approached Florence about a licensing deal and eventually it secured the master for national release.[1]

"I Met Him on a Sunday" was not a major national hit. It was very popular in New York and other big city markets. The highest it reached on *Billboard*'s Hot 100 was only #49. Its importance, however, was considerable: the song was an early manifestation of the girl group sound that would become popular by the start of the next decade. Two years later, in 1960, the Shirelles would boast their first #1 record, "Will You Love Me Tomorrow" and go on to become the quintessential girl group until the rise of the Supremes in the mid-1960s.

"I Met Him on a Sunday" was not the first proto–girl group song released in 1958, nor was it the most successful. Just a few months before the Shirelles walked into a recording studio, another group of African American teenagers got an opportunity to cut a record and they, too, made the most of it. Like the Shirelles, the quintet known as the Chantels were from the New York metro area; they lived in the borough of the Bronx. The girls met in the junior choir of Anthony of Padua, but took their name from a rival school, St. Francis de Chantal. The young ladies, who were born in the years 1940 to 1943, included lead singer Arlene Smith plus Sonia Goring, Renee Minus, Jackie Landry, and Lois Harris.

According to Jackie Landry, the girls were discovered by accident in 1957. They were coming back from seeing a concert. They were all dressed the same, and when they walked past a recording studio someone asked if they were singers. They said yes and the man who asked the question brought them into the studio to prove it. Who should come by but some members of the doo-wop group the Valentines, including songwriter Richard Barrett, who would later become their manager. The girls looked so young Barrett wasn't sure they were singers, but as Landry told writer John Clemente, "they broke into a street version of a song that would become 'The Plea.'" Barrett was so impressed that he recommended the girls to George Goldner, who recorded them on his new label, End Records. One of the songs from the Chantels' first recording session charted, at #71. That was good enough for Goldner to bring them back for another try in 1958. For that session, the girls recorded their signature song, "Maybe," which was the first successful song of what would become the girl group sound.

As Clemente wrote, "'Maybe' is one of those songs that was a trend-setting first. No other record sounded like this before. From its thunderous piano intro, through Arlene's emphatic lead, to its call and response ending, the performance is truly captivating."[2]

"Maybe" did much better than "I Met Him on a Sunday" climbing all the way to #15 on the pop chart and #2 on the R&B chart. Neither of those two proto–girl group songs were yet audience-accepted enough to dent Billboard's Top Ten.

But, one girl group did.

Like the teenagers who formed the Shirelles and Chantels, three girls—Toni Clistone, Karen Topinka, and Patti McCabe—met while attending high school (Brush HS in Cleveland) and decided to form a group. They were white girls and their group name, The Poni-Tails, reflected their ethnicity. The Poni-Tails' singular major hit "Born Too Late" outperformed both "I Met Him on a Sunday" and "Maybe," going all the way to #7 on the Billboard Hot 100 and remaining on the chart for twelve weeks. The strength of the song, besides the three-part harmony, was that it was unabashedly a girl's tune. Thematically, the song was about a teenage girl's lament that the boy she's crushing on is years older and doesn't even know who she is. The sadness is obvious in the lyrics: "Born . . . too late, for you to notice, me / to you, I'm just a kid, that you won't date / Why was I born too late?"

Asked why "Born Too Late" resonated with record buyers, Poni-Tails' Patti McCabe told *Billboard*, "It's a message song. Lots of girls fall in love with an older guy. It's like the junior high school girl who secretly loves the senior who's the football captain. Or the high school girl whose boy is away in college. 'Born Too Late' gets very close to home with a lot of girls for that reason and for that reason we think the girls bought our record."[3]

The Poni-Tails got their start by signing with a local record company, which released one single with a song the girls wrote, "Que La Bozena," as the B-side. "Your Wild Heart" was the A-side. Not much happened. Karen Topinka dropped out and LaVerne Novack joined to complete the trio. They were signed to a bigger label, ABC-Paramount, where they recorded a song called "Just My Luck to be Fifteen," which ended up as downtrodden as the song title. The message—teenage girl angst— was there; it just needed to be massaged better. And it was, in the next recording, "Born Too Late."

The Poni-Tails' career was brief, yet they were around just long enough to get thumped about in the usual 1950s mess involving songs with potential. The Poni-Tails' first song "Your Wild Heart" was covered by another teenager singer, Joy Layne, who recorded for a much bigger company, Mercury Records. Yes, bigger is sometimes better, especially when it comes to promotion and investment. Layne, whose singing style obviously aped Teresa Brewer, with Mercury backing her, turned "Your Wild Heart" into a Top Twenty hit in 1957. Then Layne got her own comeuppance. In her session for "Your Wild Heart," Mercury had her record a couple of other singles, including one called "After School." None of these charted. One of the reasons for the lack of follow-up was that Coral Records called Teresa Brewer into the studio to take a shot at "After School," which was part of larger strategy to have her go after the teenage market. The opening lyrics were the abyss: "Yesterday, I waited for you at the corner candy store, the way I always do [chorus: after school] / The hours passed, the gang went home and I was left there all alone." Brewer valiantly tried to take the song to a higher place; she couldn't because the arrangement was so insipid it bordered on novelty. The song was never released as a single, but was included on her 1957 album *For Teenagers in Love*. The target audience was obvious, especially with the cover photo of teenagers gathered round a cute Teresa busting out of a white tank top. The album included some of Brewer's hits like "Empty Arms," covers such as "Dark Moon," and throwaways "After School" and "Lula Rock A Hula."

One song with a strong girl group sound did make the Top Fifty in 1958, except the group that made the song didn't consist of just young ladies, it was actually one girl supported by two boys. Coming in at #44 for the top songs of 1958 was "To Know Him Is to Love Him" by a group called the Teddy Bears.

Once again, three classmates, this time from Fairfax High School in Los Angeles, got together to sing. The driver of the group was Phil Spector, who promised schoolmate Annette Kleinbard he would write a tune for her to sing. He recruited friend Marshall Leib to complete the trio. They recorded the song, "To Know Him Is to Love Him," at Gold Star Studio in Los Angeles and it was released on the Doré label. The song is all about the female voice, with Kleinbard in the lead and backup support by Spector and Leib. The lead singer fronting backup singers structure, borrowed from doo-wop, would become popular with most girl groups in the early 1960s. "To Know Him Is to Love Him" shot to #1 on the pop chart for three weeks and remained on the chart for twenty-three weeks. Marshall Leib would disappear from music history. Annette Kleinbard would change her name to Carol Connors in homage to her favorite girl group singers Patti Page and Doris Day with alliterative first and last names, and become a successful songwriter, including two Oscar nominations.[4] Phil Spector would become one of the most successful record producers and songwriters, especially known for his "wall-of-sound" recordings such as "Be My Baby" (Ronettes), "He's a Rebel" (Crystals), and "You've Lost that Lovin' Feelin'" (Righteous Brothers).

Except for "To Know Him Is to Love Him," all these proto-girl group songs were substantial hits but without enough airplay or sales to make it to *Billboard*'s Top Fifty songs of the year. Indeed, with the coming of rock 'n' roll, the record market had turned arid for women artists in general. The New York station that had become the beacon for rock 'n' roll in the 1950s and '60s, published its Top Forty songs. Not one was by a woman.

From 1950 through 1956, there was never a year without a song by a female soloist in the *Billboard* Top Ten tunes of the year. Then, in 1957, the ladies were exorcised. Only "Tammy" by Debbie Reynolds statistically saved the year for women coming in at #12, the only song by a female in the Top Twenty tunes of the year. Then 1958 rolled through and all the honeysuckled air had been sucked out of the radio stations—not one song by a woman in the Top Twenty, the first time that had happened in the whole decade. In 1957 only four songs by women made the Top Fifty chart. The same draught persisted through 1958; only four songs by the female voices made the list—and that includes the gender-mixed group the Teddy Bears, which had a female lead. That song came in at #44. To be fair, "To Know Him Is to Love Him" would have appeared higher on the list, but the song peaked in December so sales and airplay were split over 1958 and 1959.

Otherwise, the McGuire Sisters' "Sugartime" took the highest position for ladies, coming in at #27. This was followed by the Chordettes' "Lollipop" at #37 and finally by newcomer Connie Francis with "Who's Sorry Now" at #39.

Francis is the lone woman soloist on the list. What makes her appearance unique is that she is not a female crooner; Connie Francis is the first female soloist of the rock 'n' roll generation to make the list. Her version of "Who's Sorry Now" rose as high as #4 on *Billboard*'s Hot 100 and was #1 on the UK Singles Chart.

Connie Francis (Concetta Rosa Maria Franconero) was born December 12, 1937, in Newark, New Jersey. As a child she sang and played the accordion, gradually moving up to assorted television shows that featured kids including the *Paul Whiteman Show* in Philadelphia when she was eleven. From there it was on to *Arthur Godfrey's Talent Scouts*, where she was one of four juveniles to appear on Godfrey's Christmastime special. When he couldn't wrap his tongue around Franconero, he called her Connie Francis instead. He also told her to lose the accordion. He wasn't the only one to give her that recommendation. In 1951, her father drove Connie into Manhattan to try out for a show called *Startime Kids*. For her audition she sang Kay Starr's "Bonaparte's Retreat" while playing the accordion. After the song, producer George Sheck said, "Connie, now put the accordion down and let's hear you sing a number."

Francis appeared on the *Startime Kids* show for four years. When she turned fourteen, she was hired to make demonstration records (demos) for music publishers. It was her first experience in a recording studio.

"Sometimes the publisher would have a particular singer in mind for a certain song," Francis recalled. "At a demo session a publisher would say to me: 'Connie, try to give us a little more of that great Patti Page sound, will you?' Another day, he'd want me to sound like Teresa Brewer, another day like Joni James, or Kay Starr, or Jo Stafford, or Kitty Kallen, or Rosemary Clooney. . . . I began to sound like every female singer in the world."

In 1955, Francis was signed by MGM Records. She recorded eight singles without success and was on the verge of having her contract canceled when she walked into what appeared to be her final recording session. On her father's insistence, she recorded an updated version of the 1923 song "Who's Sorry Now" just before session hours concluded. The song debuted on *Dick Clark's American Bandstand* and by mid-year had sold over a million copies. Her career was launched.[5]

The problem for the Poni-Tails, who looked like they were destined for stardom, was that they didn't want to be rock 'n' rollers, they wanted to be the McGuire Sisters. "Born Too Late" resonated, said the Poni-Tails' McCabe, "Not because it's rock 'n' roll, because we don't sing rock 'n' roll." The Poni-Tails thought the McGuire Sisters were "the end," the ultimate compliment in the 1950s.[6]

There was nothing wrong with trying to emulate the very successful McGuire Sisters and disparaging rock 'n' roll except that the latter was the future and the McGuire sisters were the last successful advocates of a particular sisterly, close harmony sound that began in the 1930s with the Boswell Sisters. Not that others didn't keep trying. In 1957, when such female singers as country's Patsy Cline with "Walkin' After Midnight," pop music's Joy Layne with "Your Wild Heart," and rhythm & blues' Ruth Brown with "Lucky Lips" were quickly rising up the respective charts, Billboard's spotlight on up-and-coming talent included the Jaye Sisters. The magazine's reviewer wrote: "From the Midwest comes a trio of nineteen-year-olds who, like the McGuire Sisters, got a big original boost via the Godfrey Talent Scouts. The trio could follow the McGuires right up the ladder with their strong delivery, vocal charm and smart arrangements."[7] It didn't happen.

It's tempting to call the McGuire Sisters the last of the great sister acts, after the Boswells and the Andrews Sisters, but the ladies have as many detractors as fans. Their importance was that they were able to bridge the space between traditional pop and rock 'n' roll when there was so much new going on in the world of music. In turbulent times, they boasted a stable, steady career with occasional flashes of brilliance, such as 1958's "Sugartime."

The McGuire Sisters, Christine, Dorothy (Dottie), and Phyllis, were born in Middletown, Ohio, in the years 1926 to 1931. Their father worked at Armco Steel and their mother was a minister of Miamisburg First Church of God. Around 1935, mother-minister had her daughters singing in the choir. Phyllis, the youngest, was only four years old. Jim Stewart, a friend of the McGuire Sisters, grew up in Ohio and remembers his mother saying she attended country churches in the 1940s with mom leading the congregation and the three teenage girls singing hymns.[8] "They had a very religious upbringing," comments David Williamson, Dorothy's son.[9]

Middletown is near Dayton, and the McGuire Sisters, who sang at all sorts of religious functions including revivals, became well-known locally and began to pick up gigs outside of the church. As expected, conflict occurred between parents and teenage children, who were very obedient but very much wanted to sing pop music. In the end, the parents relented, clearing the way for the girls' first big gig at the Hotel Van Cleve in the big city of Dayton. They also sang on a local radio show.

With wider aspirations, the girls traveled to New York. Breaking into the Big Apple music scene was a struggle until they got a job on the daytime Kate Smith show. Then Ted Collins, a friend of Kate Smith, put them in touch with the Godfrey show for an audition. Oddly, the format for the talent competition on the Godfrey show was to have a personal representative introduce the contestants. The girls chose their manager from the Hotel Van Cleve. The girls won their competition, which meant they appeared every day for a week on the Godfrey show. He liked them so much he hired them as regulars in 1952.[10]

The McGuire Sisters' first recording was with a local Ohio label called Kentucky Records. It was a ten-inch, shellac single: "I Just Went Along for the Ride"/"Don't Fall in Love with Me." As Phyllis told Stewart, "it was recorded in some guy's garage in Miamisburg. No one else was there, just this one person and us." Stewart said they also sang "Frosty the Snowman" for an Arthur Godfrey album that was recorded by Columbia Records. This must have been in 1952, because Stewart added, "they shouldn't have sung for Godfrey because they already had signed a contract with Coral. The sisters claimed they didn't know that when they signed the contract they couldn't record for other people."[11]

Bob Thiele joined Decca Records as head of the Coral subsidiary in 1952, the same year that the McGuire Sisters signed with the label. According to Phyllis McGuire, she and her sisters met singer and record producer Gordon Jenkins ("Goodnight, Irene" in 1950) in New York and he took them to meet Bob Thiele at Coral Records.[12] Thiele didn't take credit for signing the girls, but he did claim "his association with them produced over 30 hits."[13] At first, he left the McGuire Sisters to others and as Stewart said, "the initial recordings were lame." The girls recorded four singles in 1953 and all were shelved. The next year looked like it was going to be another fallow time in the studio and then came a minor hit, "Pine Tree, Pine Over Me," which the McGuire Sisters sang with Johnny Desmond and Eileen Barton. The dam finally broke and Coral Records flooded the 1954 market with seven releases, four of which were Top Thirty hits and two, "Muskrat Ramble" and "Goodnight, Sweetheart, Goodnight," that were Top Ten records. The latter song, a reworking of the R&B hit by Jesse Belvin (also by the Spaniels, who recorded the song as "Goodnite, Sweetheart, Goodnite"), went to #7 on the pop chart. It was David Williamson's favorite song by the McGuire Sisters, because his mother Dorothy used to sing him to sleep with the tune when he was a young lad.

"Bob Thiele brought more a feel for R&B and rock 'n' roll to the McGuire Sisters' recordings," said Stewart.[14] "'Goodnight, Sweetheart, Goodnight' was a big R&B song and Bob Thiele loved R&B and jazz. He knew what crossover songs fit with his white artists." "Muskrat Ramble" was first recorded by Louis Armstrong in the 1920s. Phil Harris took a shot at the song in 1950. It came to the McGuire Sisters via Murray Kane, who managed the girls and once did arranging for the Andrews Sisters. Said Stewart, "Around the later 1980s, I went to see the McGuire Sisters at the Rainbow and Stars room in New York. Phyllis left a note with the maitre d' that she had fixed me up with someone for the night. I ended up sitting with Maxene Andrews of the Andrews Sisters."

For the McGuire Sisters, 1955 was the year that was . . . take your choice of adjectives . . . amazing, extraordinary, unbelievable. Coral released fifteen

McGuire songs (including two B-side cuts that became hits) into the market. Six charted, including the Top Ten song "He" and the song that made the group famous forever, "Sincerely," a cover of the Moonglows' #1 R&B hit.

"Sincerely" was the kind of huge experience a performer (or group) could live on forever. Coral was not ready for that. In 1956, it introduced eight more McGuire Sisters singles into the market and every one charted, although there was nothing even close to a "Sincerely" in the lot. The best performer was "Picnic," which rose as high as #13 of *Billboard's* Hot 100.

The girls' trend line was suddenly headed in the wrong direction. Coral tried to maintain the pace, dropping nine more McGuire Sisters songs into the market in 1957; nothing worked. It was as if the McGuire Sisters, two years after "Sincerely," were forgotten in the swirl of rock 'n' roll. Then when all looked lost, at the end of 1957, Coral released a little song called "Sugartime"—by singer Charlie Phillips.

"Sugartime" was first given to the Coral newcomer Phillips, a country-pop singer the label had under contract. In mid-November, the *Cash Box* featured the new release under its "Country Reviews." The reviewer liked the song immensely, writing: "Coral introduces newcomer Charlie Phillips on a tremendous debut pairing that has the necessary ingredients to carry the artist into the 'magic circle' of hits pop and country-wise. And one listen to either end of the platter should readily convince everyone that the artist has what it takes in the talent department. Top end, 'Sugartime' is a contagious, romantic rocker that he belts out in sparkling style."[15]

Coral was famous for undercutting its own performers by having multiple versions of a song recorded by different personnel it had under contract. As it turned out, there was a method to its madness. On rare occasions the Coral A&R department did end up looking like geniuses. Certainly it did with "Sugartime," which had also been given to the McGuire Sisters, who made the song slightly less country and more pop.

When *Cash Box* got hold of the McGuire Sisters version of the song, it was if the reviewer had never heard of Charlie Phillips and discovered gold in a played-out stream. The ecstatic review of the new "Sugartime" read like this: "The McGuire Sisters delve into the country music catalog and come up with a choice gem that should earn a heap of loot in the coming weeks. It's far and away the most inviting side the gals have offered in months and it should be tremendous hit. Titled 'Sugartime,' the tune is a cornball footstomping novelty with a contagious melody chanted with some wonderful harmony by the McGuires and a chorus. Great overall sound deejays will go for in a big way."[16]

Two weeks later, Coral realized it had a hot hand and posted a two-thirds-of-a-page promotion in the trade magazines with an eye-catching cartoon that featured the climax of a horse race. Mimicking the words to the song, the ad read: "Sugar in the morning, sugar in the evening, sugar at the finish line, disk jockies are on a winner, when they ride, 'Sugartime.'" If, perchance, the readership didn't get the joke, at the bottom of the promotion was a picture of a tout whispering "It's even money that 'Sugartime' by the McGuire Sisters will be #1 in a few weeks . . ."[17]

That was a good bet. "Sugartime" became the McGuire Sisters second and last #1 song. In February 1958, the song sat in the top spot, pushing out "At the Hop" by Danny and the Juniors.[18]

Outside of "Sugartime," 1958 was otherwise a fallow year for the McGuire Sisters." It was getting close to the end of the big ride for the girls.

Other old-school singers would peak in 1958 as well, some of whom would brag busier years than the McGuire Sisters; for a couple of ladies, two of the best-ever tunes by female crooners would happen that year—very late in their careers.

During the era of the female crooner, two singers named Morgan were active and although their performance names were similar, Jaye P. Morgan and Jane Morgan, the two ladies weren't related and their careers arced in vastly different ways. The year 1958 remained as dissimilar as their recording careers had been over the first half of the decade.

The more well-known of the two, due to her lengthy career on television, was Jaye P. Morgan (Mary Margaret Morgan). She was born in Mancos, Colorado, on December 3, 1931, and by the age of three was recruited into the family vaudeville act, the Morgan Family, composed of father, five brothers, and one sister. At the age of four, the family migrated to Los Angeles, where opportunities were greater, including regular appearances at the Million Dollar Theater. When the father died in 1945, the troupe broke up.

By the following year, when Jaye P. Morgan was just fifteen, the talented young lady landed a regular gig singing with western swing artist Hank Penny and his group. At the start of the new decade, she joined bandleader Frank DeVol as the lead female vocalist. She recorded a handful of songs with DeVol on the small Derby label, two of which charted on *Billboard*, "Just a Gigolo" at #22 in 1953 and "Life Is Just a Bowl of Cherries" #26 a year later.

Two things happened to Jaye P. Morgan in 1954, which considerably amped her career. She landed on *Stop the Music*, one of television's hit parade shows, and signed to a much bigger label, RCA Victor. By the end of year, she would have the biggest hit of her career, "That's All I Want from You," which climbed to #3 on the pop chart. With that kind of success, in 1955 RCA Victor went all in on Jaye P. Morgan, releasing thirteen new singles, six of which were Top Twenty songs.[19]

In the rock 'n' roll year of 1956, the label tried to keep the Jaye P. Morgan momentum alive, but nothing really worked. The seven cuts by her all died in the lower rungs of the pop charts. Things would only get worse; only three songs released in 1957, with no success. In 1958, RCA Victor kept up the slower pace of introducing new Jaye P. Morgan songs; three new releases and once again nothing happened.[20]

In the United States, Jane Morgan's recording career was not as rewarding as it was for Jaye P. Morgan, but in 1958 she did better.

Born in Newton, Massachusetts, on May 3, 1924, Jane Morgan (Florence Catherine Currier) was seven years older than Jaye P. However, life started similarly in that Jane Morgan's family also moved when she was young, not to Los Angeles but to Florida. Instead of working the family's vaudeville act, Jane Morgan began taking piano and vocal lessons at about the age of five. After graduating high school, Jane Morgan was accepted into New York's Juilliard School of Music as she intended to sing opera. However, to make ends meet, she sang popular songs at whatever type of gig she could get, from private parties on up to nightclubs and restaurants. Eventually she was hired at the Roseland Ballroom, where band leader Art Mooney found her. He liked her sound and presence, hired her, and changed her name to Jane Morgan. In 1948, she was hired to perform in France, where she became a star. She stayed in Europe for four years and her first recordings from the mid-1940s into the 1950s were done in London.[21]

Her career as a chanteuse moved back and forth across the Atlantic, until 1954, when David Kapp, after working at Decca and RCA Victor, decided to start his own label, Kapp Records. Two of her early signees were pianist Roger Williams and Jane Morgan.

Kapp Records began recording Jane Morgan in '54 and kept at it through 1955 to no effect. Jane Morgan was a very classy singer and over thirty years old, but Kapp was so desperate to get a hit record by her that, in 1956, he had her sing a paean to teenagerhood, "Let's Go Steady," a real mismatch of a singer's strengths with musical ineptitude. Finally, near the end of 1956, Jane Morgan teamed up with Roger Williams for "Two Different Worlds," which was her first record to chart. This was a tune that played to the strengths of both performers with a lengthy piano introduction before Jane Morgan's fine interpretation of a lush romantic ballad. The song was a mid-tier hit that was kind of an old-school, counter-programming coup against all that was going on musically in 1956.[22]

Then in 1957, came Jane Morgan's biggest hit in the United States, "Fascination," her only Top Ten record. Again a lengthy instrumental lead before the vocals of Jane Morgan, who enters with her voice in a lower register cooing, "It was fascination, I know." Again, very non–rock 'n' roll, but done so well it competed valiantly against the best of the young dynamos that year.

Finally, with real success, Kapp Records, as was the practice at the time, went big in 1958 introducing five Jane Morgan songs, only one of which charted. "The Days the Rains Came" rose to #21 on *Billboard* and #1 on the UK pop chart.

Although 1958 was Jane Morgan's last big year as a pop star, she would continue recording all through the 1960s, doing well from 1965 through 1968 on the adult contemporary chart. By then that was all background music to her later career as a nightclub singer and stage actress in Broadway musicals.

From "Great Balls of Fire" by Jerry Lee Lewis to "Book of Love" by the Monotones to "At the Hop" by Danny and the Juniors, 1958 was a fine time for rock 'n' roll. However, two of the best records of that year—classic eternal songs—were by the veteran crooners Doris Day and Peggy Lee.

In December 1958, *Billboard* published its annual disk jockey poll of the country's "favorite single" for the year. "Everybody Loves a Lover" by Doris Day was #3 on the Top Ten while #6 was "Fever" by Peggy Lee. These were two amazing cuts by ladies who had been recording for almost two decades. The commentary aside the chart read: "'Everybody Loves a Lover' by Doris Day was one of the few records of the year by a fem artist to reach the top 30 . . . 'Fever' by Peggy Lee was also an interesting side. This sultry reading of Little Willie John's former R&B click brought her way back in a big way."[23]

Since the deejays preferred "Everybody Loves a Lover," let's start there.

As noted, songwriter and lyricist Richard Adler cowrote the music to the 1954 play *The Pajama Game*, which supplied Patti Page a Top Ten record in "Steam Heat" and, more importantly, gave Rosemary Clooney a #1 song, "Hey There." The movie version of the play came to the screen in 1957 starring Doris Day.

Now, it was one year later and Adler was working with a new collaborator Robert Allen. He heard his attorney mumble a quote about all the world loves a lover. Like a good lyricist he wrote it down, misquoting the misquote (perhaps just poetic license) as "everybody loves a lover."[24]

There are a couple of versions of what happened next. In story one, Day, who was looking to record something with a light touch, talked shop with Adler, who on a visit to Los Angeles presented her with the song, "Everybody Loves a Lover," which Day loved and wanted to record.

David Kaufman, in his biography of Doris Day, turned up a completely different and more in-depth version of the tale. In this take, Robert Allen brought the song around to Mitch Miller at Columbia Records, who played it for Doris Day. Again, she liked the tune and wanted to record it. Then came the hitch. Doris was married to Marty Melcher, who slipped into the role of her manager and, no surprise here, created a recording company for Day, which he also headed. Melcher had a reputation for being overbearing and not necessarily a person who played with a clean deck of cards. Without telling his wife, Melcher went to Miller and said, "She'll only do it if I can publish the song." So, Miller went back to Robert Allen, who exclaimed, "Hell no, I'm going to publish it myself. I wrote the song—why should I give it to him?" Miller delivered the news to Melcher, who said his wife wouldn't record the song. The very next day Miller got a call from Day, who told him "I'm not going to walk away from a hit. I'm going to do the song."[25]

Here the story gets better. Over his long career, Frank De Vol worked not only with Jaye P. Morgan but with a slew of women vocalists, including Kay Starr, Margaret Whiting, and Dinah Shore. He got the call to produce "Everybody Loves a Lover" and who did he bring in to add a modern touch to the song? Drummer Earl Palmer, the dean of rock 'n' roll session musicians, who could be heard on everything from "I'm Walkin'" by Fats Domino to "Summertime Blues" by Eddie Cochran to "La Bamba" by Ritchie Valens to "You've Lost That Lovin' Feeling" by the Righteous Brothers and many more.

Cash Box got a preview copy of the record and on June 28, 1958, in its "Record Review" column made "Everybody Loves a Lover" the Disk of the Week. The unnamed reviewer got everything right about "Everybody" when he scribbled: "Guitar, bass, drums and snapping finger supply a fabulous beat for Doris Day's sensational new Columbia platter, 'Everybody Loves a Lover.' It's the canary's most exciting side in many moons and should be her biggest seller since "Que Sera, Sera." Terrific novelty bouncer that jockeys will wear out. The portion where the lark harmonized with herself on double tracks is just great. Sounds like a smash."[26]

The song would climb all the way to #6 on the pop chart. It would be Doris Day's last major hit record.

In 1962, the Shirelles were on a three-year run of great songs, from "Will You Still Love Me Tomorrow" in 1960 to "Soldier Boy" at the beginning of '62. To cap the latter year, the group's producer, Luther Dixon, brought them a song not custom written for them. He chose for their next record the old Doris Day tune "Everybody Loves a Lover." Dixon updated the tune with a steal—listen closely and one can hear a duplication of the instrumentation of Barbara George's hit from the year before, "I Know (You Don't Love Me No More)." "Everybody Loves a Lover" was a major hit in the Northeast, recalled original Shirelle Beverly Lee: "They always loved us in the New York metro." It was liked elsewhere as well, and rose to #19 on the pop chart. It would remain one of the more popular Shirelles tunes for Lee in her long years on the oldies circuit.[27]

If there was a singer who had a better track record in the 1940s than Doris Day, it was Peggy Lee, who had thirty-three records in the Top Thirty including two #1s, "Somebody Else Is Taking My Place" in 1942 and "Mañana" in 1948. By the next decade, her output slowed and there were no real standout records. From 1950 to 1956, she charted fourteen more records, with her best performance coming in 1952 when "Lover" climbed to #3 on the pop chart. She didn't have a song that charted in 1957, but then there was the astounding "Fever" in 1958.

The song was a cover of Little Willie John's version in 1956, which was a #1 tune on the R&B chart and crossed over to the pop charts, where it peaked at #24. Ruth Brown, who had a number of songs "covered" by white singers, didn't disparage the trend. What she protested against was "duplicates," which were the exact same arrangements and sound as the original. Brown had nothing against taking an existing song and reworking it as something that was your own. This is what Peggy Lee did to "Fever," turning it inside out and pulling from the core the song's torrid, sensual heart. Many would say the Peggy Lee version of "Fever" makes Little Willie John's rendition pallid by comparison—not that his recording was bad. It wasn't; his version was snappy-bluesy. Peggy Lee, instead, seduced you, when she sang: "Now you listened to my story / Here's the point that I have made / Chicks were born to give you fever / Be it Fahrenheit or centigrade." Peggy Lee was all "chick."

Peggy Lee (Norma Deloris Egstrom) was born May 25, 1920, in Jamestown, North Dakota. Her first singing gig was on a local radio station in nearby Valley City. In 1937, she was invited to audition for WDAY in Fargo, the biggest radio station in the state. She was hired immediately, but the programming director decided she needed a better stage name and dubbed her Peggy Lee. Later that year, at the age of seventeen, she traveled to California for work, got sick, returned to North Dakota, and after healing returned to California, where she found regular work in Palm Springs. A Chicago nightclub owner caught her show and invited her to sing at his club, and that was where Benny Goodman discovered her. It wasn't by accident. His female vocalist Helen Forrest was leaving and Goodman had been looking for a replacement.[28]

In 1942, Lee scored her first #1 record and inadvertently helped kick-start Frank Sinatra's solo career. Benny Goodman and Peggy Lee were booked at New York's Paramount Theater for New Year's Eve. Bob Weitman, manager of the theater, had heard that Sinatra, who had left the Tommy Dorsey band earlier that year, had headlined at the Mosque Theater in Newark, New Jersey, and the young girls in the audience positively swooned. At the last minute he decided to put Sinatra on the undercard with the Benny Goodman and Peggy Lee show. Much to Goodman's surprise, the young ladies in the audience screamed in appreciation when Sinatra was introduced. It was one thing to be big in Newark, but it was another to be big in New York.[29]

As for Lee, she got married and left the Benny Goodman band. Her intention was to settle down into married life, but that she was such a hot singer it was tough to step away. She signed with Capitol Records and remained a busy and successful recording artist into the early years of the 1950s.

Lee signed with Decca in 1952 and her pace of recordings slowed considerably. From 1952 through 1956, she charted eleven songs, only one of which was a Top Ten hit: "Lover" was a #3 song in 1952. So, she went back to Capitol, where she recorded "Fever."

Peggy Lee was also a successful songwriter. In fact, she wrote the lyrics to her #1 record, "Mañana (Is Soon Enough for Me)," in 1948. After "Fever," she was more successful as an album artist. Still, she embraced rock 'n' roll, recording Lennon/McCartney tunes as well as Carole King.

As for singles? While Lee did well on adult contemporary into the 1960s, her days as a pop singer recording artist were over. Or it seemed so until 1969. Then, out of nowhere came "Is That All There Is?' a strange, bleak, talk/tune that captured America's attention. One didn't know if it summed up Peggy Lee's worldview or was a reflection of her own life, but it was such an outlier song in the Age of Aquarius that deejays played it and even teenagers bought the record. It ended up as a #11 song on *Billboard*'s Hot 100.

If anything, the song reflected the dispirited aging of rock 'n' roll wunderkinds Jerry Leiber and Mike Stoller, who had been writing hit songs since before the new music was given the name rock 'n' roll: "Hound Dog," "Yakety Yak," "Love Potion #9," and so many more. By 1969, Leiber and Stoller had tired of writing for teenagers and drifted instead into to the dark, smoky world of European cabaret to write a song of disillusionment: "And then I fell in love / . . . then one day he went away and I thought I'd die, but I didn't / and when I didn't I said to myself / is that all there is to love?"

The song was first given to Leslie Uggams for an album release. In 1969, Peggy Lee recorded it with an arrangement by Randy Newman that was "subtler and queasier," wrote music historian Ken Emerson. "She insisted that Capitol Records release it as a single despite the company's initial resistance, and was rewarded with her last major hit . . . and that's all there was."[30] The refrain still haunts: "Is that all there is, is that all there is? / If that's all there is my friends, then let's keep dancing"—like the doomed castle inhabitants at the end of Ingmar Bergman's black-and-white soul-searcher "The Seventh Seal."

"Queasier" is not generally used to describe the release of songs or even a particular song. Yet 1958 was not over before one last queasy scrimmage occurred among the female crooner set—and it was all about one of the most pointless songs any of the singers were forced (or opted?) to record in their long careers.

The circular hoop had been a child's toy for centuries. Then in the 1950s a wide, hollow plastic version was introduced under a new sobriquet, Hula Hoop. The first word of the toy came from the Hawaiian dance, because the hip movement to keep the hoop circulating around the waist resembled the hula.

It was one of the greatest toy fads of modern history, popping up everywhere in 1958. Through the summer over 25 million Hula Hoops were sold at $1.98 each; over 100 million were sold globally that year.[31]

Novelty songwriters quickly jumped into the market in the form of hoop-la delirium and that ended up on the music sheets for female crooners. Music historian Ed Ward picked up the action: "In September [1958], the country was suddenly in the grip of the Hula Hoop craze . . . the impact on the music business was violent. The first to cut a Hoop disc was Atlantic. Over a weekend Trinity Music publisher-songwriter Charlie Graen wrote "Hoopa Hoola" with Bob Davie. On Tuesday, September 2, Grean flew to Chicago where he recorded Betty Johnson . . . Atlantic rushed out deejay acetates the following day while a pretty Trinity secretary visited New York disk jockeys to demonstrate Hoop swinging."[32]

Graen had been active in the music industry since the big band era, eventually ending up as producer for RCA Victor Records. He was also a novelty songwriter of distinction, having written "The Thing" for Phil Harris in 1950.

He was also briefly married to singer Betty Johnson, voice of his "Hoopla Hula" song. His lyrics were timely but strained: "I never seem to want to do the stroll anymore / and western movies really are becoming a bore / 'cause now I discovered there's a new way to wing / I'm getting all my kicks in a big round ring." The rhythm track was Hawaiian music mashed into a basic 1950s rock 'n' roll beat. If Connie Francis heard Betty Johnson's song, she would have been so glad because finally someone was trying to imitate her.

Betty Johnson was the Varetta Dillard of the female crooner set. As good a singer as Dillard was, she never quite found the promised land of Ruth Brown, Etta James, and LaVern Baker. Her biggest hit was "Mercy, Mr. Percy," which landed at #6 on the R&B chart in 1953. However, if she is known for anything today, it's her 1955 song "Johnny Has Gone," dedicated to the late, great Johnny Ace.

Betty Johnson never climbed to the pantheon of the female crooners either, and is best known, if at all, for the 1954 novelty song "I Want Eddie Fisher for Christmas," which, of course, was all about the sexy young singer.

Betty Johnson was born March 16, 1929, in Guilford Country, North Carolina. Her father organized the Johnson Family Singers, which included her parents, three brothers, and herself. It was a successful act, performing on radio and making records from 1938 to 1951. By 1948, Betty had her own fifteen-minute radio programs and thereafter appeared on stage, radio, and television. In 1954, she signed with Columbia Records and then RCA Victor and finally Bally Records. She bagged a few minor hits including "I Dreamed" and the novelty song "Little Blue Man."[33]

"Hoopa Hula" was not a hit for Betty Johnson, partly because she got snuffed by Georgia Gibbs, who recorded a different novelty ditty, "The Hula Hoop Song" and was able to get a slot on *The Ed Sullivan Show* the first week in September.

Gibbs was recording for Roulette Records, notorious for its ties to the New York mafia while being a very successful label producing #1 songs in the 1960s such as "Peppermint Twist" by Joey Dee and the Starlighters and "Hanky Panky" by Tommy James and the Shondells. Roulette's creative team was led by songwriters Hugo Peretti and Luigi Creatore, and it was Peretti who composed and arranged "The Hula Hoop Song," which boasted such scintillating lyrics as "Hula Hoop, hula hoop / anyone can play the Hula Hoop / anyone can play from three to one hundred and ten." The writers were unknowns, Carl Maduri and Donna Kohler.

According to Ed Ward, the same day that Gibbs was recording at Roulette, Teresa Brewer was cutting the same song at Coral Records. Now it became a horse race between Georgia and Teresa—an actual race between the two record companies as to who could get their acetates into the hands of disc jockeys first.[34]

In the end, Gibbs just out-hustled Brewer in this duel. "The Ramblings" column in the *Cash Box* of October 18, 1958, noted, "Georgia Gibbs, whose first hit for Roulette, 'The Hula Hoop Song,' is a best seller, was designated 'Star of the Week' on the NBC radio show of the same name."[35] The next month, Gibbs was in Toronto where the press reported, "Georgia Gibbs in town for TV appearances and to visit DJs with her current click, 'The Hula Hoop Song.'" And by December Roulette announced, "the Hula Hoop Song" was on its way to becoming the label's top hit of the year overseas.[36]

The major difference between the Gibbs and Brewer versions of the same song was that the songwriters were listed as Maduri and Kohler for Roulette, but as Kohler and Maduri for Coral. Still, with Gibbs hustling harder, her version of the song rose to #32 on the record chart narrowly beating out Brewer, whose version went to #38.

It would be the last hit record for Gibbs. Brewer would continue recording into the 1960s, scoring a few more mid-tier hits including "Heavenly Lover" in 1959 and "Anymore" in 1960. Despite spending many hours in the recording studio across the decade of the 1960s, Brewer's glory days as a hitmaker were over.

CHAPTER TEN

BLAME IT ON THE BOSSA NOVA
(1959 AND BEYOND)

TERESA BREWER—TONY BENNETT—MINDY CARSON—
DINAH SHORE—PATTI PAGE—EYDIE GORMÉ—
STEVE LAWRENCE—BOB THIELE—ROSEMARY CLOONEY

It was a beautiful photo of Teresa Brewer. She looked determinedly over her right shoulder at the camera. A full bouffant streams into curls below the nape and mingles with a fluffy collar. Her lips are full, brows finely arched over the eyes, and pupils parked in the right corner staring at the camera. The headline over the photo reads "Gets Own Show at Last" and the brief caption explained: "TV show of her own will come to Teresa Brewer, the song star, when she takes over the Perry Como Show for the summer. She begins as soon as she finishes current engagement at Las Vegas. Under $25 million deal signed by Perry, he pays for his replacement show."

The newspaper clip was pulled by Bill Munroe from an unknown newspaper, probably late spring 1959, and it wasn't exactly correct. Brewer was one of three acts that would replace Perry Como during his summer hiatus. The other two performers were Tony Bennett and the singing group the Four Lads.

Como, a hugely successful pop singer, had been performing on radio since the mid-1930s, finally getting a show of his own in 1943. He was so good at it that with the arrival of television, he simply moved his show, *The Chesterfield Supper Club*, to the new medium in 1948, often with female regulars such as Jo Stafford, Peggy Lee, and the Fontane Sisters. In 1955, he was lured to NBC, where he updated his schmoozy-crooning format into *The Perry Como Show*.

Like many female singers in the 1940s and '50s, Brewer was given the opportunity to star in motion pictures or early television. In 1953, when she was a young, bright songstress, Paramount Pictures invited her to come to

Hollywood to try her hand with another young singer, Guy Mitchell, in a Rhonda Fleming movie called *Those Redheads from Seattle*. A couple of old pros including Agnes Moorhead were in supporting roles, director Lewis Foster, and costume designer Edith Head were enlisted as well in what was billed as the first musical to be released in 3-D. In the movie, Brewer sings "Baby, Baby, Baby," which Coral Records released as a single. It did very well, climbing to #12 on the record chart despite competition from Mindy Carson. (In 1958, Carson released an album called *Baby Baby Baby*.)

According to a *Variety* review, Brewer "comes over the screen like a million bucks." Paramount was pleased and offered her a contract, but Brewer turned it down. As she later said, "The movie was filmed on the Paramount lot in 1953. They did the location shots without us. I had never acted in my life when I did that and they wanted to give me a seven-year contract! I was going to be a starlet, but I already had two kids and was expecting a third, so I thought that was ridiculous. I said, 'no, thank you.'"

Brewer preferred to stay on the East Coast. She was living at the time in New Rochelle, about a half-hour drive from New York City. This was a better personal decision because she could raise her family and make the occasional trip into Manhattan to record.

It was in also in 1953 that Brewer was invited to emcee her first television show. In the early days of television, one of the oddest formats was the back-to-back, fifteen-minute musical shows. The self-contained programs were led by different hosts. This particular show was called *Summertime U.S.A.* and it was the seasonal replacement for the *Jane Froman's USA Canteen*. Brewer and cohost Mel Tormé were placed in different simulated resorts twice a week. So viewers would see Brewer and Tormé, perhaps, in Niagara Falls, Havana, or Rio de Janeiro. The show was slotted for only one season.

Brewer's popularity was such that when Dick Clark moved from his afternoon *Bandstand* spot to the *Dick Clark's Saturday Night Beechnut Show* in 1958, one of the first season's guest stars was Teresa Brewer, who with Annette Funicello, were the first females in a group that included Neil Sedaka, Eddie Cochran, Sam Cooke, Fats Domino, Little Richard, and Tab Hunter.

Although she appeared on many variety shows throughout the 1950s, in 1959, it had been six years since she cohosted a television slot. She was an old pro by this time and so was Tony Bennett, who she liked personally.[1] Even the Four Lads had been recording since the early 1950s, so everyone should have known their places.

Brewer was originally engaged to sing every week on the show for thirteen weeks while Como was on vacation. After the first seven weeks the producer would be replaced by Henry Howard, an assistant director of the show who would soon become producer of the NBC show *Perry Presents*. In 1956, Howard produced *The Patti Page Show* and the year before that *The Julius La Rosa Show*. He had known Como since Perry Como's Kraft Music Hall show in 1948. Howard had been around singers for a long time, but for some reason he and Brewer did not get along. They fought it out in the press.

Brewer had been getting along just fine with the first producer for four weeks. Then she told a reporter, "But a certain person said things that weren't exactly complimentary to me. He was rude to people who visited me on the set and wouldn't allow a reporter in to interview me. He threw my press agent out."

Howard told the press, "Miss Brewer was difficult to work with because she thought she should get billing over her co-star, singer Tony Bennett."[2]

Back to Brewer. "I never spoke two words to him. I never saw him do anything but sit around in a chair and watch. But he is to become producer of the summer show on July 24, and I was told that he said he didn't like my talent."[3]

Howard also kept punching. "I guess if you get Tony Bennett and Teresa Brewer together, you are bound to get trouble. Both of them want to be the star. We tried to make them co-stars, but she kept complaining that he had bigger arrangements and more lavish sets and was getting more to do."[4]

One of Brewer's complaints was that Howard was rude to her agent. But who was the agent in question?[5]

Howard explained that "Miss Brewer," through her "husband and agent" Bill Monahan, had complained about her material and that Bennett was getting bigger songs.[6]

The brouhaha came to a head—almost—when newspapers on July 6, 1959, reported that Brewer had handed in her notice and would leave the show after her appearance on July 25. In other words, she would have completed seven of the thirteen weeks. That wasn't good enough for Howard, who appeared a bit spiteful about what happened, and fired her immediately. Brewer told reporters, that her professional agency, Music Corporation of America, later known as MCA, was informed by an attorney for the producers of the show, "If she is that unhappy she need not report for rehearsals this week and will be considered finished with the show as of last Saturday." The producers of show would pay her through the July 25 date.[7]

Brewer had been caught by surprise, telling reporters she was stunned. Asked if she considered that she was fired, Brewer answered, "I do. I have to," and "I've never been fired before. I'm very sorry it happened this way."

She continued, "I had no idea this was going to happen. I had picked out my songs for Saturday night and my gowns and I was ready to rehearse. Now I don't know what to think. I'm caught off guard. I had turned down several nightclub dates so I could be on the show. Now I hope I can get them back."[8]

Men moved successfully between the music world and Hollywood. Bing Crosby and Frank Sinatra were singers first before they became Oscar-winning actors. By the late 1940s, singer Doris Day was already a successful Hollywood transplant, while going in the reverse direction was Debbie Reynolds, from Hollywood to a singer with a #1 record.

Of the female crooners, Rosemary Clooney performed in a handful of movies during the years 1953 and 1954, most famously with Bing Crosby in *White Christmas*. Patti Page was in fewer movies, but she did nab a nice supporting role in *Elmer Gantry*, for which Burt Lancaster won an Academy Award for best actor.

It wasn't Hollywood but the new medium of television that created the most opportunities for female crooners. That was partly because in the earliest days of television it was easy to transfer what was a successful radio format—a show emceed by a well-known singing host who also introduced other singers—to television. Some of the men such as Perry Como and Andy Williams did this well. For the most part, women were also good emcees, but they rarely lasted more than a season. Nevertheless, so many female crooners, from the little-known to the well-known, got a chance to host that, for the most part, the movement across media helped sustain the female crooner moment as well as individual careers.

Highlights from the 1950–60 decade include *The Rosemary Clooney Show* in 1956, *The Georgia Gibbs Show* in 1957, and *The Jo Stafford Show* (United Kingdom) in 1961. Lesser-known singers with television slots include Jane Froman with two eponymous shows *Jane Froman's U.S.A Canteen* in 1952, which morphed into *The Jane Froman Show* in 1953.

One of the earliest attempts at creating a singing/television career involved Mindy Carson, born July 16, 1927, in New York City. In 1946, the teenage Carson won an audition for the radio program *Stairway to the Stars*, and the next year Paul Whiteman gave her a featured spot on his radio show.[9] She began her recording career with another bandleader, Harry Cool, and by 1949, she was a hot enough commodity that NBC inked her to a five-year contract calling for a "combined build-up via radio, television and RCA Victor Records." The deal had a potential $50,000 per annum value (big money in those days) for Carson, if the television and radio shows were picked up. Exclusive of the deal were any royalties she would receive from recordings.[10]

The trouble was, Carson's recording career never really took off. She had a few minor hits in the early 1950s, but RCA Victor dropped her in 1952. Still, she landed on her feet because in December of the same year, she was signed by NBC to do *The Mindy Carson Show*, sponsored by Embassy Cigarettes. She then signed with Columbia Records, which had her duet with Guy Mitchell for the single "Cause I Love You, That's A-Why," which climbed to #24 on the pop chart in 1952. Her television show lasted a year, and that was it for Carson until 1955, when "Wake the Town and Tell the People" reached #13 on the pop chart. Otherwise, a couple of minor hits and then it was all over.

The busiest of the female crooners was Patti Page, who hosted her first show in the 1952–53 television season. It was on NBC as a fifteen-minute program and called *Scott Music Hall* because it was sponsored by Scott Tissues. In the early 1950s, a brand would often include its product name in the title of the television show it sponsored. Page was out of television for about a year; then in 1955 Oldsmobile sponsored *The Patti Page Show*. These shows only lasted one season, as did Page's next venture *The Big Record* (1957–58), another music variety series, this time on CBS. Oldsmobile was the main sponsor and Page sung the Oldsmobile jingle. Again one and done. Then Page switched networks again, this time to ABC, for *The Patti Page Olds (Oldsmobile) Show*, which also lasted one season.

The most successful of the female singers to host a television show was Dinah Shore. The singer was the epitome of a femme crooner; however, her most prolific and successful days were in the 1940s. She continued into the 1950s with occasional successes—just nowhere near to being the recording queen she had been the decade before. Part of the reason for that was she was the one woman singer to master the art of television, hosting variety shows in the 1950s and 1960s, and then came back in the 1970s to star in a series of daytime talk shows. When she was in her seventies she even had a show for three years on cable television. In 1991, she was inducted into the Television Hall of Fame.

Dinah Shore (Fannye Rose Shore) was born in 1916 in Winchester, Tennessee. By the time she was in fifth grade the family moved to Nashville. When she was in college at Vanderbilt University, she made her radio debut on WSM radio in Nashville. She eventually moved to New York, where she was hired as a vocalist at radio station WNEW. There she sang with Frank Sinatra before moving up to a series of more important radio shows. Her first recordings were in 1939 and by the next year, with RCA Victor, enjoyed six songs that were Top Twenty-Five hits. She was prolific, unveiling twenty-one new singles just in the year 1942. Her first #1 record, "I'll Walk Alone," arrived during 1943 and her second, "The Gypsy," in 1946, on her new label Columbia Records. The following year was a truly banner one, with twenty-one more singles, including the #1 hit "The Anniversary Song," Her last #1 was "Buttons and Bows."[11]

In the early to mid-1950s Shore recorded often, just not as successfully. Her biggest hits in the decade came in 1950 and 1951 with the #3 songs "My Heart Cries for You" and "Sweet Violets." Her last good year as a pop singer was in 1957 when three songs ("Fascination" #15, "Chantez-Chantez" #19, and "I'll Never Say 'Never Again' Again" #24), were Top Twenty-Five hits. If Shore had any impact on rock 'n' roll, it was her recording of the 1930s tune "Dream a Little Dream of Me," which was the B-side to her mid-tier hit "Can Anyone Explain? (No! No! No!)" from 1950. The 1968 hit version of the song by Mama Cass of The Mamas and the Papas closely adheres to the Shore pacing, although it loses some of the etherealness of Shore's big-band styling.

Shore married actor George Montgomery in 1943 and that union lasted almost twenty years before divorce. According to gossip columns, Shore kept an active dance card in her single years including romantic duets with Frank Sinatra in the 1950s and Eddie Fisher in the 1960s. The latter affair was a bit ironic because Fisher's first date with Debbie Reynolds was to a dinner at Dinah Shore's home.[12]

All that was just noisy backdrop to the other thing Dinah Shore was really, really good at—television.

As the decade of the 1950s began, Shore made a guest appearance on an NBC Bob Hope television special. A year later, NBC offered her a slot of her own, which became *The Dinah Shore Show*. That morphed into *The Dinah Shore Chevy Show*, which ran from 1956 to 1963. Shore had a couple of things going for her. America was slowly changing, settling down after World War II, while culturally dividing into "squares" and "hipsters." As noted, the music scene was slowly evolving with influences from country & western and rhythm & blues. With any change there are many who always prefer the older melodies, which is why the post-swing, crooner crowd was able to hold on for so long. David Sarnoff, who ran RCA and NBC, adored Shore's very conservative song choices and middle-of-the-road presence. If there was any flamboyance to her shows, it was her exuberance in singing the Chevrolet jingle, "See the USA in your Chevrolet" and sweeping air-kisses to her audience, live and on the airways, at the end of her show.[13]

Kids may have preferred, in the early 1950s, song shows such as *Your Hit Parade* and then later in the decade, *American Bandstand*, but their moms and dads loved their conservative, buttoned-down hosts Perry Como, Andy Williams, and the rare female success story, Dinah Shore.

All things change, and the variety show, a staple of 1950s television, slowly withered until there were just a few that carried on, including the most famous, *The Ed Sullivan Show*. Changing music tastes by the younger generation, which was considered a large consumer target, was one factor for the change, but different types of shows grew in popularity. There is one theory that the western killed off the variety format. In 1955, the first wave of westerns landed on television and by 1959 a viewer had a choice of thirty different shows in the format.[14] With the demise of the variety show, that particular outlet, which served the female crooners well throughout the 1950s, came to a close.

Also coming to a close for the old-style crooners were the record charts. In 1959, not one of the post–big band singers made *Billboard*'s list of Top

Fifty songs. Nor did close harmony groups such as the McGuire Sisters and Chordettes make the list, effectively ending the phenomenon of the white sister acts, a staple of the pop charts for thirty years.

The one thing that didn't change in 1959 was the limited amount of turntable minutes for female singers in the time of rock 'n' roll. Of the top twenty-five songs for the year 1959, only one female singer made the list, teenager Dodie Stevens, who warbled a jaunty novelty record "Pink Shoe Laces." She was only fourteen at the time of her success, yet she wrapped her whimsy of a voice around the key lyric "He wears tan shoes with pink shoelaces / a polka dot vest and man, oh, man / tan shoes with pink shoelaces / And a big Panama with a purple hat band."

Doing well that year were two other songstresses of the teenage market, who also did novelty tunes: Connie Francis with "Lipstick on Your Collar" at #28; and Connie Stevens, teaming up with TV star Edd Byrnes for "Kookie, Kookie (Lend Me Your Comb)," at #37. The female side of the song market was saved from absolute silliness by two stalwarts of the blues/jazz world who crossed over to the pop chart: Della Reese with "Don't You Know" at #43, and Dinah Washington with "What a Diff'rence a Day Makes" at #45.

This isn't to say the female crooners had completely given up the singles market; at least a half a dozen of the ladies were still making records. Rosemary Clooney, whose last major hit, "Mangos," was in 1957, released three songs in 1959 and none of them charted. The next year she would unleash four more singles, but only one would make it to the record chart, at a lowly #84. She would never reach the *Billboard* Hot 100 chart again.

Jaye P. Morgan was very busy in 1959, releasing six new singles, only two of which made it to the lower reaches of the Hot 100. Like Clooney, Jaye P. Morgan would have just a single record reach the bottom regions of the record charts in 1960, the last time for her as well.

Another very active singer was Patti Page, who boasted four new singles in 1959, all of which charted in the lower region of the Hot 100. Her recording career didn't die as quickly, however. She would have another fifteen songs hit the *Billboard* Hot 100 chart in the 1960s, including the title song to the movie *Hush, Hush Sweet Charlotte*. By the end of decade she was covering popular songs such as "Gentle on My Mind," "Little Green Apples," and "Stand By Your Man," which did well on the more specialized adult contemporary chart.

Like Page, Teresa Brewer unleashed four new singles for 1959, two of which made it to the *Billboard* Hot 100, including "Heavenly Lover," which made it to #40. Brewer did better the next year, when "Anymore" reached #31 on the pop chart. She managed five more singles in 1961, only one of which, "Milord," reached the netherworld of pop charts. Although recording into the 1990s, she was never again to see one of her songs on the *Billboard* Hot 100.

The most successful of the old-style crooners in 1959 were the redoubtable McGuire Sisters, who introduced five new records, one of which, "May You Always," reached #11 on the chart.

Nothing much happened for the McGuire girls the next year. However, they came back strong in 1961 with a Top Twenty hit "Just for Old Time's Sake" and barely making the charts with two songs that sounded like R&B covers, but weren't, "Just Because" and "Tears on My Pillow." It was the end of line for the McGuires as hitmakers. The ladies retired from public appearances in 1968.

Another female singer from the 1950s also offered to the 1960s market a couple of solid records. Eydie Gormé's first two songs released in 1953 disappeared without a trace. The same could not be said for Gormé, who had one of the stranger careers of all the female crooners. So much so that she is rarely put into the same category. Her biggest hit, "Blame It on the Bossa Nova," came in 1963, in the midst of the girl group era, and she is sometimes lumped into that group although she started out singing with the big bands. She was certainly no teenager discovered singing a cappella on a street corner. When she finally hit it big, she was past thirty years in age.

Eydie Gormé (Edith Gormezano) was born August 16, 1928, in the Bronx, New York. Singer and songwriter Neil Sedaka is always mentioned as her first cousin, but the family relations are tenuous. As Sedaka said, "Our grandmothers were related somehow. At best first cousins once removed."

When Sedaka, who was eleven years younger, was growing up, he wasn't aware that he had a relation that was famous. Then his aunts said to him, "Hey that's Eydie Gormezano, we grew up with that family in Turkey." Both the Gormezanos and Sedakas were Sephardic Jews who came to the United States from Turkey. Both families spoke Spanish at home and in later years Eydie Gormé recorded a couple of Spanish-language albums with Trio Los Panchos. These were huge hits in Latin America. Needless to say, Eydie Gormé didn't pass along any helpful hints about the music business to her "cousin" Neil, who had his first hit as a teenager in 1958.[15]

While attending City College of New York, Gormé sang with local bands, including one where the trumpet player was Ken Greengrass, who would become a well-known manager of musicians, including Eydie Gormé. From local groups, Gormé steadily moved up. In 1950, she was singing with the Tommy Tucker Orchestra, which had been around since the 1930s. After Tucker, Gormé sang with the more well-known Tex Beneke, fronting his own swing band after a long association with Glenn Miller, who went missing in 1944 while flying to France from England.

Coral Records signed Gormé in 1952, getting her into the studio quickly and releasing her first songs in 1953. She cut five singles (ten songs including

B-sides) that first year. Nothing really happened with those cuts except that a song called "Frenesi" charted in Canada. The first US hit arrived the next year when "Fini" became a Top Twenty record. The more interesting cut was the weirdly named B-side "Gimme Gimme John," which was a quick-tempo finger-snapper.[16]

Bob Thiele had joined Coral in 1952 in the course of the label signing numerous female acts. He either couldn't find the right mix for Gormé or had too many other ladies to handle, and she slid quietly through the cracks. She caught a break and signed with a bigger label, ABC-Paramount, in 1955, which released five Eydie Gormé records the following year, two of which were standouts, "Too Close for Comfort" and "Mama, Teach Me to Dance," both Top Forty hits. ABC-Paramount at least gave Gormé some fine writers to work with. Among the tunesmiths for the post-swing "Too Close for Comfort" was Jerry Brock, who that same year of 1956 composed the score for the Broadway show *Mr. Wonderful* starring Sammy Davis Jr. ("Too Close for Comfort" was from that show).

As for the Latin-beat "Mama, Teach Me to Dance," the tune was composed by some familiar names: Dick Manning and Al Hoffman. Together the two wrote "Allegheny Moon" for Patti Page. Manning, working with Robert Colby, scribed "Jilted" for Teresa Brewer and "Fascination," recorded by both Dinah Shore and Jane Morgan.

"I thought she had a magnificent voice," said Sedaka. "I put her in the same category as Streisand, Celine Dion, Edith Piaf, or Shirley Bassey. She had that full voice; a belting sound. What happened to her career was she had a great voice for standards, a great singer of the American songbook, but she came along just when rock 'n' roll was happening. Those songs were not written for her kind of voice. When you saw her in concert, you realized how great she was."

Steve Allen, who had been Gormé's labelmate at Coral, began hosting a late-night program, which would evolve into *The Tonight Show*. He invited Gormé to be a regular. He already had a young male singer named Steve Lawrence and in 1953 decided he needed to balance the programming with a pretty young female. In 1954, Coral released an Eydie Gormé single with two songs from the play *Peter Pan*, "Make Yourself Comfortable" and "I've Gotta Crow." The male voice on the record "Make Yourself Comfortable" is Steve Lawrence. The two singers made themselves so comfortable together they were married in 1957, and the following year they hosted *Steve Allen Presents the Steve Lawrence–Eydie Gormé Show*, a summer replacement for *The Steve Allen Show*.[17]

Rock 'n' roll was taking over radio plays. Gormé's sing-the-standards approach to song managed to cut some sway in 1956, so ABC-Paramount tried the all-in strategy, sending five new Gormé records to market in 1957 and four more in 1958. Although six of the nine charted, only two made a substantial impact. "Love Me Forever" reached #24 on the chart in 1957 while "You Need Hands" tapped a #11 slot in 1958.

Meanwhile, from the other side of the marriage, Steve Lawrence's career finally seemed to be taking off as well. He started recording with King Records in 1952 with two well-received singles "Poinciana," a #21 record that year, and then "How Many Stars Have to Shine," a #26 record on the chart the next year. He switched to Coral Records in 1954, the old label of Eydie Gormé. As ABC-Paramount flooded the market for Gormé in 1957, Coral did the same for Lawrence with eight new songs, six of which charted including a cover of Buddy Knox's "Party Doll." It became Lawrence first Top Five recording. He would continue going forward as an inconsistent hitmaker, with some releases going Top Ten but most barely charting or not charting at all.

Then came the 1960s and the story changed for both Gormé and Lawrence. The couple were regulars at both the Brill Building and 1650 Broadway, two midrise office buildings where most of the young songwriters of the day (including Neil Sedaka) made their offices. It was an odd business, defined by lyricists and tunesmiths who toiled together to make records. Sometimes the duos were two men such as Burt Bacharach and Hal David or Doc Pomus and Mort Schuman, but more often than not, it was a couple such as Carole King and Gerry Goffin, Jeff Barry and Elle Greenwich, or Barry Mann and Cynthia Weill. In addition to the songwriters, many record producers kept offices in the building. They all saw so much of each other that inevitably, close friendships formed.

Don Kirshner, who boasted his own record labels but was better known as the co-owner of the influential music publishing company Aldon Music, had a handful of premier songwriting teams under contract, including Mann and Weill and Goffin and King. Kirshner became close friends with Gormé and Lawrence and let them tap into his songwriters. The first strike was Carole King and Gerry Goffin. They had written a song called "Go Away Little Girl," which Bobby Vee recorded for Liberty Records but was not released as an A-side single. It then fell to Lawrence, who was recording for Columbia Records. That version shot all the way to #1 in January 1963 and stayed for two weeks before getting bounced by the pop-folk song "Walk Right In" by the Rooftop Singers."

Next to strike were Barry Mann and Cynthia Weill. The duo hadn't done as well as King and Goffin, who with "Go Away Little Girl" had four #1 records under their belt. Mann and Weill would get their first #1 in 1964 with the Righteous Brothers singing their tune "You've Lost that Lovin' Feelin.'" Mann and Weill boasted their first hit in 1961, a song called "Bless You" sung by Tony Orlando, and then came a string of top-tier records including "Uptown" by the Crystals, "My Dad" by Paul Peterson, and "On Broadway" by the Drifters.

Predating Chubby Checker's "The Twist" in 1960 and even the Diamonds' "The Stroll" in 1958, the first female crooner to introduce a dance song with an R&B rhythm was Mindy Carson, who had a song called "The Fish." She chirped, "What is this new dance, I'm asking you, man / they call it the fish . . ." It was Eydie Gormé's turn in 1963. The traditional Latin dance called the samba swayed to a particular beat, which a new generation of Brazilian songwriters and singers modernized with a relaxed syncopation. The new style was called the bossa nova or the bossa nova beat and it exploded worldwide starting in the late 1950s and early 1960s. Stan Getz introduced the bossa nova to the United States with a couple of hit records, "Desafinado" with Charlie Byrd in 1962 and "The Girl from Ipanema" with Astrud Gilberto in 1963.

Mann and Weill didn't get anywhere near the boss nova beat with a record called "Blame It on the Bossa Nova," but it did at least have the phrase in the title and lyrics. The song was intended for Bobby Rydell, who back in 1961 cut a dance record called "The Fish," which didn't swim in the same pond as Mindy Carson's song of the same name. It doesn't appear that Rydell ever recorded "Bossa Nova," so Eydie Gormé was happy to take a shot at it. It was a smart move. The song danced its way to #7 on the pop chart becoming Gormé's only Top Ten hit. When her follow-up singles quickly deflated, she tried to tap the well one more time in 1964 with "Can't Get Over (The Bossa Nova)," but America was already over the Brazilian-beat craze. The oddity in all of this was that Gormé was not the first of the female crooners to discover the bossa nova and record a song with that phrase in the title. That distinction belonged to Kay Starr, who in 1962 recorded the ridiculously titled "Bossa Nova Casanova." It's doubtful the tune was ever released.

"When Barry and Cynthia wrote 'Blame It on the Bossa Nova' it allowed Eydie to get out of her niche," Sedaka said. "'Blame It on the Bossa Nova' was trendy and it was danceable. Barry and Cynthia were great writers. It was more of a pop song and Eydie had never really had something like that."

Recording separately, Steve Lawrence and Eydie Gormé released a total of seven songs in 1963. Gormé sang three, all of which charted, but none reached "Bossa Nova" level. The songs became very minor hits although "Don't Try to Fight It, Baby" was written by Gerry Goffin (with Jack Keller) and "Everybody Go Home" by Gerry Goffin and Carole King.

"After you have a tremendous record, the second or 'sophomore record' is very hard to write and produce," Sedaka commented, and he would know, being one of only a handful of recording artists to have a Top Ten record over decades.[18]

Ken Emerson, who wrote *Always Magic in the Air: The Bomp and Brilliance of the Brill Building Era*, was not a fan of either singer, writing: "The staid show-biz sweethearts [Steve Lawrence and Eydie Gormé] did not bring out the best in Aldon's youthful songs, yet these were the biggest hits the couple ever had . . .

Even double-tracked, Lawrence's demure vocal diminished sexual temptation in "Go Away Little Girl" to goody two-shoes. 'Blame It on the Bossa Nova' bore scant resemblance to the latest twist on the samba and Gormé gropes for several notes, but enlivened by Mann's presence in the band (playing organ) and the Cookies back-up vocals, it showed a bit of pizzazz."[19]

As back-up singers, the Cookies were popular with the Kirshner circle of friends such as Neil Sedaka and Gerry Goffin and Carole King. "I remember them saying 'get the Cookies because they catch on so very fast. You can tell them what you want done and they do it,'" Margaret Williams, one of the Cookies, recalled.

When the Cookies were called in to back up Eydie Gormé, who no longer was an ingénue, she was startled at the three young Black girls who walked into the recording studio. Gormé stared at Williams and blurted out, "How old are you?" Older Cookies singer Dorothy Jones cut in, "She's seventeen going on eighteen." Gormé responded, "You look about twelve or thirteen." The Cookies went over to the piano where Barry Mann was sitting. He showed them what he wanted them to do, basically just by giving the Cookies the notes to sing. They backed up two songs. The Cookies were so quick and so good it took just a couple of takes to get "Blame It on the Bossa Nova" perfect. Williams laughed, "When we heard the song on the radio, we were shocked it was a hit."

Williams holds very fond memories of Eydie Gormé because she had their back when a racial incident kept them away from a gig. It all started when Steve and Eydie were hired to do a telethon in Manhattan. They wanted the Cookies to be their back-up singers. It was a last-minute decision and the girls lived in the outer boroughs of New York, so they quickly grabbed their performance clothes and jumped into a taxi to take them to Manhattan. They ran to the back door of the studio, knocked, and a tall white guy opened the door. The Cookies explained they were the back-up singers for Steve and Eydie. The guy looked over the three young Black girls and said "yeah, right" and slammed the door in their face. The girls were stunned and unable to contact Steve and Eydie to tell them they had arrived. In the end, they took a taxi back to their homes. Carole King called Dorothy Jones, asking 'What happened?" Dorothy explained. Carole then called Eydie who exclaimed, "Get them back here, everyone is waiting for them." So, back in the taxi went the Cookies. "When we got back to the studio Eydie was so upset with that guy, she cursed him out," Williams said. "She yelled to him, 'You should have checked with somebody. These are my girls who do background singing for me.' The guy turned beet red, but you know this was the early sixties and there was a lot of prejudice. He just figured we were just random black girls trying to put one over."[20]

Gormé was a singing heroine to another up-and-coming teenage singer, Donna Loren, who in the early 1960s would star on the television show

Shindig! "When I was growing up, I practiced singing to the album *Gormé Sings Showstoppers*," she said. The 1959 album featured a dozen songs from recent Broadway hits to standards. Loren particularly recalled singing to "Johnny One Note" and "Hello, Young Lovers." Remembering her teenage years, Loren noted, "These were Broadway standards I could sing along with. I wore that vinyl out."[21]

Although after 1963 neither Lawrence nor Gormé were hitmakers again, as a duo they became more well-known than ever. The Steve and Eydie act was extremely popular; the married duo were successful nightclub performers, guests on television shows, and occasionally on stage as well. Like a few of the female crooners, Gormé along with Lawrence mixed well with the Hollywood crowd. They befriended a wide of circle of actors and singers, from Frank Sinatra to Carol Burnett to Dick Van Dyke.

Gormé's attorney Mark Sendoff was also a big fan. "She was adorable, couldn't have been more fun. And she was very generous to those who she liked and appreciated. She raised two kids and took care of her husband. She was divine," he said.

One of Sendoff's favorite anecdotes about Steve and Eydie occurred in the 1990s. They were performing in Cerritos, California, and hired a bus to take friends to the show, including the Don Rickles, the Dick Van Dykes, the Bob Newharts, and the Dick Martins (*Laugh-In* television show). On the way to the performance, Dick Martin suffers chest pains indicating a heart attack. They drop him off at a hospital and the bus goes on to Cerritos. When it was all over and everyone was boarding the bus, Steve Lawrence said, "We have to go back and pick up Dick." And they did.[22]

Neil Sedaka finally became close to his "cousin" Eydie after both became big stars. One time Eydie was singing Neil's song "Breaking Up Is Hard to Do" on the Johnny Carson show and when she concluded the song, a young man from the audience surprised everyone by walking onto the stage and thanking her for singing that particular song. It was Neil Sedaka.

"We would hang out in Vegas between shows," Sedaka recalled. "Eydie and Steve and my wife and I. In New York, they had a big beautiful apartment with a grand piano." Sedaka went to that apartment with a couple of songs for Eydie. The first was "Teach Me How," and Eydie, a perfectionist, had Sedaka play it for two hours so she could get the exact intonation of the song. She eventually recorded it along with another song, "My World Keeps Getting Smaller," which Neil wrote with his writing partner Howard Greenfield. The latter song was a powerful Dusty Springfield–type ballad, perfect for Gormé, who nailed it. The song was released in 1970 and Gormé was forty-three years old; she missed the youth market and it was slotted into adult contemporary, which is the market where she ended up within a year after "Blame It on the Bossa Nova."[23]

Eydie Gormé wasn't the only female crooner to reinvent herself after her hit-making years. Teresa Brewer did also—and as with Gormé, it was because of her husband. Not Bill Monahan, but her second husband Bob Thiele.

In 1961, Thiele had been with Coral Records, what he called the "black sheep" division of Decca Records, for nine years when it and he had a falling out over $50, which was the amount of raise Thiele was looking for and denied by the label's execs. So, when a rival label called, Thiele entertained leaving Coral. Somehow the trade publications got hold of the story, which was read by the Coral mavens, and suddenly the $50 raise was granted. Thiele noted, "I stayed at Decca a little while longer." Not much longer, though. He left either later that year or early in 1962 to take over a jazz label called Impulse! Records, where he recorded John Coltrane. He would remain close to many important jazz artists for the next decade.[24]

Coincidentally, or not, soon after Thiele left Coral, so did Teresa Brewer. In 1962, she signed with Philips. While the hits stopped coming, she didn't quit recording. According to Bill Munroe, she recorded one hundred songs and eight albums for the label. "Some Brewer fans like the Philips years because they feel her voice was at its best," Munroe asserted. Meanwhile, her fourth child, another girl, had been born in 1958, and she spent much of the sixties raising her family and watching her marriage fall apart. She didn't enjoy the travel, but liked doing Vegas because she could settle in for a week or so. She also did the occasional television appearance. "She was family centered," Munroe continued. "I had the feeling that her first manager Ritchie Lisella was a hustler and would get her engagements. In later years, she didn't actively seek work. If an offer came her way and it sounded attractive, she would accept it. She was never consumed or obsessed by her career."[25]

Then came the divorce from Bill Monahan and a quick turnaround marriage to Bob Thiele. The newlyweds were two veterans of different sides of the entertainment world; they understood the music industry and, most importantly, understood who they were in regard to the wider universe. This was a marriage that worked. They said their vows in 1972 and remained married until Thiele's death in 1996.

By the early 1970s, Thiele was deep into jazz, owning a handful of labels: Flying Dutchman, Blues Time, and Amsterdam. Knowing Brewer's range and ability to sing in any genre, Thiele made the big leap, inviting his wife to sing with some of the more famous jazz musicians he had recorded or befriended over the years.

This is how Thiele explained it: "To continue making pop records, I also had a label named Amsterdam, on which I recorded my soon to-be-wife Teresa Brewer, while I began to produce jazz dates with her and many of the musical legends who were my friends. These sessions paired Teresa with such giants as

Earl 'Fatha' Hines, Benny Carter, and Count Basie and soon compelled an entire worldwide constituency of fans and critics to become her loyal supporters."[26]

The first time Brewer worked with a jazz band was in 1973, the year after she married Thiele. As she explained, her husband asked her if she would like to record an album with Count Basie. Her response was, "Oh, my goodness, would he do one with me?" As it turned out he certainly would and the two started by recording Bessie Smith songs. "I was scared stiff, but he [Count Basie] was so professional and so nice," she later told a reporter. "He was helpful, didn't rush, and we'd get the songs in one or two takes. "

That same year, through her husband, she met Duke Ellington, who had heard about the Count Basie album. Jokingly, he asked when she was going to do an album with him. That intro led to an album with the Duke. Later she worked with Clark Terry, Stephane Grappelli, Wynton Marsalis, and even Dizzy Gillespie.[27]

Writing about his career, Thiele remarked that in the 1980s he went to work for a jazz affiliation of CBS Records, where he released studio productions, with among others Lonnie Liston Smith, Gato Barbieri, and Teresa Brewer, who he commented was "now a respected presence on the international jazz scene."[28]

Brewer outlived her second husband by eleven years. In 2007, she died at age seventy-six of a rare brain disorder called progressive supranuclear palsy. For almost seventy of those years, she was an entertainer. She recorded almost 600 songs, some more than once. She also notched seventy-seven albums.

For many of the female crooners, the onset of rock 'n' roll with its R&B influence was no more than a slight wrinkle in time. At first, it gave zest to sometimes flagging careers, especially with the cover record phenomenon, but as the 1950s kicked on, it became more and more apparent that the record-buying youth of America was listening to something different from what they were singing—and they had been singing the same kind of tune for a long time, because for many their first hint of fame came during the World War II years or soon after.

For Patti Page, the coming of rock 'n' roll was an extension of her real life, because her husband Charles O'Curran was the musical director on many Elvis Presley movies. Also, during the mid- and late 1950s, Page played Las Vegas four times a year, doing four-week engagements. Since Elvis's mother was such a big Patti Page fan, he and his mother would fly there to watch Page perform. When Elvis was on location filming the movie *Blue Hawaii*, Page took a break from her busy schedule to join her husband. After shooting, they would all have dinner and the sit around and sing old songs. As a reward for being there, Elvis put Page in the movie as an anonymous extra. As she noted, "Just as a gag, I took part in a big wedding scene where the major characters are coming down a waterway in canoes . . . you won't see my name in the credits, but if you look I'm there in the film, in a boat with one of Elvis' cousins." So knowing Elvis personally, the whole rock 'n' roll thing slid past her without affecting her career that much.

Although she might have privately winced at a lack of a big hit since "Left Right Out of Your Heart" went Top Ten in 1958, she was still as busy as ever, releasing at least four new singles a year through the early 1960s, having a thriving nightclub career, and making occasional television appearances.

Then came the Beatles. What's odd about the British Invasion is that Page never met the Beatles, but she saw them in concert when they played Las Vegas. Kappi Ditson Jorda, who handled Page's record promotion publicity, also did the travel arrangements for the Beatles and got her a free ticket. She was sitting next to Kappi in the middle of a large auditorium and as Page recalled: "I was scared to death at that concert. Girls were standing on seats and screaming so loudly I couldn't really hear the music. At one point I thought they would come climbing over the seats and there might be a stampede. They were pushing toward the stage and the guards, stationed at the end of every aisle, had to keep them back."

Afterward Page reflected, "We were aware of the huge changes they [Beatles] were ushering in, but I'm not sure the Beatles were aware of it. Pop music made a dramatic change. We already had rock 'n' roll, but this was different. Nobody could really pinpoint what 'it' was; we just knew things were going to be different."[29]

Nineteen-sixty-four was the year the Beatles came to America. It was also the year Page recorded a song called "Hush ... Hush, Sweet Charlotte," the title song of the gothic horror movie starring Bette Davis, which was so successful it was nominated for seven Academy Awards. How Page came to record the song is a bit unusual. The version of the tune sung over the opening credits was done by a bunch of young boys in a taunting manner and the lyrics were a bit horrific. "Chop-chop, sweet Charlotte, chop cop till he's dead; chop-chop, sweet Charlotte, chop off his hand and head." (Al Martino sang the real title tune over the closing credits.)

As could be expected, with the gruesome lyrics, no one attempted a commercial version of that version of the song. Bob Johnston, who was the A&R man at Page's label, Columbia, saw that the movie had done well and somewhat liked the soft meandering melody of the real title song as sung by Al Martino. So he called up the producer of the Academy Awards show and offered that Patti Page would record "Hush ... Hush, Sweet Charlotte" if she would be booked to sing it on the Academy Awards show. The producer agreed. Near the end of 1964, Page flew to Nashville to record, although for the commercial release, composer and lyricist Mack David, who already had five Academy Award nominations under his belt, wrote new lyrics. Page and David already had a professional relationship as he wrote "I Don't Care If the Sun Don't Shine," which became a Top Ten hit for Page in 1950. He would get a sixth nomination for his version of "Hush . . . Hush, Sweet Charlotte."

Instead of all that chop chop nonsense, the song began this way: "Hush, hush, sweet Charlotte / Charlotte, don't you cry /; Hush, hush sweet Charlotte / He'll love you till he dies."

On April 5, 1965, Patti Page sang "Hush . . . Hush, Sweet Charlotte" at the 37th Academy Awards. While, sadly, the song lost to "Chim Chim Cher-ee" from *Mary Poppins*, it climbed to #8 on the pop chart and to #2 on adult contemporary. Although she charted many more times on the country charts throughout the 1970s, the song would be Page's last big hit for the pop charts.

When all was sung and tabulated, Page could count 110 hits on *Billboard*'s singles charts, four #1 records, and thirty-nine studio albums. She sold over one hundred million records over her long career. Page died in 2013 at the age of eighty-five.

Rosemary Clooney, who had four #1 records in the early 1950s probably knew something was amiss in her career after 1954, when she boasted a Top Ten hit with "Mambo Italiano." After that it was tough to break a new record. Nothing worked except a little song called "Mangos" hit the Top Ten in 1957, and then the arid desert winds blew in once more. But, if you are recording albums and your nightclub bookings are hot and steady, how do you know when your world has changed?

Clooney could pinpoint the exact moment. She was booked to play the Kentucky State Fair in 1959, when she picked up the local newspaper to read "Fabian, new to music, helps stir interest in fair's Clooney Show." She recalled, "I never expected to need a teen sensation to attract people to my show. I sang the hits people expected to hear: 'Come On-a-My-House,' 'Botch-A-Me,' 'This Ole House,' and for balance, 'Tenderly' and 'Hey There.' The audience applauded warmly. But when 16-year-old Fabian took the mike, fans ran screaming down the aisles to the stage."

Someone liked the show. A reviewer, apparently not a youngster, wrote that Clooney's performance was "everything rock 'n' roll was not." Clooney was a realist and while she understood the line was meant as a compliment, the words were contrapuntal to the tenor of the times. In a frank summation, Clooney, looking back, commented: "The rock wave was cresting, about to break, and when it did, it would wash my kind of music right out of the mainstream. Within a decade, nobody would be able to get a contract to record the kind of music I understood and loved."[30]

Clooney would have a second career—as part of a group. In 1977, she was invited join with two other singers, Margaret Whiting and Barbara McNair, and singer-comedienne Rose Marie as a touring act called Four Girls Four. McNair bowed out early to be replaced by big-band singer Helen O'Connell. It was such a successful act, the group toured for over five years and the "girls" were on the road as much as forty weeks of the year. When some of the stalwarts began to drop out, new singers such as Kay Starr stepped in. One singer who got the call from Clooney was Teresa Brewer. The two were never close friends, although Brewer esteemed Clooney, who Brewer said was the type of person she would just like to sit in the kitchen and chat with over a cup of coffee. That was close to Brewer's mindset at the time. It was the early 1980s and she was still pretty much a homebody. Brewer declined the offer, telling Clooney she just didn't want to do all that traveling.

Rosemary Clooney died in 2002 at the age of seventy-four.

Brewer, looking back on her career, told Bill Munroe, "To be a success as a singer, you had to be tough. I was never tough. Patti Page wasn't tough. Dinah Shore, Rosemary Clooney, and all those others that seemed so easy-going, they were tough when it came to the business of show business."[31]

RESEARCH AND ACKNOWLEDGMENTS

All references to chart position of songs are from *Billboard*.

The research behind this book relies on music trade publications, general circulation newspapers, magazines, music history books, and published biographies. In addition, I personally interviewed numerous individuals who supplied me with relevant, firsthand recollections of the personalities featured in the book.

*

When I started looking into the accomplishments of what I consider the forgotten female recording stars of the early 1950s, I decided I would use Teresa Brewer as the string that would tie all the diverse singers together into one narrative. Luckily, I stumbled upon Bill Munroe, who not only headed a Teresa Brewer fanzine but was a depository of Brewer ephemera and press clippings going all the way back to the start of her career. I'm not sure I could have completed this book without Bill's help, so this is a big shout-out to the man who probably knows more about Teresa Brewer's career than even her children.

I interviewed a number of entertainment sources directly for this book. In various other encounters with recording artists and media where the names of featured singers or songs came up in recorded discussions with me, I included their comments as well.

So a big thanks to:

Tom Bialoglow of the Duprees
Mike Glynn
Beverly Lee of the Shirelles
Nanette Licari of Reparata and the Delrons
Donna Loren
Phyllis McGuire

Kathleen Monahan
Louise Murray of the Hearts and Jaynetts
Mike Palermo
Diane Renay
Neil Sedaka
Mark Sendoff
Jim Stewart
Beverly Warren of the Raindrops
Tim Weisberg
Margaret Williams of the Cookies
David Williamson

NOTES

INTRODUCTION: TENNESSEE WALTZ

1. Patti Page and Skip Press, *This Is My Song: A Memoir*, Kathdan Books, 2009.

2. Charlie Gillett, *The Sound of the City: The Rise of Rock and Roll*, Outerbridge & Dienstfrey, 1970.

3. Kitty Kelley, *His Way: The Unauthorized Biography of Frank Sinatra*, Bantam, 1986.

4. Ruth Prigozy, *The Life of Dick Haymes: No More Little White Lies*, University Press of Mississippi, 2006.

5. *Billboard* Top 100 Songs, 1949, www.billboardtop1000f.com/1949.

6. "*Billboard* year-end top 30 singles of 1950," Wikipedia, https://en.wikipedia.org/wiki/Billboard_year-end_top_30_singles_of_1950.

7. Louise Harris Murray, interview.

8. Bill Munroe, interview.

9. US Census results for 1940 and 1950, https://www2.census.gov.

10. "Teresa Brewer: Her Life and Career," Teresa Brewer Center, www.teresafans.org.

11. Philip H. Ennis, *The Seventh Stream: The Emergence of Rocknroll in American Popular Music*, Wesleyan University Press, 1992.

CHAPTER ONE: MUSIC! MUSIC! MUSIC! (1950)

1. "Benny Show's Phil Harris Dies at 89," *Los Angeles Times*, August 13, 1995.

2. Adam Bernstein, "Singer Georgia Gibbs, 87, Performed with Big Bands on Radio Shows," *Washington Post*, December 12, 2006.

3. Bill Munroe, interview.

4. "Teresa Brewer: Her Life and Career."

5. Eileen Barton, interview, www.eileenbarton.com.

6. "Ol' Man Mose—For Those Who Like 1930s Music with F-Bombs," Digital Citizen, December 26, 2011, digitalcitizen.ca/2011/12/26/ol-man-mose-for-those-who-like-music-with-f-bombs/.

7. "The Billboard Music Popularity Charts/The Disk Jockeys Pick," *Billboard*, January 14, 1950.

8. "Disk Jockey's Regional Record Reports," *Cash Box*, January 4, 1950.

9. "Disk Jockey's Regional Record Reports," *Cash Box*, January 21, 1950.

10. "Teresa Brewer: Her Life and Career."

11. "Disk Jockey's Regional Record Reports," *Cash Box*, February 25, 1950.

12. "Just Plain Bill's," *TV Show*, September 1953.

13. Stephan Weiss, Discogs.com, https://www.discogs.com/artist/758113-Stephan-Weiss.

14. "Bernie Baum; Songwriter of the '50s and '60s," *Los Angeles Times*, September 2, 1993.

15. Ennis, *The Seventh Stream*.

16. "Record Review," *Billboard*, January 21, 1950.

17. "Record Possibilities," *Billboard*, February 11, 1950.

18. "Round the Wax Circle," *Cash Box*, January 21, 1950.

19. "Wurlitzer Entertains Artists," *Cash Box*, November 11, 1950.

20. Interview with Bill Munroe, 1990.

21. David Laing, "Teresa Brewer, Popular Singer with Influential Hits on Both Sides of the Atlantic," *The Guardian*, October 18, 2007.

22. "Teresa Brewer," *Hit Parader*, July 1954.

23. "Record Possibilities," *Billboard*, March 25, 1950.

24. "Record Reviews/Disk of the Week," *Cash Box*, April 1, 1950.

25. "London's Brewer Disk of 'Music' Hits Million Sale," *Billboard*, April 22, 1950.

26. "Teresa Brewer Ears 'Choo'n Gum' Winner," *Cash Box*, May 20, 1950.

27. "Teresa Brewer: Her Life and Career."

28. "Record Possibilities," *Billboard*, October 28, 1950.

29. Mark Clague, "About Bennie and Martha," Bennie and Martha Benjamin Foundation, http://benniebenjaminfoundation.org/about-bennie-and-martha/. "Top 100 Pop Songs in 1950," Playback.fm, https://playback.fm/charts/top-100-songs/1950.

30. "Nation's Top Ten Jukebox Tunes," *Billboard*, March 18, 1950.

31. "Record Reviews/Disk of the Week," *Cash Box*, April 1, 1950.

32. Ed Ward, *Rock of Ages: The Rolling Stone History of Rock & Roll*, Summit Books, 1986.

33. Gillett, *The Sound of the City*.

34. Beverly Warren, interview.

35. Bill Janovitz, "Hank Williams: Cold Cold Heart," song review, www.allmusic.com.

CHAPTER TWO: COME ON-A MY HOUSE (1951)

1. Railroad Jack, "1950s Teens," flickr.com, https://www.flickr.com/photos/blast_of_the_past/5877853392/.

2. "Music as Written," *Billboard*, May 6, 1950.

3. "Music as Written," *Billboard*, September 16, 1950.

4. Jerome, Dan, "Too Young . . . Too Young . . . ," *TV Star Parade*, June 1950.

5. "Teresa Brewer: Her Life and Career."

6. "Teresa Brewer: The Squeak That Made Good," *Look*, April 1950.

7. Reece Choules, "The Rise and Fall of London Records," Culture Trip, https://theculturetrip.com/europe/united-kingdom/england/london/articles/the-rise-and-fall-of-london-records/.

8. Jerome, "Too Young . . . Too Young . . ."

9. "Just Plain Bill's."

10. Bill Munroe, interview.

11. "Just Plain Bill's."

12. Jerome, "Too Young . . . Too Young . . ."

13. Frances Kish, "She Follows Her Heart Home," *TV-Radio Mirror*, September 1959.

14. Dick Reddy, "What Makes Teresa Tops?" *Compact: The Young People's Digest*, December 1956.

15. "Just Plain Bill's."

16. Kish, "She Follows Her Heart Home."

17. "Teresa Brewer: The Squeak That Made Good."

18. Jerome, "Too Young . . . Too Young . . ."

19. "Record Reviews/Disk of the Week," *Cash Box*, January 20, 1951.

20. "What's Happened to the Girl Singers?," *Cash Box*, May 5, 1951.

21. Richard Buskin, "Classic Tracks: Les Paul & Mary Ford, 'How High the Moon,'" Sound on Sound, https://www.soundonsound.com/techniques/classic-tracks-les-paul-mary -ford-how-high-moon.

22. Ennis, *The Seventh Stream*.

23. Nelson George, *The Death of Rhythm & Blues*, Pantheon Books, 1988.

24. Rosemary Clooney and Joan Barthel, *Girl Singer: An Autobiography*, Broadway Books, 1999.

25. "Most Played Juke Box Records," *Billboard*, July 28, 1951.

26. "Most Played Juke Box Records," *Billboard*, July 28, 1951.

27. Clooney and Barthel, *Girl Singer*.

28. Clooney and Barthel, *Girl Singer*.

29. "Lone but Only London Has Longing for You," *Billboard*, August 4, 1951.

30. "Record Review/Sleeper of the Week," *Cash Box*, February 3, 1951.

31. "Miss Music Teresa Brewer," *Billboard*, February 10, 1951.

32. "Best Selling Pop Singles," *Billboard*, March 24, 1951.

33. "Record Review/Disk of the Week," *Cash Box*, August 4, 1951.

34. "Coral Signs Teresa Brewer; Decca Acquires New Artists," *Cash Box*, September 29, 1951.

CHAPTER THREE: YOU BELONG TO ME (1952)

1. "Juke Box Disk Purchases Up to 50,000,000 a Year," *Billboard*, January 19, 1952.

2. Johnny Whiteside, *Cry: The Johnnie Ray Story*, Barricade Books, New York, 1994.

3. "Rhythm & Blues Record Reviews," *Billboard*, August 18, 1951.

4. Whiteside, *Cry: The Johnnie Ray Story*.

5. Myrna Greene, *The Eddie Fisher Story*, Paul S. Eriksson, Middlebury, Vermont, 1978.

6. Beverly Warren, interview.

7. Clague, "About Bennie and Martha."

8. Larry Birnbaum, *Before Elvis: The Prehistory of Rock 'n' Roll*, Scarecrow Press, Lanham, Maryland, 2013.

9. Tim Weisberg, interview.

10. Tom Bialoglow, interview.

11. Pee Wee King, Country Music Hall of Fame, http://countrymusichalloffame.org/full-list -of-inductees/view/pee-wee-king.

12. "Jo Stafford & Paul Weston Wed," *Cash Box*, March 15, 1952.

13. Gene Lees, "G.I. Joe," *Singers and the Songs*, Oxford University Press, 2012.

14. "Sleeper of the Week," *Cash Box*, July 6, 1952.

15. "Regional Record Report," *Cash Box*, October 18, 1952.

16. Spencer Leigh, "Jo Stafford: Multi-million-selling hit singer who with 'You Belong to Me' was the first woman to top the UK charts," *Independent*, July 19, 2008.

17. "Biography," Paul Weston and Jo Stafford Collection, University of Arizona/Collection of Fine Arts/School Music, http://collections.music.arizona.edu/westonstafford/Jo/Biography.

18. Kitty Kelley, *His Way: The Unauthorized Biography of Frank Sinatra*, Bantam Books, 1986.

19. Geoffrey Stokes, *Rock of Ages: The Rolling Stone History of Rock 'n' Roll*, Rolling Stone Press/Summit Books, New York, 1986.

20. Virginia McPherson, "Hill-Billy Tunes Get Hot on Record Parade," *Santa Cruz Sentinel*, July 27, 1947.

21. "Jo Stafford Inks 4-Year CBS-TV, $1,000,000 Deal," *Variety*, September 16, 1953.

22. Jim Stewart, interview.

23. Record Reviews," *Cash Box*, October 18, 1952.

24. "Thru the Coin Chute: California Clippings," *Cash Box*, December 13, 1952.

25. Jim Stewart, interview.

26. "McKenzie Replaces Valli," *Cash Box*, June 6, 1953.

27. Stacia Proefrock, "Roy Hogsed," Allmusic, https://www.allmusic.com/artist/roy-hogsed -mn0000850303.

28. "Milton Kellem," Discogs, https://www.discogs.com/artist/801176-Milton-Kellem.

29. "Music Popularity Charts," *Billboard*, April 5, 1952.

30. "Teresa's Terrific on Her New Release/Coral Introduces," *Billboard*, June 21, 1952.

31. Len Brown and Gary Friedrich, *Encyclopedia of Rock & Roll*, Tower Books, 1970.

CHAPTER FOUR: TILL I WALTZ AGAIN WITH YOU (1953)

1. "Co-wrote music and lyrics for Tony winners 'Pajama Game' and 'Damn Yankees,'" Songwriters Hall of Fame, https://www.songhall.org/profile/Richard_Adler.

2. Patti Page with Skip Press, *This Is My Song: A Memoir*, Kathdan Books, 2009.

3. Donna Loren, interview.

4. Diane Renay, interview.

5. "Teresa Brewer Sings, Sings, Sings," *Cash Box*, December 24, 1951.

6. "Teresa Brewer," *Popular Songs*, February 1952.

7. "Lovin' Machine by Teresa Brewer," January 16, 2009, YouTube, https://www.youtube.com/ watch?v=BD5jDxcO-yA.

8. "Sleeper of the Week," *Cash Box*, September 13, 1952.

9. "Sleeper of the Week," *Cash Box*, November 1, 1952.

10. Kish, "She Follows Her Heart Home."

11. Reddy, "What Makes Teresa Tops?"

12. "Teresa Brewer," *Songs That Will Live Forever*, January 1956.

13. Reddy, "What Makes Teresa Tops?"

14. Bill Munroe, "A Wonderful Hobby: A Conversation with Teresa . . ." 1990.

15. Bob Thiele and Bob Golden, *What a Wonderful World*, Oxford University Press, 1995.

16. "Milt Gabler Named A&R Head of Decca; Bob Thiele Takes Over at Coral," *Cash Box*, June 6, 1953.

17. "Music as Written," *Billboard*, August 1, 1953.

18. "'Ricochet's' Ricocheting Over: Sheldon, Coral, Cap End Fuss," *Billboard*, August 22, 1953.

19. "Teresa Brewer's Ricochet," *Billboard*, August 29, 1953.

20. Kish, "She Follows Her Heart Home."

21. Bob Thiele, Bob Golden, *What a Wonderful World*, Oxford University Press, 1995.

22. "Teresa Brewer," *Hit Parader*, July 1954.

23. "Hit Parade Renewed," *San Mateo Times*, August 30, 1952.

24. Al Morton, "Television Is a Gluttonous Monster in a Field of Drama," *Delaware County Daily Times*, June 4, 1953.

25. "This Week's New Releases on RCA Victor," *Billboard*, January 19, 1952.

26. Joe Csida, "Billboard Backstage," *Billboard*, June 28, 1952.

27. "Record Review," *Billboard*, June 21, 1952.

28. Sandra Pesman, "June Valli: Heading for 2nd Time at the Top," Raleigh Register (from *Chicago Daily News*), April 30, 1975.

29. "Music as Written," *Billboard*, November 1, 1952.

30. "Joni's Musical Journey," Joni's World, www.joniejames.com.

31. Joni James, "Why Don't You Believe Me," Amazon Music, www.amazon.com/why-don't -you-believe-me-/dp/B009E7B10.

32. "Music as Written," *Billboard*, April 19, 1952.

33. "Music Popularity Charts, *Billboard*, April 16, 1952.

34. "Joni James," *Billboard*, September 27, 1952.

35. "Joni James," *Billboard*, September 27, 1952.

36. "Platter Spinner Planner," *Cash Box*, December 20, 1952.

37. "Another Smash Hit from America's Newest Singing Sensation!" *Cash Box*, December 20, 1952.

38. "Many Are Called, But Few Chosen: Few New Diskery Artists Able to Hit Big Time in '52," *Billboard*, January 3, 1952.

39. Birnbaum, *Before Elvis: The Prehistory of Rock 'n' Roll*.

40. Tom Bialoglow, interview.

41. Lindsay Planer, "Joni James: *Platinum & Gold: The MGM Years*," review, Allmusic, www .allmusic.com/album/platinum-gold-the-mgm-years-mw0000225064.

42. Phil Roura, "One from Her Heart: Joni James Returns to the Spotlight," *New York Daily News*, September 22, 1996.

CHAPTER FIVE: LITTLE THINGS MEAN A LOT (1954)

1. Bill Haley Jr. with Peter Benjaminson, *Crazy Man, Crazy*, Backbeat Books, Guilford, Connecticut, 2019.

2. "Reviews of New Pop Records," *Billboard*, May 15, 1954.

3. "Decca," *Billboard*, June 5, 1954.

4. Haley and Benjaminson, *Crazy Man, Crazy*.

5. Ward, *Rock of Ages*.

6. Marv Goldberg, "The Chords," Schooltime Compositions, 2003 and 2009, http://www.uncamarvy.com/Chords/chords.html.

7. Ward, *Rock of Ages*.

8. Richard Patterson, Bart Shevory, John Young, and Joe Matthews, "Crew Cuts," Canadian Pop Encyclopedia, https://archive.is/20120717191834/http://jam.canoe.ca/Music/Pop_Encyclopedia/C/Crew_Cuts.html.

9. Ennis, *The Seventh Stream*.

10. Birnbaum, *Before Elvis: The Prehistory of Rock 'n' Roll*.

11. "Record Review," *Billboard*, May 13, 1950.

12. Liner notes, Kitty Kallen, *A Lonesome Old Town*, LP, Decca Records, 1956.

13. Adam Bernstein, "Kitty Kallen, silken-voice pop singer of 'Little Things Mean a Lot,' dies at 94," *Washington Post*, January 7, 2016.

14. "The Nightclub Reviews," *Billboard*, July 16, 1949.

15. Jack Gaver, "Kitty Kallen Solo Star Now," United Press International/*Pittsburgh Press*, November 6, 1949.

16. "In Short," *Billboard*, January 28, 1950.

17. "Music as Written," *Billboard*, July 9, 1949.

18. "B. Granoff, TV Syndicator, Agent," *Sun-Sentinel*, May 2, 1996.

19. JC Marion, "Kitty Kallen," Wayback Machine, 2002, https://web.archive.org/web/20160305074452/http://home.earthlink.net/~jaymar41/kallen.html.

20. Kelley, *His Way*.

21. "Edith Lineman Calisch, critic and lyricist, dies," *Richmond Times-Dispatch*, December 24, 1984.

22. "Round the Wax Circle," *Cash Box*, January 8, 1955.

23. "Review Spotlight On," *Billboard*, February 5, 1955.

24. "The Cash Box London Low Down," *Cash Box*, May 21, 1955.

25. "Kitty Kallen Suffering Paralyzed Vocal Cords," Jefferson City *Daily Capital News*, January 26, 1963.

26. "Thru the Coin Chute: New England Nibbles," *Cash Box*, July 16, 1955.

27. Bernstein, "Kitty Kallen."

28. Bob Thiele and Bob Golden, *What a Wonderful World*, Oxford University Press, 1995.

29. "TV Plug Creates Unprecedented Demand for New Record; Top Names Covering 'Let Me Go,'" *Cash Box*, November 21, 1954.

30. Jason Ankeny, "Joan Weber," Allmusic, https://www.allmusic.com/artist/joan-weber-mn0000135658/biography.

31. "Girl Born to Singer Joan Weber in N.J.," *Morning News*, Wilmington, Delaware, November 24, 1954.

32. "Disk of the Week," *Cash Box*, December 4, 1954.

33. Bill Munroe, "A Wonderful Hobby: A Conversation with Teresa . . . ," 1990.

34. Thiele and Golden, *What a Wonderful World*.

35. "Round the Wax Circle," *Cash Box*, December 11, 1954.

36. "Round the Wax Circle," *Cash Box*, December 18, 1954.

37. "Disk Jockey Regional Record Reports," *Cash Box*, December 25, 1954.

38. Thiele and Golden, *What a Wonderful World*.

39. Munroe, "A Wonderful Hobby."

40. Mitch Miller, "Television Academy Foundation Interviews," Television Academy Foundation, https://interviews.televisionacademy.com/interviews/mitch-miller.

41. "Popularity Poll Winners," *Song Hits*, June 1954.

42. "Reviews of New Pop Records," *Billboard*, April 3, 1954.

43. Jerome, "Too Young . . . Too Young . . ."

44. Jack K. Paquette, *Small Town Girl*, Xlibris, 2013.

45. Seymour Rothman, "Teresa: Still Feeding Nickels in the Nickelodeon," *Blade Sunday Magazine, Toledo Blade*, November 4, 1973.

46. Wanda Cook, "Teresa Brewer: Still Toledo's Little Girl," *Blade Sunday Magazine, Toledo Blade*, November 16, 1980.

47. Thiele and Golden, *What a Wonderful World*.

48. Cook, "Teresa Brewer: Still Toledo's Little Girl."

49. Munroe, "A Wonderful Hobby."

CHAPTER SIX: DANCE WITH ME HENRY (WALLFLOWER) (1955)

1. Etta James with David Ritz, *Rage to Survive: The Etta James Story*, Da Capo Press, 1995.

2. Ward, *Rock of Ages*.

3. Gillett, *The Sound of the City*.

4. Ward, *Rock of Ages*.

5. Ruth Brown with Andrew Yule, *The Autobiography of Ruth Brown, Rhythm & Blues Legend*, Donald I. Fine Books, 1996.

6. Mark Sendoff, interview.

7. Clooney and Barthel, *Girl Singer*.

8. Munroe, "A Wonderful Hobby."

9. Karen Schoemer, *Great Pretenders: My Strange Love Affair with '50s Pop Music*, Free Press, 2006.

10. Adam Bernstein, "Georgia Gibbs, 87; Performed with Big Bands and on Radio Shows," *Washington Post*, December 12, 2006.

11. "Jo," Music in the Modern Manner—The Hudson-DeLange Orchestra (1936–38), Keep (It) Swinging.

12. "Victor Inks Gibbs, Adds Other Talent," *Billboard*, April 13, 1957.

13. Stephen Miller, "Georgia Gibbs, 87, Bubbly Singer in the 1940 and 1950s," *New York Sun*, December 12, 2006.

14. "Review Spotlight on . . . ," *Billboard*, February 26, 1955.

15. Gillian Garr, *She's A Rebel: The History of Women in Rock 'n' Roll*, Seal Press, 1992.

16. Victor Livingston, "Fontaine [*sic*] Sisters Spend Yule with Parents in Cornwall," *Newburgh News*, December 26, 1951.

17. May Okon, "They Have Hair Harmony, Too," *New York Sunday News*, February 20, 1955.

18. Television-Radio, *Billboard*, January 6, 1951.

19. "Going Strong," *Billboard*, February 17, 1951.

20. "Record Reviews," *Cash Box*, June 23, 1951.

21. "Record Reviews," *Cash Box*, March 17, 1951.

22. "The Billboard Annual Disk Jockey Poll," *Billboard*, September 15, 1951.

23. "Dot Records Ink Term Pact with Fontane Sisters," *Billboard*, April 17, 1954.

24. Ennis, *The Seventh Stream*.

25. Birnbaum, *Before Elvis: The Prehistory of Rock 'n' Roll*.

26. Gillett, *The Sound of the City*.

27. "Best Buys," *Billboard*, January 15, 1955.

28. Preston Lauterbach, *The Chitlin' Circuit and the Road to Rock 'n' Roll*, W. W. Norton, 2011.

29. "Brewer," *Billboard*, February 26, 1955.

30. Munroe, "A Wonderful Hobby."

CHAPTER SEVEN: A SWEET OLD FASHIONED GIRL (1956)

1. Munroe, "A Wonderful Hobby."

2. Cook, "Teresa Brewer: Still Toledo's Little Girl with Big Voice."

3. Munroe, "A Wonderful Hobby."

4. "Life," Teresa Brewer Center, www.teresafans.org.

5. Reddy, "What Makes Teresa Tops?"

6. "Popularity Poll Winners," *Song Hits Magazine*, June 1955.

7. "Life," Teresa Brewer Center, www.teresafans.org.

8. Reddy, "What Makes Teresa Tops?"

9. Kathleen Monahan, email interview.

10. Reddy, "What Makes Teresa Tops?"

11. Pogie Joe, "Mrs. Sandman: A Chat with the Chordettes' Lynn Evans," YouTube.

12. Ken Emerson, *Always Magic in the Air: The Bomp and Brilliance of the Brill Building Era*, Penguin Books, 2005.

13. Pogie Joe, "Mrs. Sandman: A Chat with the Chordettes' Lynn Evans."

14. Emerson, *Always Magic in the Air*.

15. John Bush, "Patience and Prudence," AllMusic, www.allmusic.com.

16. Len Brown, Gary Friedrich, Encyclopedia of Rock & Roll, A Tower Book, 1970.

17. Zac Johnson, "The Dinning Sisters," AllMusic, www.allmusic.com.

18. "Cathy Carr Launches New Carnival Policy," *Pittsburgh Post-Gazette*, May 4, 1954.

19. "Music as Written," *Billboard*, March 10, 1956.

20. "Cathy Carr Plugs 'Tower,'" *Billboard*, March 31, 1956.

21. "This Week's Best Buys," *Billboard*, March 31, 1956.

22. "Review Spotlight On . . . ," *Billboard*, April 7, 1956.

23. "Canadian Capers," *Cash Box*, November 17, 1956.

24. "Cathy Carr Skyrockets 'Ivory Tower' into Gold Mine," *Cash Box*, June 23, 1956.

25. Fred Bronson, *The Billboard Book of Number One Hits*, Billboard Publications, 1985.

26. Erskine Johnson, "In Hollywood Today," *Lawton Constitution and Morning Press*, August 4, 1957.

27. Bronson, *The Billboard Book of Number One Hits*.

28. Eleanor Knowles, "Singer, Composer Meet in S.L.," *Deseret News*, July 14, 1956.

29. "Juke Box Regional Record Report," *Cash Box*, May 19, 1956.

30. Knowles, "Singer, Composer Meet in S.L."

31. Matthew C. Foley, "Who is Kay Starr?" https://www.members.tripod.com/~Kay_Starr/biography.html.

32. Birnbaum, *Before Elvis: The Prehistory of Rock 'n' Roll.*

33. Bob Rolontz, "Rhythm & Blues," *Billboard*, March 15, 1956.

34. "Review Spotlight On . . ." *Billboard*, December 10, 1955.

35. "Honor Roll of Hits," *Billboard*, January 7, 1956.

36. "Best Selling Pop Records in Britain," *Billboard*, April 7, 1956.

37. Preston Lauterbach, *The Chitlin' Circuit and the Road to Rock 'n' Roll*, W. W. Norton, 2011.

38. Margaret Jones, *Patsy: The Life and Times of Patsy Cline*, HarperCollins, 1994.

39. Mike Palermo, interview.

40. David Kaufman, *Doris Day: The Untold Story of the Girl Nex Door*, Virgin Books, 2008.

CHAPTER EIGHT: TAMMY (1957)

1. Peter Guralnick, *Last Train to Memphis: The Rise of Elvis Presley*, Little Brown, 1994.

2. Maury Dean, *Rock 'N' Roll Gold Rush: A Singles Un-cyclopedia*, Algora Publishing, 2008.

3. "Life," Teresa Brewer Center, www.teresafans.org.

4. "Teresa Brewer: The Squeak That Made Good," *Look*, 1957.

5. "Teen Top Pop Poll," *Teen*, February 1958.

6. Patti Page with Slip Press, *This Is My Song: A Memoir*, Kathdan Books, 2009.

7. Mike Glynn, interview.

8. Page with Press, *This Is My Song: A Memoir.*

9. Mozabilly, "Barry Sisters," October 31, 2008, http://donttellyourfriends.blogspot.com.

10. Mike Glynn, interview.

11. David Dachs, "The Story behind Those Golden Records," *Rome News-Tribune*, May 10, 1959.

12. Milton Yakus, https://www.discogs.com/artist/693363-Milton-Yakus.

13. "Old Cape Cod," Wikipedia, https://en.wikipedia.org/wiki/Old_Cape_Cod.

14. Steve Desroches, "Old Cape Cod Turns 50," *Provincetown Banner*, November 29, 2007.

15. Schoemer, *Great Pretenders: My Strange Love Affair with '50s Pop Music.*

16. Bronson, *The Billboard Book of Number One Hits.*

17. Thiele and Golden, *What a Wonderful World.*

18. "Coinmen You Know," *Billboard*, June 17, 1957.

19. "Coral Records, Hot Parade," *Billboard*, July 15, 1957.

20. "Coral Records, Hot Parade," *Billboard*, July 15, 1957.

21. "Honor Roll of Hits," *Billboard*, July 22, 1957.

22. "1957 Top Tunes," *Billboard*, November 11, 1957.

23. "Golden Wax: Awards Go To 4 Coral Top Artists," *Billboard*, October 28, 1957.

24. David Tucker, *The Women Who Made Television Funny: Ten Stars of 1950s Sitcoms*, McFarland, 2007.

25. Ephraim Katz, *The Film Encyclopedia*, Thomas Y. Crowell, 1979.

26. Joseph Murrells, *The Book of Golden Discs*, Barrie & Jenkins, 1978.

27. Jeff Hannusch, *I Hear You Knockin': The Sound of New Orleans Rhythm and Blues*, Swallow Publications, 1985.

28. Rick Coleman, *Blue Monday: Fats Domino and the Lost Dawn of Rock 'n' Roll*, Da Capo Press, 2006.

29. Michael Rietmulder, "Bonnie Guitar, Pioneering Renaissance Woman in Music, Dies at 95," *Seattle Times*, January 16, 2019.

30. "Doris Day Discography," Wikipedia, https://en.wikipedia.org/wiki/Doris_Day_discography.

31. Eric Braun, *Doris Day*, Orion, 2010.

32. Carrie Rickey, "Actress Doris Day Dies at 97," *Philadelphia Inquirer*, May 13, 2019.

33. Kaufman, *Doris Day: The Untold Story of the Girl Next Door*.

CHAPTER NINE: SUGARTIME (1958)

1. Beverly Lee, interview.

2. John Clemente, *Girl Groups: Fabulous Females That Rocked the World*, Krause Publications, 2000.

3. Ren Grevatt, "On the Beat," *Billboard*, October 20, 1958.

4. Carol Connors, interview.

5. Connie Francis, *Who's Sorry Now*, St. Martin's Press, 1984.

6. Ren Grevatt, "On the Beat," *Billboard*, October 20, 1958.

7. "Review Spotlight On . . ." *Billboard*, February 23, 1957.

8. Jim Stewart, interview.

9. David Williamson, interview.

10. Phyllis McGuire, email question and answer.

11. Jim Stewart, interview.

12. Phyllis McGuire, email question and answer.

13. Thiele and Golden, *What a Wonderful World*.

14. Jim Stewart, interview.

15. "Country Reviews," *Cash Box*, November 16, 1957.

16. "The Cash Box Disk of the Week," *Cash Box*, December 7, 1957.

17. "Coral," *Billboard*, December 23, 1957.

18. "30 Popular Hits," *Billboard*, February 15, 1958.

19. "Biography," Jaye P. Morgan: The Official Website, https://jayepmorgan.com/bio/.

20. Kim Summers, "Jaye P. Morgan Biography," Allmusic, www.allmusic.com.

21. "Jane Morgan," Biography, IMDb, https://www.imdb.com.

22. "Jane Morgan Biography," Oldies.com, https://www.oldies.com/artist-biography/Jane-Morgan.html.

23. "The Billboard Eleventh Annual Disk Jockey Poll," *Billboard*, December 13, 1958.

24. Garry McGee, *Doris Day: Sentimental Journey*, McFarland, 2005.

25. David Kaufman, *Doris Day: The Untold Story of the Girl Next Door*, Virgin Books, 2009.

26. "The Cash Box Disk of the Week," *Cash Box*, June 28, 1958.

27. Beverly Lee, interview.

28. John Fordham, "Peggy Lee," *The Guardian*, January 22, 2002.

29. Kelley, *His Way: The Unauthorized Biography of Frank Sinatra*.

30. Emerson, *Always Magic in the Air*.

31. "Hula Hoop," How Products Are Made, www.madehow.com/Volume-6/Hula-Hoop.html.

32. Schoemer, *Great Pretenders: My Strange Love Affair with '50s Pop Music.*

33. Mike Streissguth, "Betty Johnson," Wayback Machine, https://web.archive.org.

34. Schoemer, *Great Pretenders: My Strange Love Affair with '50s Pop Music.*

35. "The Ramblings," *Cash Box*, October 18, 1958.

36. "Canadian Capers," *Cash Box*, November 1, 1958.

CHAPTER TEN: BLAME IT ON THE BOSSA NOVA (1959 AND BEYOND)

1. "Life," Teresa Brewer Center, www.teresafans.org.

2. "Teresa Brewer Won't Quit—NBC Fires Her," *New York Daily News* (possibly *New York Post*), July 6, 1959.

3. "'Amazed,' Says Singer: Como Show Fires Teresa Brewer," *Boston Globe*, July 6, 1959.

4. "Teresa Brewer Won't Quit—NBC Fires Her."

5. "Feelings Hurt, Singer Fired Before She Can Quit TV," source unknown.

6. "Teresa Brewer Won't Quit—NBC Fires Her."

7. "'Amazed,' Says Singer: Como Show Fires Teresa Brewer."

8. "Teresa Brewer Won't Quit—NBC Fires Her."

9. "Torch Singer: Mindy Carson, pride of the Bronx, rockets herself into the bigtime," *Life*, September 26, 1949.

10. "Mindy Carson's 5-Yr. NBC Pact," *Billboard*, August 20, 1949.

11. Douglas Gomery, "Dinah Shore," Museum of Broadcast Communications, http://museum.tv/archives/etv/S/htmlS/shoredinah/shoredinah.htm.

12. Greene, *The Eddie Fisher Story.*

13. Gomery, "Dinah Shore."

14. "The Six-Gun Galahad," *Time*, March 30, 1959.

15. Neil Sedaka, interview.

16. William Ruhlman, "Eydie Gorme," Allmusic, https://www.allmusic.com/artist/eydie-gorme-mn0000128249/biography.

17. Saeed Ahmed, "Singer Eydie Gorme Dies at 84," CNN, August 11, 2013.

18. Neil Sedaka, interview.

19. Emerson, *Always Magic in the Air.*

20. Margaret Williams, interview.

21. Donna Loren, interview.

22. Mark Sendoff, interview.

23. Neil Sedaka, interview.

24. Thiele and Golden, *What a Wonderful World.*

25. Bill Munroe, interview.

26. Thiele and Golden, *What a Wonderful World.*

27. Munroe, "A Wonderful Hobby."

28. Thiele and Golden, *What a Wonderful World.*

29. Page with Press, *This Is My Song: A Memoir.*

30. Clooney and Barthel, *Girl Singer.*

31. Munroe, "A Wonderful Hobby."

SELECTED DISCOGRAPHY

Eileen Barton

If I Knew You Were Comin' I'd've Baked a Cake/Poco Loco in the Coco, 1950, National 9103

May I Take Two Giant Steps/If You Saw What I Saw, 1950, National 2069

Cry/Hold Me Just a Little Longer, 1951, Coral 60592

Wishin'/When You're Near Me, 1952, Coral 60651

Pretend/Too Proud to Cry, 1953, Coral 60927

Don't Let the Stars Get in Your Eyes/Tennessee Tango, 1953, Coral 60882

Toys/I Ain't Gonna Do It, 1953, Coral 61019

Don't Ask Me Why/Away Up There, 1954, Coral 61109

Pine Tree, Pine Over Me/Cling to Me (with Johnny Desmond and the McGuire Sisters), 1954, Coral 61126

Sway/When Mama Calls, 1954, Coral 61185

Teresa Brewer

Music! Music! Music!/Copenhagen, 1950, London 604 (78) & 30023 (45)

Choo'n Gum/Honky Tonkin', 1950, London 678 (78) & 30100 (45)

Longing for You/Jazz Me Blues, 1951, London 1086 (78) & 451086 (45)

Gonna Get Along Without Ya Now/Roll Them Roly-Boly Eyes, 1952, Coral 60676

You'll Never Get Away/The Hookey Song (with Don Cornell), 1952, Coral 60829

Till I Waltz Again with You/Hello Bluebird, 1952, Coral 60873

Dancin' with Someone (Longin' for You)/Breakin' in the Blues, 1953, Coral 60953

Into Each Life Some Rain Must Fall/Too Much Mustard, 1953, Coral 60994

Ricochet (Rick-O-Shay)/Too Young to Tango,1953, Coral 61043

Baby Baby Baby/I Guess It Was You All the Time, 1953, Coral 61067

Bell Bottom Blues/Our Heartbreaking Waltz, 1953, Coral 61066

Jilted/Le Grand Tour De L'amour, 1954, Coral 61152

Skinnie Minnie (Fish Tail)/I Had Someone Else before I Had You, 1954, Coral 61197

Let Me Go, Lover!/The Moon Is on Fire, 1954, Coral 61315

Pledging My Love/How Important Can It Be?, 1955, Coral 61362

Silver Dollar/I Don't Want to Be Lonely Tonight, 1955, Coral 61394

The Banjo's Back in Town/How to Be Very, Very Popular, 1955, Coral 61448

Shoot It Again/You're Telling Our Secrets, 1955, Coral 61528

A Tear Fell/Bo Weevil, 1956, Coral 61590

A Sweet Old Fashioned Girl/Goodbye John, 1956, Coral 61636

I Love Mickey (with Mickey Mantle)/Keep Your Cotton Pickin' Paddies Offa My Heart, 1956,
      Coral 61700

Mutual Admiration Society/Crazy with Love, 1956, Coral 61737

Empty Arms/The Ricky-Tick Song, 1957, Coral 61805

Teardrops in My Heart/Lula Rock-A-Hula, 1957, Coral 61850

You Send Me/Would I Were, 1957, Coral 61898

Pick Up a Doodle/The Rain Falls on Ev'rybody, 1958, Coral 62013

The Hula Hoop Song/So Shy, 1958, Coral 62033

The One Rose (That's Left in My Heart)/Satellite, 1959, Coral 62057

Heavenly Lover/Fair Weather Sweetheart, 1959, Coral 62084

Peace of Mind/Venetian Sunset, 1960, Coral 62167

Anymore/That Piano Man, 1960, Coral 62219

Have You Ever Been Lonely/When Do You Love Me, 1960, Coral 62236

Milord/I've Got My Fingers Crossed, 1961, Coral 62265

Cathy Carr

Ivory Tower/Please Please Believe Me, 1956, Fraternity 734

Heart Hideaway/The Boy, 1956, Fraternity, 743

First Anniversary/With Love, 1959, Roulette 4125

I'm Gonna Change Him/The Little Things, 1959, Roulette 4152

Mindy Carson

Candy and Cake/My Foolish Heart, 1950 RCA Victor 47-3204-B

That's A-Why/Train of Love (with Guy Mitchell), 1952, Columbia 39879

All the Time and Everywhere/Barrels 'n Barrels of Roses, 1952, Columbia 39889

Tell Me You're Mine/The Choo Buy Song, 1953, Columbia 39914

Memories Are Made of This/Cryin' for Your Kisses, 1955, Columbia 40573

Wake the Town and Tell the People/Hold Me Tight, 1955, Columbia 40537

The Fish/Bring Me Your Love, 1955, Columbia 40438

Since I Met You Baby, Goodnight My Love, 1956, Columbia 40789

The Chordettes

Mr. Sandman/I Don't Wanna See You Cryin', 1954, Cadence 1247

The Wedding/I Don't Know, I Don't Care, 1956, Cadence 1273

Eddie My Love/Whistlin' Willie, 1956, Cadence 1284

Born to Be with You/Love Never Changes, 1956, Cadence 1291

Lay Down Your Arms/Teen-Age Goodnight, 1956, Cadence 1291

Just Between You and Me/Soft Sands, 1957, Cadence 1330

Lollipop/Baby, Come-A Back-A, 1958, Cadence 1345
Zorro/Love Is a Two-Way Street, 1958, Cadence 1349
No Other Arms, No Other Lips/We Should Be Together, 1959, Cadence 1361
A Girl's Work Is Never Done/No Wheels, 1959, Cadence 1366
Never on Sunday/Faraway Star, 1961, Cadence 1402

Rosemary Clooney

You're Just in Love/Marrying for Love (with Guy Mitchell), 1951, Columbia 39052
Beautiful Brown Eyes/Shot Gun Boogie, 1951, Columbia 39212
Come On-A My House/Rose of the Mountain, 1951, Columbia 39467
Mixed Emotions/Kentucky Waltz, 1951, Columbia 39333
I'm Waiting Just for You/If Teardrops Were Pennies, 1951, Columbia 39535
I Wish I Wuz/Mixed Emotions, 1951, Columbia 39536
Be My Life's Companion/Why Don't You Love Me, 1952, Columbia 39631
Tenderly/Did Anyone Call, 1952, Columbia 39648
Half As Much/Poor Whip-Poor-Will, 1952, Columbia 39710
Botch-A-Me (Ba-Ba-Baciami Piccina)/On the First Warm Day, 1952, Columbia 39767
Too Old to Cut the Mustard/Good for Nothin' (with Marlene Dietrich), 1952, Columbia 39812
Blues in the Night/Who Kissed Me Last Night, 1952, Columbia 39813
The Night before Christmas Song/Look Out the Window, 1952, Columbia 39876
If I Had a Penny/You're After My Own Heart, 1952, Columbia 39892
You'll Never Know/The Continental (with Harry James), 1952, Columbia 39905
Dennis the Menace/Little Josey (with Jimmy Boyd), 1953, Columbia 39988
Happy Christmas, Little Friend/Christmas, 1954, Columbia 40102
Hey There/This Ole House, 1954, Columbia 40266
Sisters (with Betty Clooney)/Love, You Didn't Do Right by Me, 1954, Columbia 40305
Mambo Italiano/We'll Be Together Again, 1954, Columbia 40361
Count Your Blessings (Instead of Sheep)/White Christmas, 1954, Columbia 40370
Pet Me Poppa/Wake Me, 1955, Columbia 40579
The Key to My Heart/A Little Girl at Heart, 1956, Columbia 40619
Memories of You/It's Bad for Me, 1956, Columbia 40616
I Could Have Danced All Night/I've Grown Accustomed to Your Face, 1956, Columbia 40676
Mangos/Independent, 1957, Columbia 40835
Many a Wonderful Moment/Vaya Vaya (Go My Darling Go), 1960, RCA Victor 7754

Doris Day

Quicksilver/There's a Bluebird on Your Windowsill, 1950, Columbia
I Said My Pajamas/Enjoy Yourself, 1950, Columbia 38709
Hoop-De-Do/Marriage Ties, 1950, Columbia 38771
Bewitched/Imagination, Columbia 38698
I Didn't Slip, I Wasn't Pushed, I Fell, 1950, Columbia 38818
A Bushel and a Peck/The Best Thing for You, 1950, Columbia 39008
It's a Lovely Day/Nobody's Chasing Me, 1951, Columbia 39055
Would I Love You (Love You, Love You) (with Harry James)/Do Do Do, 1951, Columbia 39159

Shanghai/Just One of Those Things, 1951, Columbia 39423

Domino/If That Doesn't Do It, 1951, Columbia 39596

A Guy Is a Guy/Who Who Who, 1952, Columbia 39673

Sugarbush/How Lovely Cooks the Meat (with Frankie Laine), 1952, Columbia 39693

When I Fall in Love/Take Me in Your Arms, 1952, Columbia 39786

No Two People/You Can't Lose Me (with Donald O'Connor), 1952, Columbia 39863

A Full Time Job/Ma Says, Pa Says (with Johnnie Ray), 1952, Columbia 39898

Mister Tap Toe/Your Mother and Mine, 1953, Columbia 39906

When the Red, Red, Robin (Comes Bob, Bob, Bobbin' Along)/Beautiful Music to Love By, 1953, Columbia 39970

Candy Lips/Let's Walk That-A-Way (with Johnnie Ray), 1953, Columbia 40001

Kiss Me Again, Stranger/A Purple Cow, 1953, Columbia 40020

Choo Choo Train/This Too Shall Pass, 1953, Columbia 40063

Secret Love/It's Magic, 1954, Columbia 50005

I Speak to the Stars/The Blue Bells of Broadway, 1954, Columbia 40210

If I Give My Heart to You/Anyone Can Fall in Love, 1954, Columbia 40300

I'll Never Stop Loving You/Never Look Back, 1955, Columbia 40505

Ooh Bang Jiggily Jang/Jimmy Unknown, 1955, Columbia 40581

Let It Ring/Love's Little Island, 1956, Columbia 40618

Que Sera, Sera/I've Gotta Sing These Blues Away, 1956, Columbia 40704

Julie/Love in a Home, 1956, Columbia 40758

The Party's Over/What'ja Put in That Kiss, 1956, Columbia 40798

Twelve O'Clock Tonight/Today Will Be Yesterday Tomorrow, 1957, Columbia 40870

Teacher's Pet/Blues in the Night, 1958, 41103

Everybody Loves a Lover/Instant Love, 1958, Columbia 41195

Tunnel of Love/Run Away, Skidaddle, Skidoo, 1958, Columbia 41252

Love Me in the Daytime/He's So Married, 1959, Columbia 41354

Any Way the Wind Blows/Soft as the Starlight, 1960, Columbia 41569

Lover Come Back/Should I Surrender, 1962, Columbia 42295

The DeCastro Sisters

Teach Me Tonight/It's Love, 1954, Abbott 3001

Boom Boom Boomerang/Let Your Love Walk In, Abbott 3003

Fontane Sisters

Tennessee Waltz/I Guess I'll Have to Dream the Rest, 1951, RCA Victor 3979

Castle Rock/Makin' Like a Train, 1951, RCA Victor 4213

Cold, Cold Heart/I Get the Blues When It Rains, 1951, RCA Victor 42274

Happy Days and Lonely Nights/If I Didn't Have You, 1954, Dot 15171

Hearts of Stone/ Bless Your Heart, 1954, Dot 15265

Rock Love/You're Mine, 1955, Dot 15333

Rollin' Stone/Playmates, 1955, Dot 15370

Seventeen/ If I Could Be with You (One Hour Tonight), 1955, Dot 15386

Daddy-O/Adorable, 1955, Dot 15428

Nuttin' for Christmas/Silver Bells, 1955, Dot 15434

Eddie My Love/Yum Yum, 1956, Dot 15450

I'm in Love Again/You Always Hurt the One You Love, 1956, 15462

Voices/Lonesome Lover Blues, 1956, Dot 15480

Please Don't Leave Me/Still, 1956, Dot 15501

Banana Boat Song/Honolulu Moon, 1956, Dot 15527

I'm Stickin' with You/Let the Rest of the World Go By, 1957, Dot 15555

Chanson D'Amour/Cocoanut Grove, 1958, 15736

Jealous Heart/Encore D'Amour, 1958, Dot 15853

Georgia Gibbs

If I Knew You Were Comin' I'd've Baked a Cake/Stay with Happy People, 1950, Coral 60169

Simple Melody/A Little Bit Independent, 1950, Coral 60227

I Still Feel the Same about You/Get Out Those Old Records, 1951, Coral 60653

Tom's Tune/I Wish, I Wish, 1951, Mercury 5644

Good Morning Mr. Echo/Be Doggone Sure You Call, 1951, Mercury 5662

While You Danced, Danced, Danced/While We're Young, 1951, Mercury 5681

Cry/My Old Flame, 1951, Mercury 5759

Kiss of Fire, A Lasting Thing, 1952, Mercury 5823

So Madly in Love/Make Me Love You, 1952, Mercury 5874

My Favorite Song/Sinner or Saint, 1952, Mercury 5912

Seven Lonely Days/If You Take My Heart Away, 1953, Mercury 70095

For Me, for You/Thunder and Lightning, 1953, Mercury 70172

The Bridge of Sighs/A Home Lovin' Man, 1953, Mercury 70238

Somebody Bad Stole De Wedding Bell/Baubles, Bangles and Beads, 1954, Mercury 70298

My Sin/I'll Always Be Happy with You, 1954, Mercury 70339

Wait For Me, Darling/Whistle and I'll Dance, 1954, Mercury70386

Tweedle Dee/You're Wrong, All Wrong, 1955, Mercury 70517

Dance with Me Henry (Wallflower)/Every Road Must Have a Turning, 1955, Mercury 70572

Sweet and Gentle/Blueberries, 1955, Mercury 70647

I Want You to Be My Baby/Come Rain or Come Shine, 1955, Mercury 70685

Goodbye to Rome/24 Hours a Day, 1955, Mercury 70743

Rock Right/The Greatest Thing, 1956, Mercury 70811

Kiss Me Another/Fool of the Year, 1956, Mercury 70850

Happiness Street/Happiness Is a Thing Called Joe, 1956, Mercury 70920

Tra La La/Morning, Noon and Night, 1956, Mercury 70998

Silent Lips/Pretty Pretty, 1957, Mercury 71058

I'm Walking the Floor Over You/Sugar Candy, 1957, RCA Victor 6922

The Hula Hoop Song/Keep in Touch, 1958, Roulette 4106

Eydie Gormé

Fini/Gimme Gimme John, 1954, Coral 61093

Too Close for Comfort/That's How, 1956, ABC-Paramount 9684

Mama, Teach Me to Dance/You Bring Out the Lover in Me, 1956, ABC-Paramount 9722

I'll Take Romance/First Impression, 1957, ABC-Paramount 9780

You're Kisses Kill Me/Kiss in Your Eyes, 1957, ABC Paramount 9817

Love Me Forever/Let Me Be Loved, 1957, ABC-Paramount 9863

You Need Hands/Dormi-Dormi-Dormi, 1958, ABC-Paramount 9925

Gotta Have Rain/To You, from Me, 1958, ABC-Paramount 9944

The Voice in My Heart/Separate Tables, 1958, ABC-Paramount 9971

Blame It on the Bossa Nova/Guess I Should Have Loved Him More, 1963, Columbia 42661

Don't Try to Fight It, Baby/Theme from Light Fantastic, 1963, Columbia 42790

Everybody Go Home/The Message, 1963, Columbia 42854

I Want You to Meet My Baby/Can't Get Over (The Bossa Nova), 1964, Columbia 43082

Tonight I Say a Prayer/Wild One, 1969, RCA 0250

Gogi Grant

Suddenly There's a Valley/Love Is, 1955, Era 1003

Who Are We/We Believe in Love, 1956, Era 1008

The Wayward Wind/No More Than Forever, 1956, Era 1013

You're in Love/When the Tide Is High, 1956, Era 1019

Strange Are the Ways of Love/Marjolaina, 1958, RCA Victor 47-7294

Bonnie Guitar

Dark Moon/Big Mike, 1957, Dot 15550

Mister Fire Eyes/There's a Moon Over My Shoulder, 1957, Dot 15612

I'm Living in Two Worlds/Goodtime Charlie, 1965, Dot 16811

Joni James

Why Don't You Believe Me/Purple Shades, 1952, MGM 11333

Have You Heard/Wishing Ring, 1953, MGM 11390

Your Cheatin' Heart/I'll Be Waiting for You, 1953, MGM 11426

Almost Always/Is It Any Wonder, 1953, MGM 11470

My Love, My Love/You're Fooling Someone, 1953, MGM 11543

I'll Never Stand in Your Way/Why Can't I, 1953, MGM 11606

Nina-Non/Christmas and You, 1953, MGM 11637

Maybe Next Time/Am I in Love, 1954, MGM 11696

In a Garden of Roses/Every Day, 1954, MGM 11753

Mama Don't Cry at My Wedding/Pa Pa Pa, 1954, MGM 11802

When We Come of Age/Every Time You Tell Me You Love Me, 1954, MGM 11865

How Important Can It Be?/This Is My Confession, 1955, MGM 11919

You Are My Love/I Lay Me Down to Sleep, 1955, MGM 12066

My Believing Heart/You Never Fall in Love Again, 1955, MGM 12126

Don't Tell Me Not to Love You/Somewhere Someone Is Lonely, 1956, MGM 12175

I Woke Up Crying/The Maverick Queen, 1956, MGM 12213

Give Us This Day/How Lucky You Are, 1956, MGM 12288

Summer Love/I'm Sorry for You My Friend, 1957, MGM 12480

There Goes My Heart/Funny, 1958, MGM 12706

There Must Be a Way/Sorry for Myself, 1959, MGM 12746

I Still Get a Thrill/Perhaps, 1959, MGM 12779

I Still Get Jealous/Prayer of Love, 1959, MGM 12807

Little Things Mean a Lot/I Laughed at Love, 1959, MGM 12849

I Need You Now/You Belong to Me, 1960, MGM 12885

My Last Date with You/I Can't Give You Anything but Love, 1960, MGM 12933

Betty Johnson

I Want Eddie Fisher for Christmas/Show Me, 1954, New-Disc 5082

I Dreamed/If It's Wrong to Love You, 1956, Bally 7-1020

Little White Lies/1492, 1957, Bally 1033

Little Blue Man/Winter in Miami, 1958, Atlantic 1169

Kitty Kallen

Juke Box Annie/Choo'n Gum, 1950, Mercury 5417

Our Lady of Fatima/Honestly, I Love You, 1950, Mercury 5466

Aba Daba Honeymoon/I Don't Want to Love You, 1951, Mercury 5586

Are You Looking for a Sweetheart?/A Little Lie, 1953, Decca 28904

Little Things Mean a Lot/I Don't Think You Love Me Anymore, 1954, Decca 29037

In the Chapel in the Moonlight/Take Everything but You, 1954, Decca 29130

I Want You All to Myself (Just You)/Don't Let the Kiddy Geddin, 1954, Decca 29268

Sweet Kentucky Rose/How Lonely Can I Get, 1955, Decca 29708

Go On with the Wedding/The Second Greatest Sex, 1956, Decca 29776

If I Give My Heart to You/The Door That Won't Open, 1959, Columbia 41473

My Coloring Book/Here's to Us, 1962, RCA Victor 47-8124

Peggy Lee

The Old Master Painter/Bless You, 1950, Capitol 5218

Show Me the Way to Get Out of This World/Happy Music, 1950, Capitol 6140

(When I Dance with You) I Get Ideas/Tonight You Belong to Me, 1951, Capitol 7565

Be Anything (But Be Mine)/Forgive Me, 1952, Decca 28142

Lover/You Got to My Head, 1952, Decca 28215

Watermelon Weather/The Moon Came Up with a Great Idea Last Night, 1952, Decca 28238

Just One of Those Things/I'm Glad There Is You, 1952, Decca 28313

River, River/Sans Souci, 1952, Decca 28395

Baubles, Bangles & Beads/Love You So, 1953, Decca 28890

Where Can I Go Without You/Go You Where You Go, 1954, Decca 29003

Let Me Go, Lover/Bouquet of Blues, 1954, Decca 29373

Mr. Wonderful/Crazy in the Heart, 1956, Decca 29834

Joey, Joey, Joey/They Can't Take That Away from Me, 1956, Decca 29877

Fever/You Don't Know, 1958, Capitol 3998

Light of Love/Sweetheart, 1958, Capitol 4071

Alright, Okay, You Win/My Man, 1959, Capitol 4115

Hallelujah, I Love Him So/I'm Lookin' Out the Window, 1959, Capitol 4189

I'm a Woman/Big Bad Bill, 1962, Capitol 4888
Pass Me By/That's What It Takes, 1965, Capitol 5346
Is That All There Is?/Me and My Shadow, 1969, Capitol 2602

Gisele MacKenzie

Le Fiacre/Tuh Pocket Tuh Pocket (Mississippi River Boat), 1952, Capitol F1907
Adios/Darlin', You Can't Love Two, 1952, Capitol F2156
Don't Let the Stars Get in Your Eyes/My Favorite Song, 1952, Capitol F2256
Hard To Get/Boston Fancy, 1955, X 4X-0137
Pepper Hot Baby/That's the Chance I've Got to Take, 1955, X 4x-0172
The Star You Wished Upon Last Night/It's Delightful to Be Married, 1956, VIK X-0233

The McGuire Sisters

Pine Tree, Pine Over Me/Cling to Me (with Eileen Barton, Johnny Desmond), 1954, Coral 61126
Goodnight, Sweetheart, Goodnight/Heavenly Feeling, 1954, Coral 61187
Muskrat Ramble/Not as a Stranger, 1954, Coral 61258
Lonesome Polecat/Uno, Due, Tre, 1954, Coral 61239
Christmas Alphabet/Give Me Your Heart for Christmas, 1954, Coral 61303
Sincerely/No More, 1955, Coral 61323
It May Sound Silly/Doesn't Anybody Love Me?, 1955, Coral 61369
Something's Gotta Give/Rhythm 'n' Blues (Mama's Got the Rhythm—Papa's Got the Blues),
    1955, Coral 61423
He/If You Believe, 1955, Coral 61501
Give Me Love/Sweet Song of India, 1955, Coral 61494
Missing/Tell Me Now, 1956, Coral 61587
Picnic/Delilah Jones, 1956, Coral 61627
Weary Blues/In the Alps, 1956, Coral 61670
Ev'ry Day of My Life/Endless, 1956, Coral 61703
Goodnight, My Love, Pleasant Dreams/Mommy, 1956, Coral 61748
Around the World in 80 Days/Interlude, 1957, Coral 61856
Sugartime/Banana Split, 1957, Coral 61924
Ding Dong/Since You Went Away to School, 1958, Coral 61991
Volare/Do You Love Me Like You Kiss Me, 1958, Coral 62021
May You Always/Achoo-Cha-Cha, 1959, Coral 62059
Summer Dreams/Peace, 1959, Coral 62106
Livin' Dangerously/Lover's Lullaby, 1960, Coral 62162
The Last Dance/Nine O'Clock, 1960, Coral 62216
Just For Old Time's Sake/Really Neat, 1961, Coral 62249
Tears on My Pillow/Will There Be Space in a Space Ship, 1961, Coral 62276
Just Because/I Do Do Do, 1961, Coral, 62288

Jane Morgan

Two Different Worlds/Nights in Verona, 1956, Kapp 161
Fascination/Fascination (Whistling Instrumental), 1957, Kapp 191

The Day the Rains Came/Le Jour Ou La Pluie Viendra, 1958, Kapp 235
With Open Arms/I Can't Begin to Tell You, 1959, Kapp 284
Happy Anniversary/C'est La Vie, C'est L'amour, 1959, Kapp 305

Jaye P. Morgan

Just a Gigolo/Wasted Tears, 1953, Derby 964
Life Is Just a Bowl of Cherries/Operator 299, 1954, Derby 988
That's All I Want from You/Dawn, 1954, RCA Victor 5896
Danger! Heartbreak Ahead/Softly Softly, 1955, RCA Victor 6016
If You Don't Want My Love/Pepper Hot Baby, 1955, RCA Victor 6282
Not One Goodbye/My Bewildered Heart, 1955, RAC Victor 6329
Get Up! Get Up!/Sweet Lips, 1956, RCA Victor 6441
Lost in the Shuffle/Play for Keeps, 1956, RCA Victor 6505
Johnny Casanova/The West Point Dress Parade, 1956, RCA Victor 6565
Just Love Me/The Call of the Wild, 1956, RCA Victor 6653
Mutual Admiration Society/If'n (with Eddy Arnold), 1956, RCA Victor 6708
Are You Lonesome Tonight/Miss You, 1959, MGM K12752
I Walk the Line/Wondering Where You Are, 1960, MGM K12924

Patti Page

I Don't Care If the Sun Don't Shine/I'm Gonna Paper All My Walls with Love Letters, 1950,
    Mercury 5396
All My Love/Roses Remind Me of You, 1950, Mercury 5455
Back in Your Own Backyard/The Right Kind of Love, 1950, Mercury 5463
Tennessee Waltz/Boogie Woogie Santa Claus, 1950, Mercury 5534
Would I Love You (Love You, Love You)/Sentimental Music, 1951, Mercury 5571
Down the Trail of Achin' Hearts/Ever True, Ever More, 1951, Mercury 5579
Mockin' Bird Hill/I Love You Because, 1951, Mercury 5595
Mister and Mississippi/These Things I Offer You, 1951, Mercury 5645
Detour/Who's Gonna Shoe My Pretty Little Feet, 1951, Mercury 5682
And So to Sleep Again/One Sweet Letter, 1951, Mercury 5706
Come What May/Retreat, 1951, Mercury 5772
Whispering Winds/Love, Where Are You Now, 1952, Mercury 5816
Once in a While/I'm Glad You're Happy with Someone Else, 1952, Mercury 5867
I Went to Your Wedding/You Belong to Me, 1952, Mercury 5899
Why Don't You Believe Me/Conquest, 1952, Mercury 70025
How Much Is That Doggie in the Window/My Jealous Eyes, 1953, Mercury 70070
Now That I'm in Love/Oo! What You Do to Me, 1953, Mercury 70127
Butterflies/This Is My Song, 1953, Mercury 70183
Father, Father/The Lord's Prayer, 1953, Mercury 70222
Changing Partners/Don't Get Around Much Anymore, 1953, Mercury 70295
Cross Over the Bridge/My Restless Lover, 1954, Mercury 70302
Steam Heat/Lonely Days, 1954, Mercury 70380
What a Dream/I Cried, 1954, Mercury 70416

Let Me Go, Lover!/Hocus Pocus, 1954, Mercury 70511
Piddily Patter Patter/Every Day, 1955, Mercury 70657
Croce Di Oro/Search My Heart, 1955, Mercury 70713
Go On with the Wedding/The Voice Inside, 1955, Mercury 70766
My First Formal Gown/Too Young to Go Steady, 1956, Mercury 70766
Allegheny Moon/The Strangest Romance, 1956, Mercury 70878
Mama from the Train/Every Time, 1956, Mercury 70971
Repeat After Me/Learnin' My Latin, 1956, Mercury 71015
A Poor Man's Roses/The Wall, 1957, Mercury 71059
Old Cape Cod/Wondering, 1957, Mercury 71101
I'll Remember Today/My, How the Time Goes By, 1957, Mercury 71189
Belonging to Someone/Bring Us Together, 1957, Mercury 71247
Another Time, Another Place/These Worldly Wonders, 1958, Mercury 71294
Left Right Out of Your Heart/Longing to Hold You Again, 1958, Mercury 71331
Fibbin'/You Will Find Your Love, 1958, Mercury 45255
Trust in Me/Under the Sun Valley Moon, 1958, Mercury 71400
The Walls Have Ears/My Promise, 1959, Mercury 71428
With My Eyes Wide Open, I'm Dreaming/My Mother's Eyes, 1959, Mercury 71469
Goodbye Charlie/Because Him Is a Baby, 1959, Mercury 71510
The Sound of Music/Little Donkey, 1959, Mercury 71555
Two Thousand, Two Hundred, Twenty-Three Miles/Promise Me Thomas, 1960, Mercury71597
One of Us (Will Weep Tonight)/What Will My Future Be, 1960, Mercury 71739
I Wish I'd Never Been Born/I Need You, 1960, Mercury 71695
Don't Read the Letter/That's All I Need, 1960, Mercury 71745
A City Girl Stole My Country Boy/Dondi, 1961, Mercury 71792
Mom and Dad's Waltz/You'll Answer to Me, 1961, Mercury 71823
A Broken Heart and a Pillow Filled with Tears/Dark Moon, 1961, Mercury 71870
Go on Home/Too Late to Cry, 1961, Mercury 71906
Most People Get Married/You Don't Know Me, 1962, Mercury 71950
The Boys' Night Out/Three Fools, 1962, Mercury 72013
Pretty Boy Lonely/Just a Simple Melody, 1963, Columbia 42671
Say Wonderful Things/I Knew I Would See Him Again, 1963, Columbia 42791
Hush, Hush, Sweet Charlotte/Longing to Hold You Again, 1965, Columbia 43251
You Can't Be True/Dear, Who's Gonna Shoe My Pretty Little Feet, 1965, Columbia 43345
Gentle on My Mind/Excuse Me, 1967, Columbia 44353
Little Green Apples/This House, 1968, Columbia 44556

Patience & Prudence

Tonight You Belong to Me, 1956, Liberty F55022
Gonna Get Along Without Ya Now/The Money Tree, 1956, Liberty F55040

The Poni-Tails

Born Too Late/Come On, Joey, Dance with Me, 1958, ABC-Paramount 9934
Seven Minutes in Heaven/Close Friends, 1958, ABC-Paramount 9969
I'll Be Seeing You/I'll Keep Tryin', 1959, ABC-Paramount 11047

Debbie Reynolds

Ada Daba Honeymoon/Row, Row, Row (Carleton Carpenter), 1950 MGM K30282
Tammy/French Heels, 1957, Coral 9-61851
A Very Special Love/I Saw a Country Boy, 1957 Coral 9-61897
Am I That Easy to Forget/Ask Me to Go Steady, 1959, Dot 15985
City Lights/Just for a Touch of Your Love, 1960, Dot 16071

Dinah Shore

Bibbidi-Bobbidi-Boo/Happy Times, 1950, Columbia 38659
It's So Nice to Have a Man Around the House/More Than Anything Else in the World, 1950, Columbia 38689
Can Anyone Explain? (No! No! No!)/Dream a Little Dream of Me, 1950, Columbia 38927
My Heart Cries for You/Nobody's Chasing Me, 1950, RCA Victor 3978
A Penny a Kiss/In Your Arms (with Tony Martin), 1951, RCA Victor 4019
Sweet Violets/If You Turn Me Down, 1951, RCA Victor 3997
The Musicians/How D'Ye Do and Shake Hands, 1951, RCA Victor 4225
Delicado/The World Has a Promise, 1952, RCA Victor 4719
Salomee/Let Me Know, 1953, RCA Victor 5176
Sweet Thing/Why Come Crying to Me, 1953, RCA Victor 5247
Blue Canary/Eternity, 1953, RCA Victor 5390
Changing Partners/Think, 1954, RCA Victor 5515
Pass the Jam, Sam/I'll Hate Myself in the Morning, 1954, RCA Victor 5622
If I Give My Heart to You/Tempting, 1954, RCA Victor 5838
Whatever Lola Wants/Church Twice on Sunday, 1955, RCA Victor 6077
Love and Marriage/Compare, 1955, RCA Victor 6266
Stolen Love/That's All There Is to That, 1956, RCA Victor 6370
I Could Have Danced All Night/What a Heavenly Night for Love, 1956, RCA Victor 6469
Chantez-Chantez/Honky Tonk Heart, 1957, RCA Victor 6792
Fascination/Till, 1957, RCA Victor 6980
Cattle Call/Promises Promises, 1957, RCA Victor 6897
I'll Never Say "Never Again" Again/The Kiss That Rocked the World, 1957, RCA Victor 7056

Jo Stafford

Scarlet Ribbons (For Her Hair)/Happy Times 1950, Capitol 54-785
Diamonds Are a Girl's Best Friend/Open Door, Open Arms, 1950, Capitol 824
Play a Simple Melody/Pagan Love Song, 1950, Capitol 1039
Sometime/No Other Love, 1950, Capitol 1053
Goodnight, Irene/Our Very Own, 1950, Capitol 1142
Tennessee Waltz/If You've Got the Money, I've Got the Time, 1951, Capitol 39065
If/It Is No Secret, 1951, Columbia 39082
Somebody/Allentown Jail, 1951, Columbia DCH 107
In the Cool, Cool, Cool of the Evening/That's Good! That's Bad!, 1951, Columbia 39466
Kissing Bug Boogie/Hawaiian War Chant, 1951, Columbia 39529
Shrimp Boats/Love, Mystery and Adventure, 1951, Columbia 39581

Pretty-Eyed Baby/That's the One for Me (with Frankie Laine), 1951, Columbia 39388

Gambella (The Gamblin' Lady)/Hey Good Lookin' (with Frankie Laine), 1951, Columbia 39570

Hambone/Let's Have a Party (with Frankie Laine), 1952, Columbia 39672

A-Round the Corner/Heaven Drops Her Curtain Down, 1952, Columbia 39653

Tonight We're Settin' the Woods on Fire/Piece A-Puddin' (with Frankie Laine), 1952, Columbia 39867

You Belong to Me/Pretty Boy, 1952, Columbia 39811

Jambalaya/Early Autumn, 1952, Columbia 39838

Keep It Secret/Once to Every Heart, 1952, Columbia 39891

Chow Willy/Christmas Roses (with Frankie Laine), 1953, Columbia 39893

(Now and Then There's) A Fool Such As I/Just Because You're You, 1953, Columbia 39930

Without My Lover/Smoking My Sad Cigarette, 1953, Columbia 39951

Just Another Polka/My Dearest, My Darling, 1953, Columbia 40000

Way Down Yonder in New Orleans/Floatin' Down to Cotton Town (with Frankie Laine), 1953, Columbia 40116

Make Love to Me/Adi-Adios Amigo, 1954, Columbia 40143

Indiscretion/April and You, 1954, Columbia 40170

Thank You for Calling/Where Are You, 1954, Columbia 40250

Teach Me Tonight/Suddenly, 1954, Columbia 40351

Suddenly There's a Valley/Night Watch, 1955, Columbia 40559

It's Almost Tomorrow/If You Want to Love, 1955, Columbia 40595

All Night Long/As I Love You, 1956, Columbia 40640

Love Me Good/Perfect Love, 1956, Columbia 40745

With a Little Bit of Luck/One Little Kiss, 1956, Columbia 40718

On London Bridge/Bells Are Ringing, 1956, Columbia 40782

Wind in the Willow/King of Paris, 1957, Columbia 40832

Kay Starr

Bonaparte's Retreat/Someday Sweetheart, 1950, Capitol 936

Hoop-Dee-Doo/A Woman Likes to Be Told, 1950, Capitol 980

Mississippi/He's a Good Man to Have Around, 1950, Capitol 1072

I'll Never Be Free/Ain't Nobody's Business but My Own (with Tennessee Ernie Ford), 1950, Capitol 1124

Oh Babe/Everybody's Somebody's Fool, 1950, Capitol 1278

Come On-A My House/Hold Me, Hold Me, Hold Me, 1951, Capitol 1710

Oceans of Tears/You're My Sugar (with Tennessee Ernie Ford), 1951, Capitol 1567

Angry/Don't Tell Him What's Happened to Me, 1951, Capitol 1796

Wheel of Fortune/I Wanna Love You, 1952, Capitol 1964

I Waited a Little Too Long/(Ho Ho Ha Ha) Me Too, 1952, Capitol 2062

Kay's Lament/Fool, Fool, Fool, 1952, Capitol 2151

Comes A-Long A-Love/Three Letters, 1952, Capitol 2213

Side by Side/Noah, 1953, Capitol 2334

Half a Photograph/Allez-Vous-En, 1953, Capitol 2464

When My Dreamboat Comes Home/Swamp Fire, 1953, Capitol 2595

Changing Partners/I'll Always Be in Love with You, 1953, Capitol 2657

The Man Upstairs/If You Love Me (Really Love Me), 1954, Capitol 2769

Am I a Toy or a Treasure/Fortune in Dreams, 1954, Capitol 2887

Good and Lonesome/Where, What or When, 1955, RCA Victor 6146

Rock and Roll Waltz/I've Changed My Mind a Thousand Times, 1956, RCA Victor 6359

Second Fiddle/Love Ain't Right, 1956, RCA Victor 6541

The Things I Never Had/The Good Book, 1956, RCA Victor 6617

Jamie Boy/A Little Loneliness, 1957, RCA Victor 6864

My Heart Reminds Me/Flim Flam Floo, 1957, RCA Victor 6981

Foolin' Around/Kay's Lament, 1961, Capitol 15194

I'll Never Be Free/Nobody, 1961, Capitol 4583

Four Walls/Oh Lonesome Me, 1962, Capitol 4835

Gale Storm

I Hear You Knocking/Never Leave Me, 1955, Dot 15412

Memories Are Made of This/Teen Age Prayer, 1955, Dot 15436

Why Do Fools Fall in Love/I Walk Alone, 1956, Dot 15448

Ivory Tower/I Ain't Gonna Worry, 1956, Dot 15458

Tell Me Why/Don't Be That Way, 1956, Dot 15474

Now Is the Hour/A Heart Without a Sweetheart, 1956, Dot 15492

My Heart Belongs to You/Orange Blossoms, 1956, Dot 15515

Lucky Lips/On Treasure Island, 1957, Dot 15539

Dark Moon/A Little Too Late, 1957, Dot 15558

June Valli

Strange Sensation/So Madly in Love, 1952, RCA Victor 4759

Crying in the Chapel/Love Every Moment You Live, 1953, RCA Victor 5368

I Understand/Love, Tears, and Kisses, 1954, RCA Victor 5740

Tell Me, Tell Me/Boy Wanted, 1954, RCA Victor 5837

Unchained Melody/Tomorrow, 1955, RCA Victor 6078

The Wedding/Lunch Hour, 1958, Mercury 71382

The Answer to a Maiden's Prayer/In His Arms, 1959, Mercury 71422

Apple Green/Oh Why, 1960, Mercury 71588

Joan Weber

Let Me Go, Lover!/Marionette, 1954, Columbia 40366

INDEX

"Eddie My Love," 116, 120, 125
Edsels, 153
Edwards, Tommy, 39
Eisenhower, Dwight, 7
"El Choclo," 109
Ellington, Duke, 8, 183
Emerson, Ken, 166, 179
"Empty Arms," 139, 155
Ennis, Philip H., 38, 87
"En-Thuz-E-Uz-E-As-M," 71
Ertegun, Ahmet, 86
Ertel, Janet, 124
Etting, Ruth, 114
Evans, Dale, 72
Evans, Lynn, 124, 125
Evans, Ray, 137, 145
Everly Brothers, 125
"Everybody Go Home," 179
"Everybody Loves a Lover," 163, 164
"Eyes Wide Open," 142

Fabian, 185
Faith, Percy, 27, 41, 67
"Fascination," 162, 173, 177
Ferguson, Burt, 38
Ferrer, José, 42
"Fever," 163, 165, 166
"Fini," 177
"Fish, The," 179
Fisher, Carrie, 144
Fisher, Eddie, 49, 51, 52, 61, 77, 81, 88, 116, 144, 145, 174
Fisher, Todd, 144
Fitzgerald, Ella, 20, 24, 39, 150
Fitzgerald, F. Scott and Zelda, 5, 85
Five Keys, 39, 92, 134
Five Satins, 120
Flamingos, 54
Fleming, Rhonda, 52, 76, 170
"Flying Saucer," 119
Foley, Red, 8, 14, 98, 113
Fontane, Bea, 112, 115
Fontane, Frank, 112
Fontane, Geri, 112, 114, 116
Fontane, Marge, 112

Fontane Sisters, 7, 107, 111–16, 118, 121, 124, 134, 169
"Fool, The," 119
Ford, Glenn, 85, 86
Ford, Tennessee Ernie, 10, 26, 54, 106, 119, 134
"Forgetting," 132
Forrest, Helen, 165
Fosse, Bob, 66
Foster, Lewis, 170
Four Aces, 88
Four Esquires, 58
Four Girls Four, 185
Four Hues, 128
Four Lads, 61, 169, 170
Francis, Connie, 132, 157, 167, 175
Franklin, Aretha, 24
Freed, Alan, 51
Freeman, Stan, 42
"Frenesi," 177
Friedrich, Gary, 127
Froman, Jane, 67, 172
"Frosty the Snowman," 159
Fulton, Jack, 128
Funicello, Annette, 170

Gaar, Gillian, 111, 112
Gabler, Milt, 74, 75, 84
Gale, Sunny, 54, 95, 97, 135
Gardner, Ava, 91
Garvin, Clint, 89
Gaver, Jack, 90
Gaylords, 88
G-Clefs, 130
Gene & Eunice, 87
"Gentle on My Mind," 175
George, Barbara, 164
George Shearing Quintet, 57
Gibbs, Georgia, 43, 62, 64, 77, 79, 104–11, 112, 116, 168
Gilberto, Astrud, 179
Gillespie, Dizzy, 183
Gillett, Charlie, 5, 25, 26, 106, 115
"Gimme Gimme John," 177
"Girl from Ipanema, The," 179
Gladiolas, 153
"Glad Song, The," 71, 72

ABOUT THE AUTHOR

Photo courtesy of the author

Steve Bergsman has contributed to a wide range of magazines, newspapers, and wire services for more than thirty years, including the *New York Times*, *Wall Street Journal*, *Barron's*, *Toronto's HomeFront*, *Black Enterprise*, *Oldies*, *The Australian*, *Phoenix Magazine*, *Chief Executive*, and Reuters, Inman, Copley, and Creators' Syndicate news services.

His fourteen books fall into four categories: music, travel, memoir, and business. In regard to music, his books include *Chapel of Love: The Story of New Orleans Girl Group the Dixie Cups* (with Rosa Hawkins); *I Put a Spell On You: The Bizarre Life of Screamin' Jay Hawkins*; *The Friends of Billy Preston*; *The Seduction of Mary Wells*; and *The Death of Johnny Ace*.

Steve Bergsman's travel books are: *Hobnobbing with Ghosts: A Literature and Lyric Junkie Travels the World* and *Hobnobbing with Ghosts II: A Lyric and Literature Junkie Travels the World*.

His sole memoir is *Growing Up Levittown: In a Time of Conformity, Controversy and Cultural Crisis*.

Finally, Steve Bergsman's five business books are *Maverick Real Estate Investing: The Art of Buying and Selling Properties Like TRUMP, ZELL, SIMON and the World's Greatest Land Owners*; *Maverick Real Estate Financing: The Art of Raising Capital and Owning Properties Like Ross, Sanders and Carey*; *After the Fall: Opportunities and Strategies for Real Estate Investing in the Coming Decade*; *Passport to Exotic Real Estate: Buying U.S. and Foreign Property in Breathtaking, Beautiful, Faraway Lands*; and *Transforming Dirt into Gold, Land Investments: Finding Opportunity Where Others Fail to See It* (with Ronald McRae).

Printed in the USA
CPSIA information can be obtained
at www.ICGtesting.com
LVHW051439240124
769422LV00019B/85